HENRY

RUN TO SURVIVE

Vittorio Terranova

Dedicated to my wife, Kathy, for the her support in making this book possible.

Contents

I

A Hot Morning in Late Spring in Southern California, 1987

At the sound of the alarm clock, a beautiful busty Latina woman got out of bed and went to the kitchen to prepare coffee. After putting the coffee pot on the stove, she quickly took a shower and got dressed.

As she finished, she finally spoke to the man in bed, "Last night was great, but I must get to work. SHIT! It's half past eight and I'm already late. I have an important appointment at nine, and I probably won't make it."

Quickly, she put on her shoes and headed to the door. Before leaving, she stopped and abruptly asked the man, still half asleep and tired from a night of debauchery, "By the way, what is your name?"

"HENRY," he mumbled.

"Well! Bye Henry, it was a pleasure to meet you."

"Can we meet again tonight, or one of these evenings?" he asked as if afraid she was just a passing vision, or a creation of his mind.

"I don't think so! Tonight, I have a commitment with another man, and tomorrow morning I will leave for Tucson for two weeks, but I can see you later, sometime soon. Goodbye for now."

"Hey! Wait, what is your name? And..."

"I put a business card near your trousers. Please close the door before you leave. Goodbye again," she answered abruptly irritated by the questions and left without adding anything else.

Henry stayed in bed and fell asleep. When the alarm clock rang, he swore, looked at the hour and discovered it was already half past eleven. Henry quickly got up, went to the bathroom, washed his face, and got dressed. When he put on his pants, he saw a business card had fallen to the ground. Remembering what it was, he took it and read: "Dolores Lopez travel agency manager, 20234 Palm Spring Avenue, Grand Terrace, CA."

"Dolores is a nice name," he thought. He tried to remember her but couldn't recall anything, except meeting her in a pub the evening before, while both were stoned and drunk and the sexual spark did the rest.

Henry put the business card in his wallet, put on his shoes and walked out of the house, carefully closing the door behind him.

The dazzling sunlight blinded him. Slipping on his sunglasses, he mounted his 1981 Honda 450 and headed home.

In less than thirty minutes, he reached his home in Redlands. As he opened the door, a couple of Budweiser cans by the entrance rolled on the floor.

Henry's house was worse than a pigpen, littered with beer cans, and overflowing ashtrays, newspapers, books, and clothes scattered everywhere. On the small table in front of the television he saw an ashtray with a half joint.

He wasted no time and smoked it greedily, sitting on the dusty sofa and turning on the TV. After repeatedly changing the channels, he realized nothing interesting was on and turned it off.

Remembering the mail, he went to get it, hesitant and anxious. He hadn't picked it up for three days, and now it was time. The letterbox was full, stuffed with advertising coupons for fast food restaurants and department stores. In the middle of the pile, there were four letters.

He opened the first letter and read:

Smith & Davinson Lawyers
San Bernardino

Dear Mr. Henry R. Dawnin,

This is an eviction notice for the end of the month, due to not paying rent for four months. You must leave Mr. Goodwill's home by the twenty-eight of May.

Thank you.

Henry was deeply discouraged. He had to leave the place he had called home for almost four years. But why? He had phoned Robert Goodwill two weeks earlier and promised to pay as soon as possible. Goodwill had reassured him that he would wait some time for the payment. Instead, now the son of a bitch was evicting him, after Dawnin had always paid on time and even repaired part of the small, ugly house.

That bastard Goodwill, a construction engineer and builder, was full of money and owned half of the town in Palm Springs, but despite his rich financial status, Henry was evicted for a mere $350 of unpaid rent. Yes, it had accumulated to almost $1400, but still, what a cheapskate. Shouting in anger, Henry opened the second letter, already knowing what it was.

It was the trimester bill for the school in Santa Barbara where his sixteen-year-old daughter Chris lived with her mother.

Relations between Henry and his former wife, Nathalie, were far from friendly. They had not spoken in a long time and could barely tolerate each other. Nathalie had left Henry several years ago to marry a wealthy lawyer in Santa Barbara, and now she taught literature at the university. Despite not needing the money, Nathalie had obtained a court order for child support, so Henry had been paying the tuition for their daughter's expensive Catholic school.

Until a year ago, Henry had no financial problems. Not that he swam in gold, but he lived comfortably. In fact, he had a cute, crowded pub back then, co-owned with a friend, Jim White. Despite his last name, Jim was black. Henry often teased him about it. They argued frequently, but their quarrels always ended with a hug and a good drink.

Jim was the muscle and Henry the brains behind the operation, and their pub was thriving to the point of expansion. Jim was Henry's best friend—a cheerful, helpful, polite, friendly, and caring guy. His only flaw was his talkativeness; once he started, no one could stop him. A strong, tall, athletic man, Jim had played college football and stayed in shape by going to the gym and running. They had been pals since childhood, their families close, and they grew up playing together. Jim lived a few blocks away from Henry, and their families often spent holidays together.

Though they were classmates in elementary school, Jim attended a different high school, and they lost touch until after graduation. Their old friendship rekindled as strong as ever, leading them to start the pub together. It was a wonderful period for Henry. Their pub was like a little jewel in town. It was not very big, but cozy and busy. Music was played on a regular basis, with different bands of blues, jazz, classic rock, folk, and bluegrass, making the pub trendy and popular.

However, a year and eight months ago, Jim died in a car accident under mysterious circumstances, leaving Henry deeply shocked. It wasn't just the loss of his best friend; Henry believed something was wrong with the accident and wasn't convinced the authorities had identified the right cause.

In the weeks before his death, Jim's behavior had been peculiar. He seemed troubled, worried, and gloomy; his usual cheerfulness gone. He barely talked, and when Henry asked what was wrong, Jim never gave a straight answer or revealed his worries.

Despite this painful event, Henry continued to move on but suffered a total collapse three months after Jim's death, when his girlfriend Theresa, complaining of incompatibility, broke up with him. At least that was what she told him, while putting her clothes in the suitcase before leaving.

Henry still loved Theresa. They often spoke on the phone and sometimes went out to eat together. Since the two most important people in his life, in one way or another, had abandoned him, Henry had changed for the worse. He was a different person.

He no longer worked zealously, and had started drinking more than normal, and smoking 6-10 joints a day. Fortunately, he never was hooked on the hard drugs, limiting himself mostly to smoking reefers and cigarettes and drinking too much. However, what really ruined him was the gambling.

Henry had started to play with very dangerous people, wise guys of the area, and the poker games were financially ruining him. One day, in a drunken stupor, he bet his pub and lost it to a shady character from San Bernardino.

To make ends meet, Henry got a job as a bartender in a local restaurant but was fired five months ago when he was found drunk. After an argument with the manager, Henry punched and broke his boss's nose. The result: he was fired immediately, spent three days in jail, and received a $1000 fine.

After that day, Henry was truly a wreck with no money, ideas, morals, or desire to work or even live. He spent his days loitering, talking to fools like himself, drinking in bars, and picking up any kind of woman.

After a long pause, he opened the third envelope.

The letter was from Theresa, who was in New York. The woman told him about the trip to the city and the concrete possibility of moving there. Theresa was a well-known occupational therapist. This news made him shudder. In fact, although they were separated, he liked and rejoiced in her presence during the few times they saw each other.

He opened the fourth and only letter with no return address and read: *"Be ready! I'm coming C. L."*

"What the hell is this letter?" He spontaneously exclaimed.

Still perplexed, he checked the postmark: *Seattle, May 17.*

The letter had been sent four days earlier.

He stared at the letter for a few seconds while mumbling, "Be ready, I am coming C.L.... what the hell does that mean? Who is it? I don't know anyone who lives in Seattle. It's probably a joke, I wonder if it is a ruse, for sure I will be asked for money. Surely, I will get another letter and then another, and if I don't answer, what happens to me? Do I get "syphilis" after five days? Fucking idiots! Don't people have other things to do?"

Henry trashed the letter in the garbage, put on loud Led Zeppelin music and went to take a shower. As soon as he got out, he heard someone literally kicking the front door. He quickly put on a towel and ran to open the door.

"Henry Dawnin?" A big, strong black man asked with an unfriendly glare.

"In person," he replied.

From a black limousine, parked across the street, two people got out, the man and woman approaching him. The man was dressed elegantly in a blue suit and tie. The woman, a thin, tall, beautiful blonde, dressed casually in jeans and a yellow t-shirt.

The man greeted him in a friendly tone, "Henry! Son of a bitch, how are you?"

"Charles!... Charles Lewis, is that you?"

"In person, you bastard! Let me hug you. Fuck! It's been a lifetime since we saw each other, how are you? This is Cindy... Cindy Hyatt, Henry Dawnin."

"Nice to meet you Henry," said the woman smiling.

"The pleasure is all mine," Henry replied, shaking the hand of the beautiful girl.

"Henry! That's Doug, who works for me."

"Hello! How is it going?" he said to the powerfully built, giant athlete who responded with a nod.

"Please come in and take a seat! And don't pay attention to the mess. In this period, I have been so busy I haven't been able to clean up."

"What do you say brother? We are family, no?" Charles said with a sneer.

The three people entered and sat in the living room.

Henry asked. "Do you want something to drink, guys? Beer, rum, bourbon, coke, sprite?"

"Fuck! Henry! Are we still in kindergarten? Coke, sprite. Give us something good, rum for me."

"And for you, Cindy?"

"Beer, thank you."

"Also, for you Doug, a beer? Ok!"

"Man! How long since we've seen each other, Charles, ten years, fifteen?"

"Something like that, and even longer," Charles replied, getting a big joint out of his pocket, and lighting it.

"How the hell did you find me? And why are you here?" Henry asked curiously.

"Ray Brown has kept me informed of what you and other friends have done over the years."

"Old Ray, Christ! I haven't seen him in more than three months."

"Yes! Old Ray! He always gave me your news... of highs... and... lows of your existence. He told me about your partner, your pub, how you lost it, and about Nathalie, and your former girlfriend, Theresa. I know everything, dear Henry, you cannot escape from me, ah! Ah."

Having said that, Charles, in an imperious and arrogant way, passed the reefer to Cindy, who greedily smoked a puff.

"You didn't answer the other question I asked, why are you here?"

Henry said not hiding his curiosity and annoyance.

"Why am I here...why am I here? I'm here for business, very important business."

Cindy, after taking another puff, passed the joint to Henry.

Charles, after stopping momentarily, resumed talking, "Henry, I know you're in shit, deep shit. You don't have money, you don't have a job, you don't have a dick. You spend your days fucking yourself with dope and alcohol, going from bar to bar picking up the sluts and tarts that give you their bodies and maybe... even AIDS. But you don't care, you always want to prove you are a 'macho man', a cool dude and so you prove it to them. I know you don't even have the money to pay the rent, so you'll be evicted from this house at the end of the month. You don't have the money to pay your daughter's school tuition. And dear Henry! You have no ideas and no purpose in life. You are a failure, a poor loser, who has never done anything good, and you will continue to be so, for the rest of your life and forever. I pity you, poor little, pathetic man."

"Fuck! No more talk. What do you want from me? Charles! Why are you here? Why are you breaking my balls?" Henry shouted furiously, interrupting the insulting monologue.

"Well! Well! Look Cindy! Incredible! Someone comes to help a friend... an old friend in need, and this is the result. Kicked in the face and nothing more but look at this guy. I left Seattle for this reason. If I had known, I would have stayed home. And then one says *friends*, *friends*, but look what friends I have. I do everything for them trying to help and instead I get kicked in the ass and that sucks."

"Why are you here? Charles! Why are you here?" Henry continued to scream furiously.

"I'm here for you, to help and offer a job."

"A job?"

"Yes! Henry! A job for which you will be well rewarded, and which can change the rest of your life. We're talking about $200,000, no trifle."

"Two hundred thousand dollars, did I hear it right?"

"Yes! $200,000 you will have to earn, as it won't fall from the sky. You will have to take risks. That's the point." Charles seriously, going to the core, and not mocking anymore.

"What is it?"

"It's a mission. You will have to face a risky mission."

"What kind of mission is it?"

"Go to a *wholesaler* and buy certain goods."

"What goods? Don't tell me its drugs?" Henry asked abruptly.

"Henry, you are smart, bravo! How did you guess?"

"Because I know you, it's about drugs, isn't it?"

"100% pure cocaine, stuff of connoisseurs, and marijuana that if you smoke it, you will go into orbit for a couple of days."

"Christ! Charles, who the fuck do you think I am, your private pusher? I hate doing these things. I have never been involved in any drug dealing, I might be a user, but never a seller." Henry said irritated.

4

"Are you sure? Look! We're talking about $200,000. For someone who will be evicted in ten days, I think the money will be useful, what do you think Cindy?" Charles exclaimed with his usual, mocking, and arrogant tone.

Cindy smiled and after a childish giggle, exclaimed with no spontaneity, "What in the world! For $200,000, I would do anything, it's a huge sum," then laughed loudly.

"You'd certainly sell even yourself for that amount, poor idiot," Henry thought, looking at her silly behavior. Then dark thoughts appeared in his mind. $200,000 would solve his problems very well. He was in deep trouble, and his living situation wouldn't improve. So why not ask for more information?

And so, he did. "Okay, Charles! What is this about?"

"Finally, this is the Henry Dawnin I know. It's very simple. It's just a matter of going to Tijuana and picking up certain goods for me. I will give you the address and money you need for the trip, then wait for further instructions. By the way this is the code you use to make phone calls, every word is calibrated for the mission."

"What about money? Do I have to pay? Or do I go there and pick up the goods without doing so?"

"Bravo! That's a good question. No! You must pay, but of course you won't bring money with you. So, once you get to Mexico, you'll go to a place that I'll tell you later. Follow my directions carefully and you'll find some briefcases."

Henry was frightened by the trip and the possible outcome. In fact, he knew it could be very dangerous. However, he needed the money desperately, and desperate people often do things they regret later. On the other side, if the mission went well, he would get a lot of cash. But something smelled very fishy to him, oh yes! Something smelled worse than rotten cod in this mission.

At the end, after a short reflective pause, putting the rest of the reefer in his mouth and with resolution, Henry said, "Okay Charles! I am in! When do we start?"

"Yes! This is the Henry I know. You see Cindy, all my friends have balls, and big ones. You will leave in less than a week, and I will call to tell you when. Here are the documents with locations and people you will contact, memorize them and burn everything. I recommend you be cautious and wish you success."

Charles got up from the couch, followed by his friends, and shaking Henry's hand, said, "Good luck, my old man. Think about how your life will change after the success of this enterprise."

"Thank you! And we will talk soon. Bye," Henry replied coldly, with an unhappy look.

Charles, Cindy, and Doug left the house and returned to their sleek black limousine. As they drove away, dark thoughts resurfaced in Henry's mind about the journey, especially about the unexpected arrival of Charles Lewis.

He had never trusted Charles, and personally preferred, a thousand times over, the company of a rattlesnake to him. A rattlesnake or a scorpion was much more loyal than that dandy, vicious person, and above all, less poisonous.

Much to Henry's dismay, Charles had not changed a bit. In fact, Charles had not gained weight or aged at all. He was in very good shape, certainly had trained in the gym like a madman, and practiced numerous sports.

Charles Lewis had the same mischievous and treacherous brown eyes as always. His nose was small and slightly potato-like, his curly black hair cut short, and his chin a little pointed with a dimple in the middle. It was as if Charles Lewis had made a pact with the devil to stay young forever.

Old, faded memories of school came back to his memory. He remembered when Charles zoomed by on his new, fancy, expensive bike at the end of school, trying to impress Nathalie, who couldn't care less about him. Or when for no reason, Charles attacked him violently, just for the desire to be a bully. There was also the time when Charles punched him in class, making his nose bleed so much that poor Henry had to leave and go home.

These memories were from the early years of high school when Charles Lewis was a notorious bully. Henry thought of Bob, the thin, shy classmate who stuttered, had twisted legs, crossed eyes, and a big, crooked nose. Bob sat in the second row in front of Charles and was often a target for his cruelty.

The poor fellow had always been a favorite victim of Charles' sadistic behavior with many nasty pranks. Henry remembered when in class Charles dried his nose snot in the hair of the poor dude, or in the bathroom where he pissed on Bob and the poor guy ran away with shame to hide in his house.

A few weeks after that incident, one day at school, Charles was in a dreadful mood because despite his efforts, he could not conquer Nathalie's heart. He tried to fool around with another girl, but she refused his sexual advances, running away, after Charles pulled out his dick and approached her by saying, "So, Jill, are you sure you don't want to race the breeze with me? Are you sure of that? Because I am a winner, I can't lose. I am Charles Lewis; I am God and God never loses. And I would love to rape you, bitch, ha ha!"

Several people heard and saw the scene and were scared by the creepy pervert. After that repellent action, Charles and some friends, during recess, went to the bathroom, where poor Bob was. The fury of Charles Lewis was unleashed, after insulting Bob for no reason. Some of them grabbed Bob, and Charles put his head in a dirty toilet and, only after several seconds, flushed it.

Bob reported the whole story to the principal, and everyone was expecting a punishment for Charles Lewis, but incredibly after a week, Bob quit school and moved with his family to a different city.

Charles Lewis was a son of a bitch, a wicked pervert, who enjoyed hurting other people. For this reason, Henry loathed Charles, because he represented everything Henry hated in the world: a spoilt, entitled, rich, evil, powerful piece of shit.

Henry could not stand any form of harassment and abuse, especially against weaker people. He wasn't a saint, just an ordinary person who always sided with the underdog, those struggling and good people who faced the wicked world daily.

In a short time, Charles had become the boss of the school and people were afraid of him and his violent behavior. Although he was not very tall, about five feet and ten, he was stocky and muscular and had powerful strength. Moreover, a series of losers had joined him in forming a bloodthirsty gang.

Henry vividly remembered when Charles and his buddies broke the noses of two boys guilty only of approaching Jane, the girlfriend of Tom Atkinson, Charles' best friend. He recalled the beatings, the blood on the boys' faces, and the enjoyment of young Lewis, who generally delivered the coup de grace by pissing on their heads.

In a short time, Charles Lewis was no longer a nasty rascal punk, but a real dangerous criminal. He was dealing cocaine, LSD, heroin and marijuana. Rumors swirled that he had even killed people, but no one ever tried to stop him. Not even when he slashed the wheels of the principal's car and was caught red-handed. Then Mr. Harold Lewis, the father of the young delinquent, appeared in person with a personal driver and a long white limousine and everything was silenced, as in Bob's case.

Charles Lewis had always been untouchable, and no one had ever understood why. Meanwhile, poor Jimmy Jones, who gave a raspberry to the philosophy professor, was expelled for a week, while Charles merely received a timid reprimand for groping Alice, the attractive physical education teacher. Despite his many flaws, Charles had his limits. In fact, even after many attempts to be cool with girls, he had not been successful, and Nathalie was the first on the list. Charles was totally infatuated but she hated him. Despite the numerous attempts he made, the more time passed Nathalie hated him more. Lewis could not bear the insult, he, the brat who had everything in life, could not have the girl on the third bench on the right. It was a real affront to his reputation.

Especially after he had a bet with some of his henchmen, he would soon split in two the little slut, to use his language. However, more time passed, and the situation did not improve, indeed worsened considerably.

Tom bet $100 that Charles would never get together with Nathalie. The situation deteriorated further when Charles realized that Nathalie seemed to have a soft spot for Henry Dawnin. In fact, the two spent hours together talking and ... contemplating. Contemplation in a short time became love and Charles spat out bile. He had never lost anything, so he did not want to lose once.

He would never give up the woman of his life. Nathalie was more than a crush; it had become an obsession. He could no longer bear the idea she had a relationship with a loser, half-hippy, idealist like Henry Dawnin.

Charles made other attempts, and still rejected by her, he decided on a stronger approach. One day he and his henchmen stopped Henry in the street and beat him badly. This time, the young thug made a big mistake. His rival was not a twit or a coward; he had shady friends.

After calling some of the right *friends,* Henry had the satisfaction of putting a gun in the mouth of the young punk and slapping him publicly several times in the face. However, Henry did not take pleasure in this. He had always been a caring, friendly, gentle person, though he had a hidden part of his personality that sometimes scared him.

When Henry could no longer tolerate abuse and harassment, he could lose his temper and become very angry. He tried to avoid reaching this point by defusing his temper with deep breaths, taking walks, and avoiding confrontation as much as possible.

That time with Charles Lewis was a great example of how the beast hidden inside his soul was unleashed. Hence, he proposed a simple, stupid pact: "Leave me alone and I will leave you alone."

Charles, after all, was a perfect coward and understood this was the best solution. From that day on, the two continued to endure each *other.* Charles got used to the idea that Nathalie was involved in an intimate relationship with Henry, while Henry promised not to bother him in his business.

In conclusion, although many argued Charles had sworn revenge, it seemed things had settled down.

Nathalie became Henry's wife, while Charles disappeared from circulation. Someone said he would continue to do his father's job, even though no one knew what work Mr. Harold Lewis did.

All those memories, buried for years and years, came back to his mind just as the black limousine quickly disappeared from the horizon.

He was scared to death, but what more did he have to lose?

Meanwhile, in the black limousine, Cindy asked, "What a strange guy, this friend of yours is. He was almost naked with that towel the whole time. Do you trust a person like this, Charles?"

"Henry?... ha... ha...ha. Dear Cindy, in this world, you must start understanding how people are made. I am great at judging people and human behaviors. It's part of my winning personality, those nuances that make me special, and always above the others." Charles exclaimed with the most arrogant tone in the world.

"See! He is a poor jerk who believes in ideals, ideologies, and other similar bullshit. Yes! I trust him for the mission because he will do his best, for the rest ... I want this bastard dead."

"But how is he not your friend?" "A friend, him? Don't make me laugh. The day I see him dead will be the best of my life. I hate this son of bitch."

"Charles! You scare me."

"Don't worry, Cindy, think of something else, and leave Henry alone... he has already been fixed. His time is coming, late but better than never. Ha-ha."

II

The next day, despite everything, Henry felt surprisingly good. He felt alive and motivated, which was a great step forward. In fact, he hadn't been like that for months or... maybe years. For this reason, he swore to himself that after the mission, he would go straight to the Caribbean to soak up the tropical heat. He had meticulously studied the material Charles gave him and had learned it by heart. Now, all he needed was some rest and a beautiful joint.

Charles had given him a code to memorize and a series of addresses. The first stop was in Tijuana, at a downtown bar where he needed to contact Ramon Gomez, the manager. Henry had transcribed the essentials onto a sheet of paper he kept in his wallet.

Now, it was time to have fun. He had spent too much energy on all those preparations. He headed to the kitchen, opened a can of Miller Genuine Draft beer, and rolled a reefer, trying to relax and not think about his troubles.

After about forty-five minutes, he left home and got on his motorcycle.

Henry was one of those guys who rode his motorcycle at maximum speed, living for the thrill and whizzing past like a madman. He was tearing down the highway full throttle when he spotted a beautiful girl on the side of the road, holding a big camera. The vision was so fleeting it felt like a flash: a stunning brunette, possibly Asian, in a jean jacket, was all he could recall.

After parking his bike, he noticed the familiar figure of Ray Brown passing by. Henry remembered what Charles had told him, that Ray had basically been his "confidant". So driven by curiosity, he called him.

"Henry! How are you? It's been some time since we saw each other. What are you doing right now? Old friend," Brown replied friendly.

Ray was in a good mood, probably having already had a fair amount to drink. Henry realized this the moment he shook his hand, as Ray's breath reeked of alcohol. Deciding to turn this into an opportunity, Henry sacrificed the last pennies in his pocket to buy Ray a drink and hopefully glean some useful information.

Ray was always happy to have a drink with someone, especially when it was on someone else's tab. He had been that way since their school days, often leaving his wallet at home or conveniently forgetting his money, which meant someone else always ended up paying for him. Henry had fallen victim to Ray's tactics more than once back then.

However, despite this, Henry had always liked the guy. He earned the nickname "Old Ray" because, even though they were peers in high school, Ray always looked much older than the rest of the students, seemingly by a decade.

He was a tormented soul. It was evident in his dark, melancholic eyes, like something had bothered him during life. However, being a very private person, Ray never confided his demons to anyone. And he had been a hard drinker since their school times.

The two of them entered the nearest pub.

"What's going on Ray? How are you doing?" Henry asked nicely.

"Nothing new, Henry, just work and hassles. I am in a bad mood these days. But by the way! Do you know who called me a short time ago asking about you?"

"No, Ray, who?"

"Charles Lewis, that bastard," Ray replied with anger.

"Coincidentally, Charles came to my house yesterday with a big scary bodyguard and an annoying little slut."

"Ah yes! I haven't heard from him for years, and mysteriously this asshole called me asking, above all, about you and how you are doing. That bastard... for all my life. I will remember that night... that damn night... ah! That night... that night."

Old Ray seemed to be under a spell. He repeated the word "night" continuously.

Henry thought that Ray was dazed and confused, but despite being drunk, something was holding him back from expressing his real thoughts.

"What damn night are you referring to, Ray? I don't understand?"

"That night... that night... that night... that..." Ray stammered, but before he could continue, he was violently shoved. Two big guys, one so blond he looked albino and the other Latino, had pushed Ray. One of them began to swear, "Watch where you're going, son of a bitch. You stepped on us, asshole."

"What?" Ray answered, shocked.

"You stepped on my foot, old, drunk bastard," the albino yelled in anger.

"I... I... I... did nothing... nothing," Ray exclaimed fearfully.

"Shut up, asshole," the other intervened, pushing Ray to the ground. While Ray lay there, the man struck him with a solemn kick in the stomach that almost split him in two.

"HEY! WAIT! You are exaggerating guys! STOP! Leave my friend alone," Henry said with an aggressive tone.

"WHO THE FUCK ARE YOU? The defense lawyer? Mind your business! Otherwise, I will break your bones too," the albino shouted furiously with a threatening look.

Meanwhile, a crowd had gathered around. The bartender, Joe, whom Henry had known for some time, called the police. Henry, not caring about anything, angrily shouted, "It is my business when someone beats a friend of mine, and it's my business when two pieces of shit, like yourself, do not let me finish my beer in peace."

"Ah, yes?" the blond man replied, quickly approaching Henry and landing a violent punch that sent him crashing to the ground. At the same time the Latino gave a strong kick in Ray's face.

Henry was dizzy, felt blood gushing from his nose and fell to the floor. But despite the intense pain, he slowly rose again.

The albino laughed wildly, "The asshole is here again, Scott. Do I kick his butt?" The Latino asked.

"No, that's enough. Let's go away, I am fed up with this fucking place, and it is getting late."

Before leaving the room, the albino knelt beside Brown, who was still on the ground, exhausted and in pain, and whispered something in his ear. Henry was too far away to hear it, but despite his own suffering from the punch, he couldn't ignore the look of anguish and dismay on Ray's face. Ray's eyes were squinted, his mouth shriveled, and his fingers were cut and bleeding from clutching the shards of a broken glass.

All this took place in just a few seconds. The albino quickly got up and headed for the exit, followed by his friend.

Suddenly the guy turned to Henry and said, "You're lucky today because I can't slit your throat like a chicken, but next time I'll make meatballs from your flesh, you bastard."

The two men left the bar still cursing, while remotely, the police cars with their sirens on were approaching the place.

Henry crawled over to Ray on his knees. "How are you?" he asked, very concerned.

Ray did not answer.

It seemed as if he were in another world, and he trembled incredibly.

Henry helped him to get up and cordially urged him to forget what had happened. "Forget it, Ray. They're just two nasty freaks. Let's drink a good beer and don't think about it anymore."

Brown kept shaking and didn't hear him, still deep in shock. After a few moments, Ray stumbled to his feet and walked away, leaving the room.

Henry was still massaging his sore jaw when Joe asked him, "How are you doing? Are you okay? And who the hell were those jerks? Violent lunatics! They caused so much damage to the room that at least it will cost me 300 dollars to repair it."

"I'm fine, thank you. I've never seen these assholes before. What's weird is that they seemed to have it out for old Ray, like they wanted to scare him to death. They were odd guys, and they weren't from here. The blond had an East Coast accent, like New Jersey... Damn them!" Henry replied.

He paid Joe for the last beer he didn't drink, and before the police arrived and started asking questions, he quickly walked away from the pub, got on his motorcycle and left. He had just engaged the third gear when he again had a fleeting vision, of a brunette, beautiful, on the corner of the street. It seemed as if she was watching him carefully, trying to be discreet. The woman wore a jean jacket and appeared to be Asian.

Only after returning home did Henry remember that this woman might be the same one he had seen for a few seconds on the highway. After grabbing a beer and heading to the bedroom, he noticed the red voicemail light flashing. He had a message.

It was Charles who ordered him to leave within a couple of days, to be ready for the new upcoming directives.

After hearing the message three times, Henry bitterly regretted having accepted that damn *mission*. The pay would be good if he survived, but he hated what he was about to do, and he didn't trust Charles at all.

Perhaps for the first time in a year, Henry had thought a little about his situation. After all, it was he who wanted to be in deep shit. Ever since Theresa had left him and Jim had died, he had totally abandoned himself and surrendered.

His physical condition had also worsened considerably. When you smoke joints until you're completely stoned, day and night, and drink until you burst, the body suffers. He noticed this in the pub when that big thug violently hit him in the face.

Oh yes, Henry Dawnin was ready for an early retirement, due to age and debilitated physical state. And it was sad to know that. Henry had been a good athlete, a great tennis player, a black belt in karate, and even decent at basketball despite not being very tall.

But now, at thirty-eight, it was time to think differently and start living the life of the retired and... failed. That punch and the fall to the ground like a sack of potatoes had awakened him from a state of torpor that had prevented him from reflecting for a long time. Henry seemed to have woken up from a long hibernation.

Almost involuntarily, he entered the bathroom, turned on the light and looked at himself in the mirror. For the first time in months or years, Henry carefully examined his face, and what he saw disturbed him. He looked old and haggard. His long brown hair had a touch of gray, his unkempt beard matched, and his blue eyes were dull and inexpressive. Wrinkles began to line his face, particularly around his eyes, tracing the contours like furrows in a field.

As he stared into the mirror, disgust with himself began to well up, and anger and nervousness boiled within him. To relax, he needed something that gave him peace, relaxation, and joy. So, he rolled a humongous joint, Bob Marley style, and decided he didn't care about anything else.

III

The morning after, Henry woke up with a dry mouth, bad breath, a bitter taste, and a pounding headache. The extravagances are paid dearly, and Henry always paid the bill.

The evening before, the initial reefer had tripled, and four beers, several shots of rum and half a pack of Marlboro cigarettes had done the rest.

He looked at the alarm clock and saw that it was half past noon. After taking a shower and getting dressed, Henry felt ravenously hungry. Opening the fridge, he realized he had nothing to eat.

He was forced to go out to eat a bite or go shopping, so he got on his Honda and rode hastily towards the town. He had barely finished parking his motorcycle when a boy of about thirteen passed by, selling newspapers and shouting, "The latest Sun Telegram, only 25 cents, buy the Sun Telegram."

Henry instinctively gave 25 cents to the boy, having spotted a familiar photo in the pile of newspapers. He had a good eye. On the bottom of the front page was a photo of Ray Brown, accompanied by an article with the title: "Man Killed by Hit-and-Run Vehicle at Eleven in the Evening in Downtown Redlands. No Witnesses."

Henry was deeply sorry and baffled by the news. Old Ray Brown was dead, killed by a hit-and-run car in downtown, and there were no witnesses to the accident, which struck him as odd. It was crazy.

He thought back to what had happened the night before and concluded that those two thugs from the pub were certainly responsible for his friend's murder.

He had had enough. Since Charles Lewis had reappeared in his life, he had only encountered bad memories and trouble.

But despite this, he felt very motivated and rejuvenated, and for this, he wanted to discover more about the story.

Henry had just raised his head after reading the article about Ray when he noticed the same beautiful Asian woman he had seen twice the day before. She was passing quickly on the other side of the sidewalk, discreetly glancing at him. This time, he was certain it was the same person. She wore the same well-worn jeans jacket, the same red baseball hat, and had a professional camera in her hand.

Before Henry could react, the woman turned onto an adjacent street, disappearing from his sight as she walked briskly. Henry chased her for a couple of blocks, but she was gone, and he did not want to go after a ghost.

So, he walked into Joe's pub to get some lunch. The bartender asked him if he had heard about Ray, and Henry said yes. Joe was also visibly upset.

Ray had been killed just ten minutes after leaving the pub, and it was no coincidence. Joe, like Henry, suspected that those two thugs from the previous night were implicated in Ray's death. With the pub empty and nothing else to do, Joe started talking nonstop, his words blending into a seemingly endless monologue.

Henry didn't pay much attention to him, focusing instead on drinking beer and eating his burger. However, when Joe briefly mentioned Ashley Duncar and Leslie Johnson, Henry nearly choked. Oh! He had totally forgotten about that story, probably because it had happened about twenty years ago and had long since been forgotten and archived by the police.

But above all, because during that time, he was in San Francisco. Ashley and Leslie were two young girls who had been found dead in the desert after being brutally murdered. Ray Brown had been involved in the investigation, but soon after, he was cleared of all charges.

Charles's father, the infamous Harold Lewis, had been one of the key pawns in the investigation.

Henry remembered very little of this, as did Joe.

But one thing was certain, he had lost his appetite. Drinking the rest of the beer in one sip, he patted Joe on his shoulder and got up from the table.

"Where are you going? And what about the bill?"

"I'll pay you as soon as possible, so long," he replied, leaving the pub.

Henry got on his motorbike and, as usual, sped off at maximum speed, heading for the public library. After extensive computer searches, he found some news about the case in the L.A. Times and the Sun Telegram.

The bodies were discovered on September 28, 1968. Ashley and Leslie were found dead in the desert after being tortured. Their decomposing corpses were discovered three days after their disappearance. Both families had reported the girls missing on the morning of the 26th. The previous evening, around eight o'clock, the girls had gone to a disco with Ray Brown and Tom Atkinson but had not returned home.

Ray and Tom were interrogated by the police, but they had a solid alibi and were cleared of all suspicion. They admitted to accompanying their friends to the disco but left early due to other commitments. The girls had assured Ray and Tom that they had no problem getting home from the club, as they knew several people they could ask for a ride. The men claimed to have left the girls before nine o'clock.

The girls died after midnight, and at that time, the young men were in the company of Mr. Harold Lewis, his son Charles, and Mr. Andrew Martin of Washington, D.C. They had all been playing poker together until 6 am, providing them with a strong alibi.

Henry found similar information in the Sun Telegram. This local newspaper, however, also gave ample space to an article in which Mr. Andrew Martin, a distinguished and well-known businessman from Washington, D.C., defended the boys from defamatory slander.

"The police, when they do not know how to do their job, always try to harm and accuse the innocent people to have their own scapegoat. These innocent boys will not have an unjust end, at least if I am here. I will do everything necessary to defend them."

This was part of the article Henry read, along with other related pieces. The more he read, the more he wondered why the illustrious Mr. Harold Lewis had been involved in the matter, and who the mysterious Mr. Andrew Martin of Washington D.C. was.

That whole thing smelled rotten to him. Nineteen years later, after everything had been silenced, he wanted to know more. But what more could be discovered? Every newspaper he read reported the exact same news as if everyone had drawn from the same source.

Henry felt incredibly sad seeing the photos of the two girls whom he knew and especially of Ashley, who was beautiful, indeed.

Henry remembered the girl, her long black hair, vitality, dark eyes, and the fantastic body she had. If he had not been in love with Nathalie, he would probably have courted Ashley because she was the most beautiful and nicest girl in the school. Nathalie was more woman, more mature, but Ashley had a charm that few girls possessed.

Ashley was warm, sensual, sweet, intelligent and... she was dead. Her death, with that of her best friend Leslie, had been trashed in some police archive, certainly with a note: "Killed by an unknown assassin," and everything had ended there.

After some time, Henry got bored reading the same news repeatedly.

He was tired of all those memories, did not photocopy any of those articles, and came out of the library, got on his motorbike and at full throttle went home.

During that time spent at the library, he had thought a lot about the mysterious young Asian girl who seemed to be following him everywhere.

Was she involved too in the old Ray Brown accident?

Did she work for Charles Lewis? Or what else?

He was puzzled by her. Was she a friend or a foe?

The second thought was about Tom Atkinson, reading his name in that dreadful news.

Tom Atkinson was a slimy guy, bad to the bone, and probably only Charles Lewis could surpass him in being an asshole. But Tom was a great substitute for him. He always has been the number two in Charles's gang. Tom was like a bottom feeder or a catfish who eats the leftover crumbs of food at the bottom of a river. He never shone his own light but was always following Charles's directives blindly. If Charles had told him to jump from a bridge, Tom would have complied without hesitation.

At school, Henry barely interacted with him. He just stayed away from the guy.

His mean look and his nasty temper made Henry sick. Moreover, there was something not sincere about that dude, something creepy.

Arriving home, Henry found a big and surprise. A small red Chevrolet was parked in front of his house, and a well-known person was nervously smoking a cigarette in front of the door.

"Henry! Where the hell have you been? I've been waiting for you for over an hour," Cindy yelled at him, clearly irritated.

"Hi Cindy, I wasn't really expecting you. What are you doing around here?"

"I have some important news to give you from Charles."

"What's going on? Is there something new to talk about it?"

"Yes! Big news! But we better talk about it inside!"

Henry opened the front door, and the woman sat on one of the dirty and dusty armchairs. "The plans have changed. We must leave tomorrow morning, it's important."

"What?" Dawnin exclaimed, surprised.

"It's really important that we go to Mexico tomorrow."

"I understand... I understand. I'm not deaf, but what does it mean *we* have to go?" He replied in amazement.

"It means that I will come with you on this journey."

"I am very sorry, but this is impossible," he said in a decisive tone.

"What are you saying? Have you gone crazy?" Cindy shouted again with an unpleasant tone of voice.

"No, I'm not crazy. I don't want strangers. I'm used to working alone, and I'm a loner by nature. I'm sorry, but you won't come," he replied resolutely.

"I come with you and... that's enough."

"I'm sorry, Cindy, I like to work alone. I don't want distractions."

"Look Henry! For this business, I am as important as Charles. In fact, we are fifty percent partners. If you don't do as I say, you can go to hell and say goodbye to your $200,000. So, cool off and start cooperating. Do you understand? I hope so. I have no time to waste. I can easily get another person who makes less of a fuss than you and who doesn't spit on 200,000 dollars."

He felt trapped and annoyed by that whole matter and already had enough of it.

The idea of this woman accompanying him on the journey was particularly unappealing, especially since he couldn't stand her. He had felt this antipathy from the first time he saw Cindy.

Dawnin finally decided to stay in the game because he saw no other alternative. Against his will, he gave his consent to the unexpected proposal.

"Okay, Cindy, you can come."

"Oh Christ! It is time," the woman replied angrily. "Tomorrow morning, we will retrieve a jeep that I bought and go directly to Mexico. We will head to a certain location, which I know, to withdraw the money. Really, I should say *to dig* for the money because the loot is buried, and I have the map to find it. After finding the money, we will head to another area, twenty miles outside Tijuana, to buy the goods. The journey will last several days, so get used to it. You and I will stand elbow to elbow, my dear. Do we still have any problems, or is everything clear to you?" Cindy spoke with a dictatorial tone.

"Well, you didn't tell me almost anything. I don't even know where we're going, so how can I express my doubts?" Henry answered skeptically.

"Can I sleep in your house for tonight?" She asked him at the end of the brief discussion.

"Of course! Please Cindy! You can sleep in my bed and..."

"Don't be so hasty, handsome guy. We barely know each other, and you already want to take me to bed," Cindy said in a mocking tone.

"I mean, sleep in my bed while I sleep here, on the couch," he replied, annoyed. The idea of being with that woman continued to upset him.

It was time to go to sleep. Henry lay on the couch but couldn't fall asleep; he had too many troubles on his mind. Cindy walked through the living room to go to the bathroom. When she opened the door to return to the bedroom and saw he was still awake, she approached and asked, "Can I sit down?"

Henry, nodding his head, moved, giving her the necessary space.

"Do you know you're not ugly at all?"

"What do you want... say?" Henry answered surprised.

"What I just said is that you are not ugly at all; indeed, if you cared more, you could be very attractive."

"Well! Thank you... for the compliment," he replied a little timidly.

"I see you are worried. Can I know what you have on your mind?"

"I would like you to tell me where all that money comes from. And finally, what are all these mysteries, maps, and secret codes in essence? I understand that we must be more than cautious, but still, I don't get it," Henry said, upset.

"I am sorry, but I can't tell you more. However, the less you know, the better it will be for you. I'll just tell you this, it's a bigger deal than it seems."

Henry remained silent.

"Well... it's late, I'm going to sleep, goodnight."

"Goodnight Cindy."

The woman gave him one last glance before heading to the bedroom, turning on the light, and undressing without closing the door. From the couch, Henry could see everything. He watched as she lay on the bed, her beautiful naked body uncovered by sheets. Eventually, he turned to the other side, preferring to stare at the wall in front of him.

Despite her beauty, something about her still didn't sit right with him. He felt no attraction or desire for her, even knowing that the girl at that moment was... very available, and even better, he could make Charles Lewis a cuckold.

Cindy lay naked on the bed for about half an hour, reading a magazine to pass the time. Finally, she whispered angrily, "Bastard! Why don't you come here?"

Hearing snoring from the other room, she cursed under her breath, "Asshole! I'll make you pay."

She got out of bed, turned off the lights in the room, closed the door and went back to bed.

IV

The next morning, around seven o'clock, Henry and Cindy went to pick up a blue Toyota Land Cruiser off-road vehicle from a garage in the area. Then, they headed for the border. After passing customs, they drove toward their destination, traveling all morning and part of the afternoon.

Cindy spent the entire time giving Henry directions but offered no conversation, behaving as if she were bored and uninterested. Henry tried several times to start a conversation, hoping to pass the time with some small talk, but she limited herself to answering with yes or no, and sometimes not even that.

"Something wrong Cindy?" Henry asked her to try for the umpteenth time to start a dialogue.

"No! I'm fine, why?"

"I don't know, you seem... upset."

"No! I'm fine," replied Cindy, trying to act normal.

"How long have you known Charles?"

"Almost four years, why?"

"Just pure curiosity."

"Oh yes! We have been engaged for four years and will get married soon."

"Oh, I didn't know that, well... best wishes."

"Thank you!" she replied coldly.

Henry wondered what that woman saw that was special about a worm like Charles Lewis. Perhaps she had not yet known him well, although, after four years, it seemed absurd to him.

So, he opted for another hypothesis. He remembered the old motto that said: "God makes them and then pairs them." He was convinced that Cindy and Charles had to be very similar, two peas in a pod.

This was one more reason not to trust her. Even though she had behaved decently with him so far, something about her still didn't sit right. Maybe it was her look, the way she spoke, or how she moved—something in her felt false, treacherous. Henry had sensed this from the beginning. He had voluntarily refused to have sex with Cindy the night before, which said a lot about his true feelings. Henry was usually not the type to easily give up having sex, especially with a beautiful woman like her.

As he mulled over these thoughts, he suddenly felt Cindy's hand caressing his right thigh. Turning, he gave her an inquisitive look, as if to ask, "What are you doing?" But Cindy didn't seem intimidated by his fleeting glance; on the contrary.

"I think the time has come to stop and stay overnight in some motel. Do you agree?" Cindy said, continuing to massage his thigh.

Henry hesitated for a moment, considering his options. "Yes! Of course, I agree. I'm tired of driving and need a good night's sleep."

After a few miles, they found a cheap motel where they could spend the rest of the night. While Henry filled the jeep's tank, Cindy went inside to book a room in the hotel.

"We're lucky. I managed to book the last room available, a double one. You don't mind sharing, do you?"

"No problem, just let me sleep," he replied.

They entered a cheap, miserable room. Henry placed their luggage on the floor and immediately lay down on the bed, letting Cindy go to the bathroom for a shower.

When she returned, she found Henry sleeping soundly.

"Wake up! Come on, wake up! Gosh! At least take off your shoes to sleep," she shouted, but despite her insistence, Henry was so tired he couldn't even muster the energy to respond.

In a fit of frustration, Cindy yanked off his shoes and threw them against the wall. She was furious. That man was totally ignoring her, and it was driving her crazy. She had tried everything to seduce him, yet he remained oblivious.

She had even lied to him by saying there were no more free rooms when, in fact, several single rooms were available. She began to believe that Henry might be *homosexual,* but willy-nilly, that man had to pay for his affront. In fact, she had never felt so humiliated in her life.

They left early in the morning. By early afternoon, Cindy was driving the vehicle through a dusty countryside. After about thirty miles, she took a narrow road leading to the mountains. The road was in terrible condition, and in many places, they feared falling into the abyss. Some parts of the narrow road were half broken, likely due to rainwater erosion. The country road seemed to stretch on forever, but eventually, they arrived near the ruins of a church in the most remote place imaginable.

Around them, there was only silence and desolation. The church had a courtyard with a small cemetery and several graves. In the center of the courtyard, there was a well and in front of it, two slabs of white marble.

Following Cindy's instructions, Henry used a crowbar to move the tombstone from the left grave. He began to dig until he uncovered a coffin. When he opened it, he found the bones of the deceased, a sight that disgusted him.

"Shit! I got the wrong grave. It's probably the one on the right," Cindy exclaimed in surprise.

Without answering, Henry began to dig the tomb on the right. Using the same method, he removed the coffin lid, and inside, found a leather briefcase. Quickly opening it, he saw it was filled with money.

Henry was enraptured by that vision. He had never seen so much money in his life.

Bad thoughts crossed his mind. He was almost tempted to punch that bitch in the face and run away with the loot. What did he have to lose? With this money, he could afford whatever he wanted and could start a new life in a new country. But Henry wasn't like that. He was an honest person, so he resisted the temptation.

"Don't waste time counting the money. It's two and a half million. But you're going to dig again because we have something else to take."

"More money?"

"Yes, more money, Henry, this is like a bank."

"Where does all this money come from, and how much more?" Henry wondered curiously.

Cindy took him to another tomb on the other side of the well, near the northern edge of the courtyard.

"Dig into the tomb with the inscription Rosario Gutierrez," she said coldly. He carried out the order, sweat dripping from his forehead, and opened the coffin. Inside was another leather briefcase. Opening it, he saw another mountain of 100-dollar bills, symmetrically deposited inside.

Henry, overwhelmed, continued to wonder where all the money came from and what story he had been dragged into. This was not a simple story of drugs; it was something much more.

"Ah huh, Henry? Are you surprised? What's wrong? You didn't expect this, did you?"

"No, I don't understand anything, absolutely nothing..."

"You haven't seen anything yet. You must open the last tomb, the most beautiful. Start   working, come on! Move... slave, ha-ha," laughed the woman wildly. Henry stared at Cindy intently, hating her more and more.

Despite this, he did as she had ordered, heading to another tomb on the east side of the courtyard. With practiced movements, he opened the tomb and couldn't believe his eyes: two leather briefcases lay inside. Opening them, he saw another huge amount of dollars.

Henry was about to begin counting, or at least touching, grabbing, those dollars when he was interrupted by a male voice.

"It should be another five million, Henry. Don't waste time counting them."

Surprised, Henry turned back and saw Tom Atkinson, Charles's best friend, who had suddenly appeared, silent as a ghost. Perhaps Tom had been hiding there the whole time, and now, holding a gun, he approached Henry menacingly.

Henry recognized him instantly, even though it had been almost twenty years since they had last seen each other. Tom had gained about twenty pounds, sported a belly, and despite being quite tall, looked stocky and flabby. His little green, emotionless eyes were hollower than before, and his chin was even more pointed. He was slightly bald, what was left of his curly blond hair was touched with gray, and he had a short beard.

"Dear Henry! Surprised to see me? Time has passed, hasn't it?" Tom shouted at him.

"Tom, what the hell are you doing here? Why do you have that gun in your hand? What's going on? I demand an explanation," Henry screamed in fear.

"The reason is you've gotten into a bigger story than you think, Henry and I'm sorry for you, but you are in deep shit," Tom replied cynically, stopping next to Cindy and kissing her. "Kill that pig. Kill him without mercy. That swine tried to have sex and to put his hands on me," Cindy confided to him with anger and hatred as she hugged him.

"Really?"

"Yes! Throughout the trip, he did nothing but try. He is a real pervert. He almost raped me," Cindy told him with a sincere tone.

"Ugly son of a bitch! Don't worry because I would have killed him even without knowing this," Tom replied, enraged.

At the same time Henry instinctively retreated, continuing to stare carefully at the two as they spoke in a low voice to each other. At some point, his escape backward was hindered by the well. In fact, continuing to retreat, looking ahead of him, not behind, he had not noticed it. He felt trapped.

Tom finished talking to Cindy and approached with a grim face until he stopped about 25 feet from him.

Henry shouted, "Explain to me what this is all about? Please."

The two snorted and laughed.

It was Cindy who started talking, "From the beginning, I didn't want you to be part of this story. It was Charles's idea. I'm sorry, nothing personal, it's just business, and now unfortunately, you are compromised in this matter."

"Yes! Henry! It's a business we've worked on for several years," Tom exclaimed while kissing the woman at the same time.

"But! Are you the woman of Charles or not?" Henry asked, confused by Cindy.

"Aah! Ahh! He believes that I am. And he asked me to marry him, but as you can see, I have better tastes in men," she replied, laughing wildly.

"Who, Tom? I think your taste is poor in this case too. You are out of your mind. They are both assholes, dickheads," Henry shouted angrily, staring into Tom's eyes.

"I don't know what's going on, and I don't want to know it. Let's call a truce. I will leave from here, disappearing from your life and from this affair forever. You can collect the money and do whatever you want. How does that sound?" Henry added, searching for a solution to get by this dire situation.

He was waiting for an answer from Tom, but he remained silent, keeping his wicked look. That silence lasted several seconds, creating even more tension.

Finally, Tom answered him, saying, "Poor loser! Are you trying to bargain for your life? Killing you is an act of mercy. You will never be able to do anything good in life, neither now, nor ever. You suck."

Then, with extreme malice, Atkinson added, "Farewell! Henry! Have a good trip to hell, piece of shit."

At the same time, he fired two gunshots at him.

Henry was hit and falling backwards, ended up in the well.

"Now we can go, Cindy! This problem has also been solved. Now it's your job. You know exactly what you must do."

"Yes, my love," replied the girl.

Tom picked up the empty shells of the nine millimeters and then looked very carefully inside the well but could not see Henry's body. "I can't see that bastard. He must be underwater. Well, everything went as planned. Now we can go back home, to our life," he said.

Hand in hand, the two lovers left the church. Cindy got into the jeep with Tom, and in a few moments, they disappeared onto the horizon.

Solitude and silence returned to reign in the ruins of the sinister church.

V

Henry had lost track of time. His left shoulder and the edge of his chest were hurting a lot. He was bleeding, but not excessively, and it was almost certain the bullets had gone through him. And he was very lucky because they hadn't pierced his heart.

Everything seemed cloudy to him.

All those surprises in a matter of minutes and those bastards who had tried to kill him.

Why did they try to kill him?

The well was not very deep, so he could touch the bottom with his toes. He had taken a fall of about 30 feet and had hit his back, so he felt very sore. He could see the sunlight coming in from the opening. The well was quite large, built in the shape of a bottle, and the water was cold and dirty. What dismayed him most was the absence of a rope or a ladder that he could use to climb out. His fate was sealed. He would have preferred to be dead already than to face this terrible end. He shivered from the cold, and his wounds continued to bleed.

Suddenly he began to shout, calling for help, blaspheming. But nothing.

No one would come, and nobody could hear him. He stood there at the bottom of that creepy well in the desert in the middle of nowhere. He felt doomed and began to cry, desperately moving around, consuming his last remaining energy.

As he walked, tiptoeing, slowly but incessantly, from one side of the well to the other, suddenly he stumbled upon a large object.

He momentarily lost his balance, and when he got back on his feet not far, he bumped again into another object and finally into a third one.

"What the hell is that?" He was surprised. Diving, he tried to lift one but failed.

In fact, the object was too heavy for him.

Intrigued, he began to touch it from all sides, and in the end, he was certain that it was a trunk or a chest.

To open the crate, he touched something like a long stick and instinctively grabbed the object to pry and open the trunk.

Henry was amazed by its weight and texture. And by the fact that it seemed to be "porous", and different from ordinary pieces of wood. In fact, it was not. It was the humerus of a human arm. He noticed it only when he took it to the surface and with the dim light coming from above, could see its shape.

Disgusted, he threw the bone away.

By now, he was tired.

Hours had passed, and he couldn't take it anymore. Even though the wounds had stopped bleeding, he was exhausted and feverish. He realized he was about to die.

From the opening of the well, less light entered as the sun was almost setting.

The cold water had numbed him so much he no longer felt his limbs. He had the urge to vomit, but he had nothing in his stomach. His whole life was passing before his eyes: he saw his daughter Chris, Theresa, Nathalie, and finally Jim smiling at him. He would have loved to hug and kiss all of them, even Nathalie, despite their cold relationships.

Henry wished he could ask for their forgiveness for the petty life he had led and all the mistakes he had committed. Especially Chris, who needed a role model and a caring, supportive father to help her navigate life.

He bitterly regretted accepting this assignment from an enemy like Charles Lewis. He began to cry, thinking of his family, whom he would never see again. His tears ended up in that filthy, cold water that surrounded him. By now, Henry was resigned; he had closed his eyes, and only the last bit of survival instinct made him stand straight.

The water reached his mouth and the tip of his nose. Henry no longer had the strength to stand straight. He kept his eyes closed when suddenly he heard something, like a distant bell.

At first, it seemed like the fruit of his imagination, but the noise continued and slowly became louder. Eventually, Henry had no more doubts—it was the sound of bells, like those on cattle. He waited, the noise slowly approaching but always distant, while he grew weaker and weaker. Trembling from the cold and burning with fever, he screamed with all the breath left in his lungs, hoping for a miracle.

He leaned deliriously against one of the walls of the well, where the water was relatively lower due to a step. The tragic events of the past hours drifted into his mind, blending fantasy and reality in his confusion. The bell sound had now totally disappeared. Perhaps it had never existed. Henry had lost touch with reality and time.

Just as he had given up the fight and surrendered to death, a whistle awakened him from his torpor. Yes! It was a human whistle, and now he could hear voices...

Yes! He wasn't dreaming, and someone was there. Instinctively, Henry raised his head to call for help, realizing that someone was already above, looking down into the well.

With his last bit of energy, Henry shouted repeatedly, his voice echoing up the narrow shaft. He then collapsed, unconscious.

VI

"Don't move, Señor. I know your wound still hurts, but this will help you," a beautiful Mexican lady gently told him in Spanish.

Henry had just woken up and for the first time, looked around. He was in a bed in a shabby, stark room, and the woman was medicating him. He felt tired, exhausted, sore, confused, and did not know where he was and what was happening. He was about to interrogate the woman when, before he could open his mouth, two children, a boy and a girl, burst into the room, chasing each other. The little girl, about seven years old, approached the bed and asked in Spanish how he felt.

Henry spoke and understood Spanish quite well, so he replied, "Good."

The woman, without being asked anything, said to him, "This is Carmen, and he is Alfonso," pointing to the child of about five years who was staring at him curiously, "and I am Concita, Señor... Señor who...?"

"Dawnin, Henry Dawnin."

"Oh Mr. Henry! You have been sick for a long time. Fortunately, now you are finally well, and you are almost healed."

"Thank you! Concita! Can you tell me where I am? And what happened? Please."

"Oh, you were almost dead when my husband Pedro and my son Antonio found you. It was a coincidence, and you were very lucky. Generally, they stay away from that old church, like everyone else. It is well known that place brings jinx; the devil lives there, and no one in these parts sets foot there. It is a deconsecrated place. Only the Godless and the devils can go there without being burned. You are not one of them, Señor Henry, are you? Tell me, why did you go there? What happened to you?"

"It's a long story, and now I'm too tired to talk about it, but tell me... How long have I been here?" Henry said, changing the subject purposefully.

"For a week, you've been here for a week."

"A week! My God!" He exclaimed in amazement.

He was speechless.

He had been unconscious for a whole week. He himself did not believe it.

"Where am I?" Henry asked the woman concerned.

"You are in my house, Señor Henry, in the countryside. As I was telling you, Pedro and Antonio were not far from the mission when they heard gunshots and saw a jeep moving away at great speed. Intrigued by this, they decided to go and see what had happened, and luckily, they found you. You had almost drowned when they got you out of the bottom of the well. Pedro's arm was sprained getting you out. Then you were in a frenzy all this time. Luckily, I managed to get you to eat a few bites of soup during the illness, and antibiotics did the rest. I didn't take you to the hospital because it's very far from here, but Pedro called Dr. Gomez. He's good at treating sheep, and he treated your wounds and prescribed medicines. We have not called anybody and kept this matter private because we mind our own business, and I believe we have done well, don't you think? Who is Theresa, Señor Henry? Your wife? You kept calling her in your sleep incessantly."

"Oh, Theresa is just a friend whom I haven't seen in a long time. What time is it?"

"Almost six o'clock in the afternoon. My husband and my son will be here soon. Do you feel like eating with us, or do you want to stay in bed?"

Henry felt very weak and had terrible back pain. Despite this, he tried to get up but did not have any energy and felt so bad that his vision faded, and he fainted immediately.

When he woke up, he was alone in the room.

He heard several voices in the other room, including that of a man who kept joking and talking loudly. Then, he could hear cutlery on the plates. Oh yes! They were eating and the smell quickly awakened his appetite.

Suddenly, the door opened, and a man entered. He was in his forties, stocky, dark, with a big mustache, short and dirty hair, and a good-natured, friendly face.

The man was surprised to see him awake, but despite this, curiously, he approached the bedside. He was followed by a teenage boy, taller than him, thin, with an unkempt mustache, his face covered with acne and greasy hair.

"How are you? Señor Henry, I am Pedro, and he is my son Antonio."

"I'm fine, thank you. Pedro. I can't tell you how grateful I am to you and your family. Thank you! Thank you very much for your help. I hope I can go tomorrow morning because I think I've already bothered you too much."

"Don't worry about it, Señor Henry. Think about healing. Dr. Gomez told me that you will have to rest for more than a week. I really don't think you'll be able to leave tomorrow morning. Do you feel like eating a bite?"

At that invitation, he instinctively nodded his head. Pedro promptly called the wife and asked her to prepare something to eat for the guest. After about twenty minutes, the woman entered the room carrying a tray with tortillas, chicken fajitas, black beans, and fruit.

Henry greedily devoured the food, and quickly finished the abundant dinner under the watchful and curious gaze of all the family members.

When he had finished, Pedro offered a cigarette, and the two men began to talk.

At one point, Pedro asked him what had happened.

It was already the second time in a short time that Dawnin heard that question.

He didn't feel like answering because he didn't know what to say.

He hesitated, trying to change the subject, but it was Concita this time who asked him the same question.

Finally, looking into the void, Henry confided to the hosts, "I was betrayed by a woman I barely knew. She and an associate tried to kill me. I have no idea why." He did not add anything else.

Realizing his embarrassment, Pedro and Concita wisely changed the topic.

After three days of staying idle in bed, Henry felt much better. So early in the morning he rose with the intention of going around exploring the surroundings of the farm.

During this time, Dawnin had socialized a lot with the hostess, Concita. He felt comfortable talking with her and, for this reason, shared much about his past: his marriage, his daughter, the pub, and Theresa.

Concita, too, had revealed much about her life, often dwelling on her marriage. It was evident that she was tired and bored of her married life. They had become friends, and Henry found himself increasingly attracted to her beauty. She was probably one of the most beautiful women he had ever met, so gentle and polite. He felt like he was in paradise with her company.

He had wondered several times what the woman was doing there. This was not the place for her. She was not only gorgeous, but also so refined. In fact, Henry believed that she was a much more educated and sophisticated person than she had let him believe. Concita didn't look like a peasant woman, the wife of a poor, illiterate sheep farmer. These thoughts increasingly occupied Henry's mind, and he started to have concerns about the whole situation. He had been treated fantastically by them, even too well, and had nothing to complain about, yet something told him to stay alert, very alert.

That morning, looking out the window of his bedroom, Henry saw the chickens wandering around the backyard, the two children playing, and Concita, who was doing laundry and other domestic tasks.

He was on a small farm in the countryside. The house was medium in size and had five large rooms. A spacious courtyard divided the house from a chicken coop; about 100 feet from the chicken coop stood a double fence for sheep. Finally, there was a small cottage on the opposite side of the sheep enclosure. He explored the house but did not go into the bedrooms. Then he came out the main door and slowly approached the woman.

He could observe her in the sunlight while she had her back to him, intent on hanging up the laundry. Instinctively, she turned around and, seeing him coming, greeted him affectionately. Concita was 32 years old, about five feet and 10 inches tall, with long hair and dark, inquisitive eyes. She was gorgeous, indeed.

Perhaps she seemed a bit overweight, probably because of the clothes she was wearing. After greeting her, they had a pleasant conversation.

Concita was talkative, but despite being so talkative, chatting did not distract her from the work.

When they were discussing, Henry couldn't help but notice her dress. She wore a blue summer dress with a rather deep neckline that revealed a little of her chest. Underneath, she did not wear a bra.

The woman did not care at all about this. Even when she leaned down, she did it without any inhibition or shame, although when she was bent, her big boobs were often visibly on display.

Henry did not understand if there was any malice in that attitude or if she did it naturally.

"Maybe she doesn't think about it and doesn't think she's so blatantly on display. She's certainly used to being this way here, at home, and today it's incredibly hot," he murmured to himself.

Henry was very attracted and excited by her. For this reason, he could not help but give a fleeting look at her. It was stronger than him, especially when Concita bent down to pick up the laundry.

He glanced at Concita and her beauty, trying to be discreet, but the lady noticed it and seemed a little resentful by that act, so he immediately lowered his gaze and blushed.

Henry had been caught red-handed and had made the figure of the peeping tom, of the "voyeur", but he was not. Henry was simply in love and attracted to her wonderful body, and with that look, he had tried to love her in his own way without attempting anything too explicit.

A timid infatuation, born quietly, which was turning more and more towards true love.

Yes! Love!

That was what he had felt for this woman from the first time he saw her. He had felt that intensity of emotions only one time before in his whole life, and that was with Nathalie, who became his wife and the mother of his child.

If Henry had not been so shy, he would have confessed everything to Concita. He would have proposed to her to flee together away, far away.

However, he was aware of the thousand problems that stood between them, such as her family and her husband. Moreover, why would she want to abandon everything to follow an unknown adventurer like him?

No! There was no logical sense in what he was fantasizing.

Concita bent down to pick up a pair of pants and checked him with a look, but this time, he stared into her eyes, smiled amiably and then said to her, "You are beautiful."

This time, it was she who blushed when she replied, "Thank you."

Henry dared not say more. The conversation between them decreased in intensity until it stopped. It seemed they no longer had anything to talk about it.

Concita continued her housework, and Henry, despite his state of weakness, desired her more and more ardently. In the end, to escape from any temptation, he asked if he could take a shower. In fact, he felt dirty and wanted to clean up.

"Of course! Henry, but unfortunately, the water heater does not work, so you can't use the bathroom. Luckily, we have a large tub where we wash. I can warm it up with hot water, and you can bathe on the other side of the courtyard. Don't worry, it's private and who will pass by here?"

Henry was surprised because he did not expect this answer, but thinking about it… well, why not? A nice pioneer-style outdoor bath was a great idea, and above all, it would be a new thing.

In a short time, Concita prepared the hot water.

He was a bit worried about the wounds and had just finished expressing his problem, so Concita replied, "Don't worry, I'll give you a hand to wash after I'm done with the laundry."

Henry undressed and went into the tub. The wounds did not hurt very much, so he had a bath without any difficulty.

He had finished washing his hair when she arrived.

"I see you're almost done. If I had known, I would have come sooner," she said with a smile.

"My back is all yours."

Hearing those words, Concita approached, took the sponge, and gently rubbed his shoulders with soap. At that moment, Henry felt in heaven, having his ideal and desired woman there, smiling, in front of him. "Perhaps I will be lucky today. She likes me. Yes! Yes! She does. She's attracted to me," Henry thought with immense joy.

"I must try! This woman is driving me crazy. But what can I do?"

The solution to his *dilemma* came very soon. Concita moved his face to wash his back, and Henry did not miss the opportunity and kissed her gently on the left cheek. She didn't say anything. He continued to kiss her gently all over her face until he slowly reached her mouth. The woman had stiffened. Henry noticed in her a certain embarrassment, and it seemed to him as if she did not know what to do.

"Stop!" She said with little conviction. He did not obey and kissed more fervently. She did not withdraw, nor did she participate, remaining frozen.

"Come on! Stop! You know that I am a married woman," she said awkwardly after a few seconds of interminable silence.

"I know! But I can't do anything about it. You drive me crazy. You're the most attractive girl I've ever met in my life," Henry replied from the bottom of his heart.

"Really?"

"Yes! Concita! You are. And I've met a lot of women. You are the most beautiful and the sweetest."

"I also... like you!" She exclaimed as if to take off an enormous weight in the depths of her soul.

"Then kiss me."

"It's not... right."

"Why is it not right?" Henry said, interrupting the kissing.

"Because I know nothing about who you are and because I'm a married woman," she replied defensively.

"You can't command the heart."

That said, he kissed her passionately, and she gave in. They continued kissing for a while.

"Let me finish washing your back," Concita said after a few minutes.

"Please go ahead."

She started doing so, but suddenly, the soap slipped from her hands and ended up in the tub. A little hesitant, she tried to find it. She bent down so that the wide dress had no more secrets.

Henry inserted two fingers into the neckline of the dress, keeping it open.

The beautiful big breasts were there on display. Henry observed them closely, while Concita was looking for the soap.

"You have fantastic tits," Henry commented libidinously.

(Henry could no longer hold back the emotion, yet his excitement ended after Concita took back the soap and returned to wash his back).

"You're a pig," she scolded him.

"For having appreciated your breasts?"

"No! But for opening the neckline of my dress to see them. There is nothing to do! You men are all the same," she replied.

"I won't do it anymore," exclaimed Henry and at the same time, gave her a kiss on the mouth and widened her neckline again like a mischievous child.

"Okay! That's it! I'll go home. Once you get dressed, you can reach me there," she said, slightly upset by his umpteenth *joke.*

Henry quickly got dressed and went to look for his beloved lady.

He passed by the yard, where he met the children playing.

She was in the kitchen. He walked in and sat in an old armchair, didn't say anything, just contemplated her, fantasizing about her immense beauty.

It was she who broke the silence that reigned between them. "You know Henry, I often feel so lonely here and wonder why I'm in this place forgotten by God. If it was not for my children, I would have already left this house long ago. I ruined the best years of my life for nothing. It's too late for me to change places, go to a different city or make new friends in a different place. It's too late," she said with a gloomy tone.

"What do you say, Concita! You are a beautiful young woman, and you can have a decent life wherever you go, you just must believe it. How old are you?"

"Thirty-two, why?"

"You speak as if you were sixty, gosh! At thirty-two years, you have a life ahead of you," Henry said, trying to cheer her up.

"Do you really think so?"

"Indeed. Well! You can come... no, forget…" Henry said, stammering and not finishing the sentence.

"What do you mean? Come on speak? Don't be shy," she asked him curiously.

Henry nibbled his lip nervously as if he could not express his thoughts or as he was too embarrassed about what he wanted to say.

After a moment of silence, he said, "Would you like to come with me? I need a woman like you by my side. I love... and desire you."

Henry turned red with shame and did not dare to look into her eyes, so he stared at the chandelier, waiting for the answer.

"Don't you think that it is a little too early for this, and…"

"Yes, you are right. I am moving too fast in this affair," he exclaimed, interrupting her halfway, not knowing what the conclusion was.

"Henry! I'm a married woman, you remember that don't you?"

"Yes! You're right! What a jerk I've been. Please forgive me and don't think about it anymore," he said in a sad tone.

"No! Instead, I will think about it... and I will give you an answer as soon as possible. But leave me quiet to reflect."

Henry was stunned, as he did not expect that answer.

"Then all is not lost. There is some hope on the horizon," he murmured with joy.

The day had passed without any further news.

Henry had gone around the countryside, played with the children, and had, for the first time, thought about everything that happened in the last period.

He had only one regret: having betrayed Pedro's good faith by trying to take his wife away from him. However, he tried not to think about that, to focus on what had happened to him thanks to Charles Lewis and associates.

He had been tricked and almost killed like a dog by them.

Now, he wanted revenge.

Finally, Henry Dawnin found a real purpose for his existence: he had to find out what murky affair he had gotten himself into. It was time to get to the bottom and investigate the dirty matter. He could not forget that old Ray Brown, was killed by a hit-and-run car shortly after a fight with those bullies at the bar. And the old case filed, and now concluded, of Ashley and Leslie, two poor girls raped and killed by unknown persons, who perhaps were not so unknown.

Then what to think of Tom Atkinson, who had inexplicably shot him twice and almost killed him in cold blood, or the beautiful, wicked, twisted Cindy who had cheated him from the first moment of their journey.

It was also time to find out what was hidden inside that well, especially in those crates that had nearly broken his leg. Now, it was up to him to decide when and how to act.

He knew he needed to proceed without haste, waiting for the right moment. For now, he had a safe haven and believed he could repay his hosts. If his suspicions were correct, he would never again have a problem with money.

At about seven o'clock, Pedro and Antonio returned home for dinner and sat down for a frugal meal with Henry and the rest of the family.

Henry noticed that a couple of hours earlier, Concita had changed into a modest dress, completely contrasting with the one she had worn earlier in the day. She also wore a sturdy bra.

Pedro, in a good mood, talked incessantly. Suddenly, Henry interrupted to ask him what he knew about the old mission.

"That is a cursed place. Only damned souls can go there without being annihilated," replied the sheepman in a concerned tone.

"Have you ever seen something strange or abnormal?" Henry asked, intrigued.

"As a child, my father and his friends told me frightening stories of monsters and demons that roam there. No one can go there, especially at night, because the devils go out at that time to kill people and drink their blood."

"Okay, Pedro! I understand there are demons who dwell in the deconsecrated mission and kill people. Despite all the local stories and legends, have you ever seen anything strange? Abnormal? Have you seen foreign people?" Henry asked a little abruptly.

"No! I do not think so. You must understand that I always avoid that area as much as I can. When I found you, it was by pure chance, I was there because a couple of young sheep were lost and ended up in those surroundings. Hold on! A moment! A moment, now I remember something peculiar I saw that happened there. A few years ago, I was on a hill from where you can see the mission in the distance, and it was an autumn afternoon. Suddenly, a big helicopter came and landed inside the courtyard of the mission. I was very intrigued and wondered: why does a big helicopter land in a place abandoned by God? After less than an hour the helicopter quickly took off and disappeared on the horizon. I was so far away that I could see very little, indeed, almost nothing of what was happening. However, I had the impression that of the three or four men who arrived, in the end, only one left."

"What do you mean? Maybe they remained in the mission, don't you think so?" Henry exclaimed surprised.

"No! The others were gone, disappeared. Perhaps what I am telling you is just an impression that I had at the time, it may be that I am totally wrong. But I swear to you that I felt something was not right."

"Maybe you are right, or maybe not. Maybe they really disappeared as you say," Henry replied, remembering the human humerus bone he accidentally grabbed when he was inside the well.

Oh yes! Certainly, in the well, there were big surprises.

Suddenly, he interrupted Pedro, who was continuing to tell his story, asking, "I need your help. In a couple of days, when I'm better, I want to explore the inside of that well. Can you help me?"

"You're crazy! I don't want to go back to that place."

"We will go in the morning. You told me that demons come out at sunset or during the night, so we have nothing to fear, do we?" Henry exclaimed in a mocking tone.

"I don't know, it doesn't seem to me to be the case and..." Pedro answered, confused.

"Dad! What are you afraid of? We've gone there once, and we're still safe and sound, no!" Antonio said, interrupting his father's dismay and indecision.

"Come on, you won't regret it," Henry added, giving a fleeting glance at Concita, who was smiling.

"Okay, all right, I understand. We'll go there in four days on Sunday, so don't bug me anymore. Let's do it," Pedro muttered unhappily while Concita poured the rest of the bottle of beer into his glass.

After dinner, Henry went out for a walk outside and then sat in a chair on the veranda.

He was thoughtful and desired Concita more and more. In fact, despite having tried not to think about her for the rest of the day, devoting himself to something else, now he could not help but fantasize about this beautiful woman who stole his heart.

And as if he had called her, suddenly she appeared and sat next to him.

"What are you thinking about?" She asked.

"About you," he replied.

"Seriously?" She teased him.

"It's true! I fell in love like a little boy. I can't do anything about it. There is something in you that drives me crazy. Come with me! Concita! You will see that we can enjoy life... because... yes, you... you don't know that..." Henry couldn't continue the sentence.

"What do you mean? Come on! Don't be shy. Tell me?" She asked, amused.

"Well! If it's as I think, we could be rich... and have so much money we could afford what we want. And if you want, we can give a lot of money to your husband and family. Thus, they will not be too much...

afflicted by your... separation," Henry stammered, trying to calibrate the words as best he could and was feeling very embarrassed.

"Do you really want me to come with you?"

"More than ever."

"What if I came and brought the small children with me?" The woman said in a somewhat provocative tone.

Henry squinted, surprised. It was not an eventuality he had considered, and he was not happy at all with that possible outcome, although in the end, he did not reject the idea and nodded his head.

"I am more and more surprised by you, Henry Dawnin, and fascinated. I don't know anything about your past, yet I'm here, hearing your proposals, and almost... approve them. You are a handsome man, a mysterious adventurer, who came from who knows where, and I bet you are not evil but a good fellow. Anyway, tell me about this money, where do you want to go to find it? Do you want to rob something?"

"No! No robbery! The money is hidden in a safe place. At least, I think," Henry exclaimed uncertainly.

"Where? Come on! Tell me, you know you can trust me," Concita asked with great interest.

Henry looked at her suspiciously and did not reveal anything.

"I'll tell you later," he replied, cutting it short.

"I want to know one thing about you, Henry! And you must answer me sincerely."

"What?"

"Have you ever killed someone?"

"Are you kidding?"

"No! I speak seriously. Trust me! I will never betray you. I just want to know you better. That's all! I believe it is my right to know it in case I flee with you."

"I've never killed anyone, and I've never hurt even a fly. I am the most upright, honest person in the world. I swear to you! I'm not a criminal. You must believe me. I have no reason to lie to you."

"I believe you," she said.

Then Concita clutched and kissed him ardently, so much that he could not remove his lips from hers.

Finally, after a while, he stopped and said, concerned, "What in the world! Are you crazy? Your husband is at home."

"Don't worry, he is sleeping. Everyone is asleep."

They continued to kiss for a long time.

VII

SEATTLE, WASHINGTON, several days before the latest events

"Cindy! Can I know what happened to you? You arrived late, you didn't give me any explanation, talk? What the hell happened?" Charles inquired, irritated.

"That bastard of your friend Henry Dawnin betrayed us, Charles, he fucked us. And you said we could trust him. Watch! He almost killed me. Look at the bump I have on my head."

"Oh Cindy, I'm sorry, love..."

"This bump is nothing, that pig… that pig, he also raped me."

Cindy said in tears as she embraced him tenderly.

She carried on telling her side of the story. "Everything had gone as planned until we got to the old mission. There we dug and found the briefcase. While I was about to check the money, that bastard hit me with the butt of a gun. When I came back, I was tied on the ground. Seeing me awake, the bastard, before leaving with the loot, tore my blouse with violence and raped me while beating me furiously. Look at my back and my shoulders," Cindy cried, showing a series of bruises and injuries.

"That son of a bitch, may he be damned for the whole eternity. Piece of crap! So, after he got the money, he left?" Charles screamed in anger.

"Yes! Charles and it is a coincidence that I am also alive. That bastard left me tied up and gagged there in the cemetery of the mission, where not even a dog sets foot. Then, making fun of me, he left a small knife about 15 feet from me, telling me to roll like a worm to get it and free myself. I can tell you the actual words he told me before leaving, 'roll slut and with your mouth, take this knife. If you can get it and cut the ropes, well done. If not, die. If by any chance you succeed, do not forget to greet that big idiot of Charles. Tell him that I have always hated him since the first time I saw him and am so glad to steal his money that he can't imagine. And tell him not to bother looking for me because he will never find me.' That said, he walked away with the money, laughing and singing."

Charles, after listening with his mouth open to his fiancée's story, vented his anger by kicking a small table that ended up smashing onto the floor.

Then he punched a lamp that was nearby, and with a drool in his mouth, he rolled on the floor and spat on the walls of tables and chairs until he got one of the chairs and threw it out the window, shattering the glass. He was scary, beginning to swear at everything and everyone, and shouting like a madman. He swore to take revenge on Henry.

There was no place on earth where that traitor could take refuge because even at the end of the world, he would find and kill him.

The old resentment, mixed with the new affronts he received, was driving Charles crazy. He had always hated Henry for the old story about Nathalie, the only defeat of his life.

Now that man stole his money, cheated on him, and *fucked* his future wife, raped her, to be precise.

(From that selfish man who was Charles, he didn't think in the slightest about the pains, the shame, and the affront suffered by Cindy).

He didn't care about that at all.

He was convinced **Henry** had done it to spite him.

Cindy's lies had worked very well.

Henry was responsible for stealing the money.

Henry was the culprit, the villain, the traitor.

Henry was the man who had to pay for what he had not done.

Cindy, in her afflicted and sad mood, enjoyed the whole scene and was almost bursting with laughter to see Charles so furious. Everything was going the right way for her, and her partner Tom Atkinson. Charles did not have a single clue about what had really happened in that sinister abandoned church in the middle of nowhere.

THE NEXT DAY IN A LUXURIOUS BELLEVUE OFFICE

"So, Cindy was robbed, cheated and deceived by this Henry... Henry... who?"

"Henry Dawnin, Uncle Andrew. He had to be our courier for the operation. Henry was one of my classmates in high school, but sorry, this time I was wrong. I thought he would be the right man. I promised him a nice sum of money and believed that for one without a penny and a future, that would be a good reason to do the job well, yet I deceived myself. I will try everything to make up for my mistake, Uncle, I swear to you."

"Why did you come up with the idea of using this man? Charles! We have hundreds of people who can do this work and who are especially reliable and loyal. Why did you choose this Henry Dawnin?"

"Uncle! I have known him for a long time, and I cordially hate him. To be honest, he is the person I hate the most in the world..." Charles was interrupted by his uncle.

"So why did you hire him?" Andrew Martin roared in rage.

"It's simple! I thought he was the right man for the operation. In fact, he's a tough guy. I also considered him a man of honor, one of those people who, when he says something, does it despite anything that could happen. This is what discourages me. I thought he was one of them, an idealist. And finally, my best reason was that man would never pocket the promised money. In fact, Doug had the order to kill him at the end of the mission, when we would bring the goods to the predetermined place. Oh yes! This was my plan, to give a splendid death to that son of a bitch. So, I could cancel an old score, but unfortunately, the devil put his tail on it, and we lost the money and the renegade Dawnin. How do people change with time, or maybe it's me who is getting older? What do you think, Uncle?"

"Maybe... Charles, or maybe not! Don't you think Cindy could have lied to you?"

"But Uncle! How can you say that? You know who she is, don't you?"

"I know. She's almost your wife. However, there is something that does not fit for me in this whole matter. Something is fishy," Andrew said, perplexed.

"I don't understand that! Uncle! How can you doubt Cindy?" Charles exclaimed in a defensive tone.

"Yes! I know her and know her well. However, I don't know. There's something I don't like about her. You know! I generally mind my own business and keep my opinions private. However, in this case, I cannot do it for the love I have for you. Also, in your place I would not trust Tom too much. There are many sweet smiles between them. I've always told you what I think about that lad. I am convinced Tom is treacherous, very treacherous. I have never trusted him, and you know it well, since THAT... NIGHT."

"Don't worry, Uncle Andrew. Tom is an invention, a creature of mine, and he can do nothing to his *master*. He's a puppet, and I'm the one who pulls the strings to make him move. Be calm! Everything is under control."

"I hope so, Charles, you know! Since your father died, I have almost replaced him for your sake. Harold was like a brother to me. We have worked for years together at the agency, and I want for you the best there is in life," Andrew said with tenderness.

"I know, Uncle Andrew, you are my second father and always will be. You can't image how much I am grateful to you," Charles said with a sincere smile.

The only person in the world that Charles Lewis respected and feared was Andrew Martin. Andrew was the real brains behind their organization. He was incredibly smart and cunning, a man above average who could make a difference at any time.

The main difference between them was that while Charles was a crude, evil punk of mediocre intelligence who acted mostly driven by instinct, like a wild animal, Andrew, despite being as evil as Charles, had style. He was refined, well-educated, witty and a pleasant person to be around.

He was a very difficult character to describe and analyze. He could be the most ruthless, wicked person in the world against his enemies, as he could be caring, affectionate and sweet with loved ones.

Also, Andrew was a very enthusiastic food lover. His passion for Italian cuisine was well known to all. The few fortunate dudes who had the privilege to eat in his gigantic mansion had an incredible gastronomic culinary experience, enjoying those dishes that Sebastiano, the Italian chef, was preparing daily with art and devotion.

Sebastiano was a young Neapolitan man who had worked for a while in Andrew's villa. The chef had a very good salary indeed, Andrew was generous with him, and the Italian was very proud and happy with his job. The other side of the coin was that poor Sebastiano had to abide daily a series of insults and racist remarks from his boss. Being called a "slave" was one of these.

Before Charles took leave from Andrew Martin's luxurious Louis XVI-style office, the grizzled and still handsome middle-aged man asked him, "Would you like sushi?"

"Why not! Yes! I have a good appetite."

"Fantastic! I know a Japanese restaurant, not far from here, that has the best sushi in all of Seattle and its surroundings. Remember I am an expert in food. Let's go to have a nice meal."

The two men left the office to go eat... sushi.

Meanwhile, in an elegant Italian restaurant in downtown Seattle, Tom enjoyed a dish of pasta carbonara, while Cindy savored seafood spaghetti with mussels, shrimp, and clams. At the same time, they were drinking a nice bottle of Italian sparkling white wine.

In the middle of the lunch, Tom asked with malice and enjoyment, "So, he believed everything you told him?"

"Yes! Word for word. Poor idiot! Charles was dying from anger. Now, he will begin to hunt, searching for a ghost. Ah! Ah."

"Do you think he can find out we also took the other money?"

"So, what! When he revealed to me the existence of that money, he was completely stoned and drunk. He even forgot what he had for dinner. Calm down! Everything is fine. That evening, I facilitated his talkativeness with magic powders I put in his wine. So don't worry we will not have any problems, we are cool," Cindy spoke with confidence.

"I love you, Cindy. You are terrific."

Tom exclaimed, laughing cheerfully, toasting his partner.

VIII

The next morning, Henry felt fine.

He woke up around half past eight and opened the window to let in some fresh air.

It was a wonderful day.

He noticed that the sheep were not on the farm; Pedro and Antonio had gone out early in the morning. He was satisfied, as it meant he could spend the entire day with Concita without being disturbed.

He had just put on his trousers when she knocked on the door.

"Come in."

The woman came into his room and said, "Can I make your bed now or do you want to rest a little more?"

"Yes! You are welcome! Go ahead," He answered gladly.

Henry was surprised that Concita was not yet dressed. In fact, she was wearing a white, good quality, expensive and rather transparent nightgown.

(He considered her beautiful and sexy and never imagined he could admire her in this way.)

"I see that this morning you are taking it quite easy. You haven't dressed yet! Are you sick?" Henry spoke, having nothing more serious to say.

"You'll get used to me, and how I am," Concita replied with a smile.

"What do you mean?"

"You got it, don't be naïve."

"You mean that... you'll come with me," Henry exclaimed with emotion.

"Yes! I will come with you! I will be your girlfriend. I decided... I just hope I will not regret this decision," she said with a hint of dismay.

"Why will you regret it? Any place will always be better than this rathole in the desert. You will see! We will be happy together."

"I really hope so."

"If you want, we could leave tomorrow too, if only Pedro could help me explore the well! We would leave instantly," exclaimed Henry.

"You're crazy! He can't do it for several days, and besides, you're still convalescing. You must stay here," the woman replied categorically.

Henry watched Concita make his bed. He was ecstatic.

"You know! I like this nightgown you wear; it leaves very little space for imagination. Above all! I like what's... under. But what might your husband think?"

"Why do you always think of him? Think about yourself for once," she replied in a soft voice.

"Yes! You're right, I'll do it. Are you always like this, an exhibitionist?"

"I am not," she replied to the provocation.

Henry blocked her from behind and kissed her neck and lips.

After a few minutes, she jumped on him. Henry fell on the bed. Then she took off her nightgown. She had a gorgeous body. They began to make love wildly.

Her big breasts excited him. Concita was a hot and wild woman, and Henry had not had sex of this kind for a long time. Perhaps because of this, or because of his debilitated physical state, his sexual performance was quite short and unsatisfactory. After the animalistic sexual stimulus ended, Henry collapsed exhausted on the bed, recovering from fatigue. Concita got up to go to the bathroom. Henry stared at her carefully, noticing how beautiful she was. Watching her naked body in the sunlight, for the first time, he felt a strange sensation.

The woman did not look at all like the mother of three children. Her body was much more muscular, and fit than he had thought before. Probably, the large dresses she wore made her look a little heavier than she was.

Concita returned from the bathroom and put on her nightgown.

"I haven't seen or heard the children, where are they?" he asked, intrigued.

"They are at a friend's house," the woman replied without paying too much attention.

A moment of silence reigned between them.

Concita was about to leave the room, then seemed to think again, and turned around asking, "I would like to know why you want to go back down into the well. What do you think is there?"

"I don't know, but I want to find out as soon as possible. You must know while I was in there, I stumbled upon something like an iron trunk," Henry replied, a little surprised by the question.

Dissatisfied, she asked, "Could you tell me what happened to you? What story did you get involved in?"

"No! I'm sorry."

"Why? Come on, tell me?" she asked again with persistence.

"No. Maybe I'll tell you in the future, but not now," Henry exclaimed, irritated.

The woman was quite annoyed with his answer and left the room pouting.

Henry was also hurt because he had no intention of offending her. But he was also a little unnerved by her insistence.

After several hours, Concita went out to make some purchases. Before leaving, she asked if he wanted to accompany her to the village, but Henry preferred to remain alone at the farm, immersed in tranquility and solitude. However, his true reason was different.

Henry was beginning to experience those strange feelings he had at the beginning, feelings that the romantic event had only mitigated a little. Something didn't add up in the whole affair. Now that he was feeling better, he started to see events differently.

It seemed to him that Pedro and Concita wanted to keep him with them as long as possible for no apparent reason. Although he tried hard, he could not understand their motives. Concita's behavior was rather ambiguous. If she was willing to leave with him, why had she delayed him with the excuse of convalescence? And why did she always ask those same questions about the well, the church, and the trouble he was involved in? Why had they waited all those days before going into the well? They could have gone the same day instead of wasting all that time.

Above all, Henry wondered why they had trusted him so much from the beginning. After all, he was a stranger, a foreigner, an adventurer.

For any sensible person, it could pose a danger. How come they had not called the police or warned anyone, except that elusive doctor, who had come when he was in a coma and therefore had never seen? In this place, he had not met any friends or relatives of the hosts, and no one had ever visited.

And finally, this was one of his greatest points of apprehension. No man of common sense would have left his wife and offspring alone with a stranger involved in who knows what murky affair. Pedro seemed to disappear during the day to allow his wife to vent her lust.

Either he was an idiot or a naïve poor cuckold, or there was something else underneath.

He just had these thoughts when he noticed a glimmer from a hill less than a mile away from the house. Something was shining in the sun. Given the distance, it was not easy to understand what it was, but something over there continued to shine.

Henry stared carefully at that point, and in the end, was almost sure it was a binocular lens.

Someone was spying on him. He decided to go and find out what was hidden and located the exact point and route to take. Henry was not expecting that whoever was there was waiting to offer a drink, but he saw no other alternative. He had to move, and the time had arrived to discover what was going on.

The journey proved to be more strenuous than it seemed at first. The hill was difficult to climb, and he did not feel like overdoing it in his depleted physical condition.

He had lost the glimmer of binoculars for some time.

"Who knows where *the mysterious friend* ended up?" he murmured.

In two hours, after several stops, he reached the desired point.

Everything was deserted, as he had imagined, but he found important clues.

The semi-barren ground was very trampled on as if more than one person had stayed there for some time. Several cigarette butts were scattered around. He collected the cigarettes, butt by butt until he reached a total of eleven cigarettes.

He found that while all the butts were of local brands, three were Gitanes, cigarettes imported from France. "Who the hell smokes French cigarettes in the most remote place in Mexico?" he murmured, puzzled.

During his investigation, he also noticed grooves in the ground. At first, they seemed to belong to a bicycle, but Henry soon realized that there were two and always went in parallel and the same distance. They looked like wheelchair tracks. He was confused. The tracks were clearly visible, so he began to follow them. They climbed to the top of the hill. When he reached the top and saw the view, he was totally stunned.

On the other side, there was a small town, about a mile away, with streets, houses, and shops. He was amazed because he believed he was much farther from any inhabited center than he was. He stopped to observe the landscape in a careful way. He tried to locate where the sinister church was, but looking at the horizon, he could not see either the old mission or anything familiar to him.

The village was in the middle of a small valley. A long and straight road was the main artery and the only access route in the area. All the houses had been built around it. After stopping for a few minutes, he resumed following the still visible tracks, up to the point where they reached a dusty country road and disappeared.

It was simple.

The furrows of a jeep left no doubt. Those people had parked their vehicle there and then left. Who knows where they had gone now? Despite this, Henry was not disappointed because he expected something similar. Kneeling, he picked up another butt of "Gitanes". The mysterious friend had smoked a lot. He wondered if the person who had smoked "Gitanes" was the leader of the gang. It was only an intuition, but it could also be true.

He felt a little tired and was also thirsty but was in the mood for a nice cold drink and a good meal. The town was not that far away.

Henry checked the money he had and counted more than a hundred dollars, a little discolored by the dip he took in the well but still valid. "But yes! Let's go to eat," he thought.

Slowly walking on the edge of the dusty road, he reached the outskirts of the village. On the way, he was quite thoughtful and upset, but in another way, he was also excited about the whole affair. He compared himself to an investigator in search of the truth.

Finally, he arrived. Many people were walking on the sidewalks, and there was a lot of car traffic. It was clearly the downtown area.

Seeing a bank, he decided to change some of his dollars. As soon as he entered, a sturdy guard greeted him, looking at him a little suspiciously. Reciprocating the greeting, he lined up to wait for his turn. Several people, mostly women, crowded the bank, but despite the confusion, only two windows were open.

After forty-five minutes, Henry finally managed to change 50 dollars into pesos.

However, he regretted having entered the bank. In fact, he had waited a long time for a simple transaction, and it was hot, humid, and he was sweating a lot.

"Why don't you use the air conditioning? This room is hot, and staying here is unpleasant," he asked, irritated to a cashier.

"Does it really feel hot? Today, it's quite cool," the woman replied, surprised by what she heard.

Impatient, he grabbed the money and went out of that furnace. It was time to eat, drink and forget.

Walking on the main street, he saw several little restaurants. He went inside the one he liked the most. In fact, although the restaurant was full of people, he was lucky and did not have to wait for a table. He sat at a table next to a window overlooking the street, from where he could observe what was happening

He was very hungry, and after reading the menu, his hunger increased immeasurably.

While Henry was thinking about what to order, a stocky waitress brought "chips and salsa" and asked if he wanted something to drink.

"A margarita on the rocks."

"Are you American?" She asked, attracted by his accent.

"Yes!"

"From where?"

"California."

"Will you take me there, Señor?" She asked him jokingly.

"If you want! But it's not much better than here. It's just more expensive," Henry replied, smiling at her.

The waitress left in a good mood, and Henry began to devour the appetizer.

After a few minutes, the woman brought him the margarita. Dawnin did not waste time and greedily grabbed the glass, saying to himself "I will drink ten of these and fuck off to my enemies."

The idea of being alone, feeling good, and being self-sufficient made him happy.

In that moment he had shaken off all the dark events of the last period.

Henry did not think of his misadventures, and nothing seemed to disturb him anymore.

To celebrate, he ordered *carne asada,* one of his favorite dishes.

While he was enjoying his lunch, he casually glanced at the road and saw Concita's car pass by with another lad on board. The vision was like a *flash,* too fast to be well visualized, but he was sure it was her, along with an unknown friend.

"Well! Maybe it's some relative or acquaintance," he exclaimed to himself after a moment of reflection.

He resumed eating and drinking without worrying about it. Finally, seeing that it was late, he paid the bill and left the restaurant. Unhappy about going back to the farm, he decided to explore the little town.

He wandered for more than an hour, aimlessly, just to spend time. Then, it was time to go back.

On the way he made numerous stops, a little to catch his breath, a little to enjoy the moment of freedom as much as possible.

After an hour, he was at the top of the hill and could observe Pedro's house from above. Concita's car was parked under the shade of a tree. Pedro had not yet returned home. In fact, the sheep pen was empty. He sat down to contemplate the view and lit a cigarette. It was also a good excuse to lay down the plastic bag he had in his hand all that time. He had bought a bottle of red wine and one of white that he intended to offer to the hosts.

During the rest Henry reflected on the whole situation.

Perhaps he had fantasized too much, creating non-existent fears. Why would his guests organize a plot against him? Who would have wanted that? His real enemies believed he was dead at the bottom of the well. Probably Pedro was a simpleton who wrongly trusted people and his wife, which is truly unusual in a world where no one can be trusted, even the closest relatives. Regarding Concita, well, she had a beautiful, healthy and powerful body. Why was that so strange? It meant that she kept fit.

Furthermore, she was his magnificent lover, generous, smart, and sensual. Why did she want to hurt him? But why did she always ask those same questions over and over?

She was certainly too curious about him.

Henry was perplexed and hesitant and, as a part of him cast out all doubt, the other made him become fearful and alert.

After much reflection, he decided to be alert because "Trusting is good, but not trusting is better."

He returned home before seven o'clock.

Concita was in the kitchen, but there was no sign of the children.

"Look what I brought you! This Californian wine is great," he told her, giving her a kiss on the cheek.

"Oh, thank you! You're nice. Where have you been all this time?"

He told her part of his day, omitting the most important part, about the men who had spied on him with binoculars from the hill.

"See anything interesting on the way?" she asked.

"What do you mean? What do you mean by interesting? I saw a beautiful view, a couple of rabbits, hawks, and finally, beautiful women in the village where I have been. Yes! I saw many interesting things. It was a pleasant day," Henry replied gladly.

"So that's all? Nothing else interesting, unusual, strange?" The woman asked, in a slightly wary tone, as if she feared Henry was hiding something from her.

Henry marveled at that tone and became suspicious.

Why all those questions, even though they could ultimately be innocent questions?

To try to change the subject, Henry approached and kissed her saying, "I saw this morning the most beautiful woman in the world, and guess who was she? It was you."

"Thank you! I'm glad you had fun, very happy," Concita said amicably, but with a slight tone of discouragement.

"And what did you do?" He asked her, just to divert the conversation.

"Nothing special, usual things, usual life, boring life."

As Concita spoke, the sheep's trampling and bleating announced her husband's imminent arrival.

"What do you think? Can I tell Pedro that you have beautiful boobs?" he asked, mocking her.

"Tell him whatever you want. I don't care," she replied, leaving the room.

IX

"Could you accompany me to the old mission, so that I can go inside on my own, into the well," Henry asked in a firm tone to Pedro as they were eating at the table.

The man seemed surprised and confused at the request and did not know what to answer:

"But how? We didn't say... for another day... I don't know... tomorrow ... really... but... Yes!... It's true... ah, yes! Maybe I have another commitment... and...."

"Pedro you're free for the afternoon, don't you remember? At three o'clock, you have nothing to do, do you?" Concita interrupted the stuttering man with a tone of command.

Henry was impressed by the woman's tone. It seemed she was the one who decided for her husband or instructed him in the direction she wanted.

"Yes! It's true, now I remember, you're right Concita. After three o'clock, I have no commitment, it's true."

"Very well! Pedro. Great! Finally, it's time to act," Henry exclaimed with satisfaction.

"You know I really appreciated your courtesy and generosity. However, now it's time for me to go. Tomorrow afternoon, we will go to the well to find out what those mysterious crates contain, and the day after, I will be gone by dawn. I've been here too long, and I don't want to abuse your hospitality," Henry added gratefully.

While he said this, he stared Concita in the eyes with the intent of making her understand that she had to make the decision, and now it was up to her to join him or remain there forever.

However, to his surprise, the woman looked away with resignation.

After dinner, Henry spent some time with them, talking and drinking wine.

During this time, he had tried to talk several times with Concita, but for one reason or another she ignored him. He did not understand the reason.

At about 11 o'clock, he went to his room, turned off the light and went to bed, but he could not fall asleep. In fact, he had been rather hurt by her strange attitude.

He had been lying in bed for an hour without being able to close his eyes when he heard a door open and footsteps walking away into the courtyard. Intrigued, Henry went to the window and opened the curtain and saw Concita going to the small farmhouse opposite the sheep barn. When she arrived, she opened the door and entered. Shortly, he saw a light come on.

More than half an hour passed, but the light remained on, and Concita did not return.

"What the hell is she doing?" He wondered with curiosity.

To satisfy his curiosity, he decided to go there and see.

Being careful not to make any noise, he opened the window, went outside, and silently approached the shack. Although the curtain was closed, from a crack, he could see part of the room and could clearly observe Concita, who was on a cot reading a book.

After a while, the woman turned off the light.

Henry returned to his room silently.

What was she doing in the shack? Why didn't she sleep with her husband at home?

What the hell did all this mean?

He stayed awake a little longer, but no trace of her.

There was no doubt she was sleeping in the cottage.

The next morning, she woke him up at nine o'clock.

"I'm going out for an hour; do you need anything?"

"No, thank you! I don't need anything. See you when you come back," Henry replied half-asleep and heard the car drive away.

It was a godsend to remain alone and undisturbed in the house and have time to reflect. Henry felt excited and anxious, since on this important day, he could clarify many obscure points. He would finally find out if his fears were well-founded or just the fruit of his imagination. He wanted to have a gun with him, but where could he get one?

Henry didn't feel safe. However, he knew it was time to act, and he couldn't back down.

He went to the kitchen to get a cup of coffee. Then, he saw the open door of the hosts' bedroom, and after a moment of hesitation, he went inside.

Henry tended to be a discreet person who did his own business and avoided sticking his nose into the affairs of others. In normal situations, he would never think of going inside their bedroom to rummage through their belongings. But this was not a normal situation.

In fact, he was frightened for his life, and no longer trusted anyone.

Entering inside, he saw a rather shabby and modest room, without any objects of value.

The bed was next to the wall in the center of the room, opposite the front door. Two nightstands stood on the sides. A metal crucifix hung above the bed. Near the wall to the left of the door was a small table, while a large wardrobe with three drawers was on the opposite side.

He approached the bed and opened one of the nightstands.

He noticed a Bible, handkerchiefs, a rosary, and various little objects.

He went to the other nightstand and holding the cup of coffee in his hand, opened the drawer. Even here were things of little value and nothing interesting.

A little discouraged, he went to rummage through the closet.

Opening the doors, he found different clothes of modest quality. There were jeans, shirts, and a pair of tacky jackets Pedro probably thought were very *chic*.

Henry pulled the clothes apart, from left to right, and suddenly saw a woman's dress, which paralyzed him. Intrigued, he pulled it out of the closet. It was an *extra-large* size dress. He took another one and noticed the same size. All the women's clothes he found were evidently much larger than Concita's size.

He opened the first of the three drawers and saw an assortment of T-shirts, underpants, and men's socks. In the second, there were sweaters and sweatshirts. On the third, he looked at bras. But they were not ordinary bras, they were super-size, and the underpants were huge.

Concita would swim in those garments.

Dawnin was stunned, closed the drawer, trying to put everything back in place.

He went to get the cup of coffee, he had left on the nightstand, but because of his clumsiness, the cup slipped from his hands and fell to the ground, rolling under the bed and pouring all the coffee left on the floor.

"Fuck! Now I must clean."

Putting his arm under the bed to retrieve the cup, his hand touched something else.

He grabbed the object and pulled it out.

It was a large frame containing a family photo, where he recognized Pedro, Antonio, and the children. Instead, the woman portrayed alongside Pedro was not Concita, but a very fat, dark-skinned lady with a large mole on the right cheek.

She was the mother of the boys and Pedro's real wife. He was sure of it.

Then who was Concita? What did all this mean? Was she part of Charles's gang? Or what else?

He picked up the cup, cleaned the floor and went outside, heading to the shack where Concita had slept the previous night.

The curtains were still closed as well as the door.

However, this did not frighten him since Henry was determined to go inside, even breaking a window or the door. He would have done what was necessary to reach his goal.

Luckily, he noticed the door was weak and the lock ancient and managed to open it

Entering the room, he noticed the cot where the previous night Concita was lying reading. The bed had been sloppily made, and the pillow was thrown on the ground. Nearby, there was a pile of books with the most disparate titles. He noticed among these, one with the title in English: "The Terminal Man" by Michael Crichton. Looking through it, he realized it was indeed written in English.

Concita read (and understood) the English language, while with him she had always spoken in Spanish. How come?

Who was this woman who had seduced and taken him for a fool?

She was certainly not a crude, ignorant peasant who had spent her life in the countryside. Taking one of the books at random, he opened the cover and read M. S. He looked at another one, but nothing was written on it. In a third again, those initials M. S.

"Who the hell are you, M. S.?" he cursed.

Looking around, he realized there wasn't much to discover.

In fact, the room was quite stark. There was a chair with dirty clothes, a small table with a radio on it, and finally, next to the bed, a nightstand with a small drawer.

He opened it, and his gaze *froze* on a pistol.

Taking it in hand, he discovered it was an automatic Beretta 9mm, an Italian weapon used by the police forces. For a moment he had the instinct to take it with him and then use it at the appropriate time if it was necessary.

He eventually rejected the idea and put the weapon back in its place. At one corner of the small nightstand, he found a gold medallion with a heart-shaped case.

Henry opened it and saw a small photograph, which showed Concita together with another girl, a little younger than her, beautiful, and with a heavenly smile.

The photo must have been from a few years earlier, because Concita looked much younger. He was attracted to the beautiful, mysterious girl, who certainly had to be the sister because she looked a lot like Concita.

Henry stopped contemplating the beautiful maiden and returned to his grim present.

The sight of that gun made him fearful and uneasy. He cursed again the moment he had embarked on the whole affair. He could have been in some pub picking up some beautiful lady, having sex, enjoying a nice joint and drinking a cold beer.

Instead, he was entangled in a damned, murky matter.

For God's sake! His current situation was dreadful, a dead-end, an agony even worse than death itself. Above all, he was so disappointed by the mysterious, beautiful brunette who had seduced him, stolen his heart, and with whom he had made love and confided his little secrets. He had even proposed to her that they flee and adventure together, far away in remote lands.

The two of them, alone against the world.

He felt betrayed by her, even if in his heart something told him she was not an enemy but rather the opposite. She was on his side.

He could be wrong, but he believed that Concita would never shoot at him.

However, he would have discovered this in a short time.

In his search for clues, his gaze ended up on a blue, rigid suitcase branded "Samsonite". Opening it, inside, he found casual and sporty clothing. There were jeans, cotton T-shirts, skirts. Then there was underwear, a pair of athletic shoes, bras, all ordinary belongings.

Rummaging quickly through the clothes, he found a letter addressed to Maria Sanchez, but there was no precise address, only, a post office box in Puerto Vallarta. Henry opened the letter and read it. It was about three and a half pages long. It began with affectionate greetings and the premise that nothing new and important happened, but it was the only way to feel close to a loved one.

Suddenly, his curiosity was aroused by a paragraph that said exactly, "Your father, he is a little better, but still is not resigned to the situation. On my side, I pray every day to God, to perform a miracle. I weep, and go to Mass. I don't want to resign myself if there is even a small hope. The doctors are quite pessimistic about Luisa's condition, which remains the same and she is still in a coma."

Subsequently, the person who wrote, after asking for information on Maria's health, ended the letter with kisses and the wish for better times.

The signature was: "Mom".

Then there were two lines written in a nervous handwriting that said, "I hope you're well; I love you with all my heart, Dad."

Henry put the letter back in the envelope, closed the suitcase and was about to look at the table, when he heard the noise of a car, still far away but approaching.

He came out without being able to close the front door since the lock was broken, and it took some time to fix it. He didn't have any time at all.

In fact, looking out from the courtyard, he saw that Concita's car was now less than half a mile from the farm. Therefore, he tried to close the door as much as he could and ran to the opposite side of the shack to get away as quickly as possible.

Concita parked the car, and Henry appeared at the front door of the house, greeting her coldly. He was not a good actor; anyone could see he was not happy. He seemed tense, irritated, and nervous.

Seeing this, she asked, "Why are you so upset?"

Taking courage, he abruptly shouted, "I think the time has come for a clarification between us."

"What do you mean?" the surprised woman replied.

"I want to know the truth. To start with, who are you? I know you're not Concita, you're not Pedro's wife, and you're not a sheep farmer. Answer me. Who are you?"

"You are right and entitled to an explanation, and you will have it soon. And you are correct when you say that my name is not Concita and I am not Pedro's wife. I am Maria ... Maria Sanchez," the girl replied in a friendly tone, having realized her ruse was over.

"Well! Maria Sanchez, can you tell me what all this means?" Henry exclaimed, satisfied with the capitulation of the woman.

"Not now, Henry. Not now. But do not be afraid, you are not in danger. Be calm! You are with friends. No one wants to hurt you, I swear," Maria replied with a smile and a friendly tone.

Henry was not totally reassured by the answer because he still knew nothing. However, her words were encouraging and made him more relaxed and relieved. Oh yes! Why would they save him from death and then kill him? It did not make sense. After all, he had done nothing against them and was even ready to collaborate and share his findings.

"But who the hell are these mysterious friends?" He wondered curiously.

X

They had left the farm for about ten minutes, and Maria was driving the car.

Henry, to break the ice between them, asked, "So, Concit..., sorry…Maria! Are you going to find out what is inside that well or not?"

"No Henry, what was inside the well has already been recovered, thanks to you."

"Thanks to me? And... Why?"

"Because you gave us valuable information. The same day you mentioned what you found there, we went to check and retrieved it. You know, you must be fast and precise when dealing with dangerous opponents like Charles Lewis. That man is not only a poisonous snake but also very cunning."

Henry was petrified.

Maria knew about Charles.

Instinctively, he took the package of Marlboro Hard that was in the left pocket of his shirt, lit a cigarette, and took a big puff.

Then, after a moment of hesitation, he took courage and asked, "What do you know about Charles Lewis?"

"Enough! I know enough. I know he is the head of it all. It is he who pulls the strings of this whole story. We have tried to frame Lewis for a long time, but so far, we haven't had luck on our side," she replied, giving him a fleeting look to gauge his reaction.

"Do you mean arrest?" Henry asked curiously.

"Yes, just like that—arrest. You said it well, Henry. I'm a federal agent."

"Woah! You are a federal agent?" He exclaimed in surprise.

"Precisely, a federal agent of the Mexican government, like your FBI, to be clear. Charles Lewis has committed many terrible crimes here in Mexico as well. We have been hunting him for a long time but without much success."

"Of course, I am just a fool, a poor idiot who has been deceived by everyone. But why? How could I have been so stupid to be involved in this story?" Henry exclaimed in a disheartened tone, covering his face with his hands in shame.

"Do not be so severe with yourself. Anyone would have been deceived. You arrived in the wrong place, at the wrong time, and have been involved in a story bigger than you could imagine, not knowing what you were up against," Maria said politely, trying to cheer him up.

He didn't seem to be hearing her and continued his monologue.

"Everyone made fun of me, from that bastard of Charles Lewis to that bitch of Cindy Hyatt, to Pedro, who I thought was a philanthropist and instead was part of the game," Henry shouted angrily, almost crying.

Henry stopped to catch his breath, and after the brief pause, he exploded even more violently, "Above all, I have been deceived by you. You, who seduced me, showing yourself in provocative positions. The person who came to wash my back when I was bathing, behaving like a cat in heat just to achieve your purpose. You, who told me all those false, sad stories: the poor wife of a sheep farmer, raised in misery, with three children to look after and heavy domestic burdens. You, the woman who would like to change her miserable life but cannot, who would like to go to a big city instead of spending the rest of her life on a squalid farm ruining her existence. Oh Jesus! How many lies have you told me, and I was so stupid that I believed. What an imbecile I am! You, Maria! You are the biggest disappointment."

Having said that, Henry calmed down.

The silence was broken by Maria, who, in a cordial tone, said to him, "Here you are wrong, very wrong. Henry! What happened between us was authentic and real. I did not seduce you for a second purpose. I love you. I did not pretend, nor did I deceive you. I had sex because I was and still am attracted to you. I like you physically. I like your smile, your way of speaking and being. I felt this from the first moment I saw you. I can assure you I am not a tart, a loose woman who goes from bed to bed with strangers. With you, it was different. Maybe I let myself go too much, but in the end, I have nothing to complain about. I hope that our relations will remain cordial, indeed that they will improve even more."

Henry was pleasantly surprised by what the woman had just confided to him. He was flattered by the love Maria felt for him, and he had no grudge against her. On the contrary, he was falling in love even more.

However, he did not answer anything. It was then Maria who said jokingly, "I lied to you even about my age, I am not thirty-two years old, I am twenty-eight."

"See! Another lie," he exclaimed, laughing.

"Why didn't you use your real first name? Why did you call yourself Concita and not Maria? And why all that elaborate scheme?" Henry asked, intrigued.

"Well! I don't know either. It was like... a game, a fiction. When I was younger, I took acting classes, and for a certain period of my life, I hoped and wanted to be an actress. So, I changed my name, trying to identify myself as much as I could with Concita, Pedro's *false* wife. And not only that... I also changed my habits and my way of speaking and dressing. I wanted to find out as much as I could about you without arousing any suspicion at the same time. But my performance did not go as well as I had hoped." Maria exclaimed in a discouraged tone.

"That is not true. Instead, you were exceptionally good. However, in the end, you left out some small details. Perhaps, the only out-of-tune note of all your acting was the strange and unusual pairing with Pedro. How come a beautiful and refined woman like you was married to him? I mean Pedro is a good person, I have nothing against him, but he is too different from you. I know! In life, everything is possible, but not in this case."

"Why? Pedro cannot marry a... beautiful woman, as you say?"

"Of course, he can, but he didn't," Henry said, laughing.

"How come you just used the word refined? How do you know if I'm refined?"

"Intuition, Maria, pure and simple intuition, I am good at that," Henry replied by winking.

Then he added, "Your sophistication was one of your mistakes in the elaborate ruse you did, my dear." What do you mean by that?" She asked curiously.

"Simple! That morning you came to my room to make my bed, when... well!... Let us say we had fun together. You wore a silk nightgown that was sexy and of high quality. However, do you think Pedro's wife would pay 100-150 dollars for a garment like that? Or would Pedro approve of it? Never. This was your mistake, along with your body."

"My body? Why my body now? Don't you like it?"

"I love it! There is not one atom in your body I do not love. But precisely! Your body is incredibly beautiful, well-groomed and in great shape. When I saw you naked that morning, I thought, how can she be the mother of three children? You are very athletic and muscular. I am sure you trained at the gym and played different sports. Do you think Pedro's wife, with all the household activities, can spend all that time training? Yes! Your appearance made me think a lot. Sometimes it is a flaw to have a body beautiful like yours," Henry concluded with a laugh.

After an hour and a half in the car, Henry saw road signs pointing to Puerto Vallarta, twenty miles away. Another thirty minutes passed when he asked Maria how long it would take to get to their destination.

"About ten minutes," she replied.

Soon after, Maria pointed to a mansion on a hill, "That's where we're going."

She opened a sturdy iron gate with a remote control. The whole villa was surrounded by concrete walls more than twenty feet high. Both this and the total isolation of the villa from the outside world made it clear that the owners cared about their privacy. The estate was much larger than it looked from the outside. In fact, the house was quite far from the entrance. The surrounding land was planted with vegetables.

As they climbed up the street, Henry noticed several peasants plowing and sowing the land. The house was old. There was a large forecourt in front of the main door that served as a parking lot for cars. A beautiful lawn was all around the villa, as well as tall cypresses, pines and eucalyptus trees that formed thickets and created shaded areas, refreshing the environment.

Henry got out of the car, ecstatic at the beauty of the place. The chirping of birds and the singing of cicadas were uninterrupted. A light breeze blew constantly, moving the surrounding air.

The view was fantastic. Below, the entire valley was visible, where the green of the fields contrasted with the barren stony hills. A small stream flowed in a zigzag pattern until it got lost in the horizon.

The house had two floors, gray in color with terracotta tiles on the roof, in which the sparrows made their nests. There were hundreds of them.

A waiter opened the door, and the two entered.

"The master is coming, have a moment of patience. Take a seat in the living room and make yourself at home. Meanwhile, if you want to order something to drink, I will be happy to serve you."

Henry, hearing about drinking, straightened his ears, and with a slight trepidation, asked, "What do you have to drink?"

"So many things. We have rum, beer, vodka, tequila, wine, champagne, gin, and other spirits that I don't remember right now. Then we have coke, sprite, seven up...."

"Ok! Do not worry about making the list of soft drinks. Can I have a cocktail? For example, a margarita," Henry said, interrupting him.

"Certainly sir!"

"Good! So, I will take a margarita with ice and salt. Thank you."

"One for me too," said Maria.

"Excuse me," Henry politely called him.

"Yes sir," replied the waiter, stopping.

"Please put a lot of tequila in my margarita, thanks."

The man walked away, and Maria, shaking her head, smiling, said, "Do you know it is rude to ask for these things in other people's houses?"

"Why? I don't see anything special about it. I only asked for a margarita with extra alcohol. I did not insult him. After all I have been through, this is the least I can receive from this mysterious gentleman, who has already irritated me. Why all these secrets? Why didn't he show up earlier? By the way! Do you want to tell me who he is?"

"Be patient, soon you will meet him, and you will know everything."

Henry nervously looked around him.

The living room was incredibly large. It consisted of two rooms combined. The first was more formal, with two cream-colored sofas and four armchairs of the same color. A large red Persian carpet was on the floor between the two sofas and armchairs. In the center was an antique low table. On the top were magazines, silver ashtrays, a cigarette case, and a crystal cup with candy inside.

The other part was more informal, furnished with a long rectangular table surrounded by several chairs, and a couple of tall cabinets with glass panels displaying framed photographs.

As Henry looked around, he heard voices coming from outside and then a splash in the water. He approached one of the large windows overlooking the garden and saw, far away, a large swimming pool. He watched a little girl, about four years old, dive into the arms of a girl who was already in the water. A woman in her forties was sunbathing in a black one-piece swimsuit.

"That lady in the black costume is the wife of the person you're about to meet," she said.

"Maria! Are there still secrets between us? Can I trust you? And is this unknown stranger to be trusted?" Henry asked, concerned.

"Be at peace! You are among friends, the real ones, not those who shot two bullets in your body and then left."

Her tone of voice, sweet and calm, was enough to reassure him.

After a few seconds, the door opened, and a middle-aged man entered the room. He had a stern and grumpy appearance, gray hair and beard, and dark and melancholy eyes.

He was in a wheelchair. An athletic young man followed him.

"Do not worry, go ahead. I don't need you, Coco. Just close the door, please," said the austere man.

Coco closed the door, and the host approached Henry and Maria.

Despite the cold, unfriendly appearance, the man addressed the guests with great cordiality.

41

"Maria, how are you? You are more and more enchanting every time, I see you my dear."

Saying this, he kissed the woman's hand. She blushed slightly for the kind gesture.

Then, the mysterious gentleman approached Henry and affectionately shook his hand.

"Finally, I have the pleasure of meeting you, Mr. Dawnin. I am happy."

"My pleasure, mister?"

"Rodrigo Fuentes," he replied. "Please, take a seat."

The guests sat on one of the sofas, close to each other.

Henry stared at the austere character inch by inch. Looking carefully at his dull, sad eyes he read so much suffering. Certainly, Fuentes had had much pain in life. He looked like a troubled man, indeed. Rodrigo was about to start talking when he heard a knock on the door.

"Come in," he ordered.

At that command, a stocky Mexican girl dressed in a white blouse and a black skirt entered the room with a tray.

"Here are the drinks. For you, sir, I prepared the usual one," the maid said, mentioning the gin and tonic that was on the tray.

"Sir! And for you, I put triple the amount of tequila. I hope it is strong enough for your taste," She jokingly said to Henry.

"Thank you very much!" Henry replied with a smile.

"Oh yes! My dear Henry! You really need a lot of tequila not to faint while listening to the story I'm about to tell you."

Fuentes began to break the ice and try to create a cordial atmosphere.

Henry looked Maria in the eyes, and she burst out laughing, seeing his dazed and confused face.

Sipping his gin and tonic, Fuentes began his speech, "First of all, I would like to make my personal apologies, Henry, because I understand your point of view. You have been kept in the dark about all the events, and that was not nice. Maria confided to me your perplexities and fears. Maybe I was wrong not to come to you first to explain what was going on. But after all, I knew you were in a safe place, with trusted people, and nothing could happen. Finally, Maria voluntarily decided to stay with you, like a guardian angel, pretending to be Pedro's wife. As for Pedro, he is a good person, honest and loyal. I was sure that I could trust him and his family. I have been generous to him. I gave Pedro about $1500 dollars for you staying on his farm. In addition, I paid for the plane ticket for his wife to send her to Guadalajara, where she has a sister."

Stopping briefly, Fuentes pulled a package of "Gitanes" from the right pocket of his shirt and lit a cigarette.

Seeing this, Henry said in a provocative tone, "You must smoke less, Fuentes. Two packs of cigarettes a day, as strong as those, can really hurt you." Fuentes squinted his eyes and replied, a little amazed, "How do you know that I smoke two packs of cigarettes a day?"

"It is simple! Doing simple calculations, the other day, you were watching me from the top of hill. You know! Curiosity is a bad habit. At first, I had not noticed it, but after repeatedly seeing that shimmer on the hill, I was sure that it was binoculars, and someone was interested in me. Even knowing that I would never find anyone there waiting to offer me a coffee, I went to search for clues. So, I found four Gitanes butts. Calculating that if we take away meals and maybe a siesta of a couple of hours, a person is active, let's say, for ten hours, well! At that rate, you smoke no less than forty cigarettes a day. This is just my stupid impression. Maybe I'm wrong, but... I do not think so. I understand there are exceptions. Someone smokes because he is nervous, or to socialize, or to spend time, or because a friend smokes and offers a cigarette. But in this case, you had no reason to be nervous, as you were on that hill, surrounded by your men and without any danger in sight. To socialize, why socialize by spying on people? Therefore, all that remained was the third solution, to spend time, since the fourth was impossible. You smoked your own cigarettes, not another's. All the butts had the same sign. You gnaw the filter slightly at the end of the butt. You may not even know it. It's like a habit, like those who chew their nails. All the butts had the same notches. After finding these clues, I had no doubts. Anyone who smoked French cigarettes had to be the leader of the gang. When you walked into the room, I would have bet my life you were the man who smoked Gitanes, and I was right."

Fuentes was speechless like Maria. No one would have expected those incredible deductive abilities from Henry.

Rodrigo was positively surprised, so after a moment of disbelief, he said to Maria, "Well! This is the right person for us. There is no doubt about it."

"You have impressed me positively with your story, and now it's time to start mine. Everything I will tell you is the pure truth. I swear on my mother and by my honor as a gentleman. Pay close attention to what I am about to tell you. It is a damned story."

Rodrigo confided to Henry with a dramatic tone and continued, "It happened in the early eighties. In Central America, there is chaos, wars, and guerrillas everywhere: Nicaragua, El Salvador. War has always been loved by the Secret Services. In fact, selling weapons has always been a lucrative business for the CIA..."

"The CIA?" Henry exclaimed, interrupting.

"Exactly! You see Henry, I was part of that organization, of the agency. My real name is Raymond Montgomery. I changed my identity to Rodrigo Fuentes later. Now, let me continue without interrupting; I will give you a summary of what happened then.

We were in Nicaragua at the time. We had camped in a distant and remote place in the mountains. No one in the world could have found our base. I had to escort the proceeds from different operations to the main base. It was an important operation, like 15 million dollars, to be brought to safety using helicopters. I had the money loaded onto the helicopter I was in, while another military helicopter escorted us for protection.

With me were Jack Wilson, the pilot, and Rick Kemper, a twenty-five-year-old lad. Also, in this operation, there was the young Charles Lewis, son of the powerful Harold. I had known his father for years and considered him a bad person, but the son was even worse. With the young scion was another boy, Tom Atkinson. Tom and Charles were in the other helicopter, along with Brian Holtz and pilot Mark Sinclair.

We knew we would find severe weather for that night's mission, but shortly after leaving the camp, we experienced a real storm. At one point, while flying at a low altitude through the forest, Jack Wilson lost control of the helicopter and crashed into a small clearing. Rick Kemper died instantly. Wilson seemed to not be too injured, except for a wound on his forehead that was bleeding. On the contrary, I could not move my legs because they were broken, and I was hurt badly.

Among the flashes of the storm, another helicopter landed. Jack and I breathed a sigh of relief, thinking we would be rescued soon. Wilson tried to help me pull my legs out of the wreckage of the helicopter but failed. Seeing our comrades landing, he left me alone to go and ask for their help.

The helicopter landed close to us. It was incredibly dark and stormy. I barely saw Jack walk away from me, shouting at the others to help us. But it was not until a few seconds after they left that I heard three gunshots. Those were the worst moments of my life because I didn't know what the hell was going on. For a providential instinct of survival, I decided to pretend to be dead. I knew I had no chance to get away with it, but I had no other choice. I could not run away or face my opponents.

Armed with flashlights, Charles, Tom, and Brian entered the cockpit. Although I did not dare to look, I undoubtedly recognized their voices.

"Take a look at those two jerks," Charles told Brian.

Brian leaned over Rick and replied, "This one is dead, Charles."

Then he approached me, felt my wrist, and impressed by the condition of my bleeding face and my broken legs, he said, "The old man is more dead than alive. He will not have long. What do I do? Shall I give him the coup de grace?"

"No! Don't waste time. Come and help us bring these crates into our helicopter, and then set fire to what is left, and let's get out from here," Lewis replied.

Quickly, the three men loaded the money and crates with weapons into the other helicopter. Then Brian returned with a tank of gasoline and clumsily set fire to the cockpit, pouring gasoline around us.

After a few seconds, the helicopter flew away. Brian did not think about the effects of the storm. After a moment in which the fire flared up, the hard rain and the wind extinguished it before it could spread to me and destroy what was left of the helicopter.

However, fate had decided to spare me. Local people found and treated me. I lost both legs in the accident. I became a poor cripple in a wheelchair, but I did not lose the use of my brain.

From then on, I began to meditate on revenge. Charles and his companions had made a couple of huge mistakes. First, they didn't kill me. Secondly, in their hasty escape, they forgot to take away a bag full of money I had put next to the pilot's seat. Because of the impact, the bag was covered by the seat, and those bastards did not notice they had left it. In that briefcase, which I later retrieved, there was more than three million dollars.

Since then, I changed my name, no longer Raymond Montgomery, but Rodrigo Fuentes. After changing my identity, I came to settle here, in Mexico, and I have been living here for six years now. During this time, I got married and had a lovely little girl.

I invested that money, making a good profit, instead of spending it. Already having a very solid position in bank accounts abroad, I created my own organization, composed of loyal collaborators.

In these years, I never stopped, not even for a moment, controlling my old enemies from far away. As a hidden wolf is ready to catch its prey, I am ready to strike Charles Lewis and associates at the appropriate time.

Through my money and my ability to create good social relationships, I have several important friends and connections. Now, I am a prominent personality in this country. In addition, a good knowledge of Spanish helped me a lot. I owe this to my mother, who was Argentinian. It was she who, from an early age, taught me to speak this language perfectly. No one would realize or recognize that I am an American.

However, going back to what I said before about important friendships, I had the fortune and the privilege of becoming a good friend with the chief of the Mexican Secret Services. So, I discovered, and was gladly surprised, that the Mexican government was taking an interest in Charles Lewis. This was unexpected good luck for me, a godsend because it allowed me to use legal means to ensure those criminals were punished justly.

Since then, I have begun to collaborate with the anti-drug section. We exchanged the information we had about our common enemies, we studied strategies to eliminate them. In short, we started to get serious. At that time, I met Maria, who had been on the trail of those criminals for some time.

Now, I want to take a step forward to the recent events and then return to clarify other events of the past. Let's talk about the last events in which you were involved.

From some informants, I had the tip that Charles Lewis, with his beautiful companion Cindy Hyatt and the trusted bodyguard Doug Harrison, had booked three first-class seats for Ontario, South California. This news interested me a lot. I knew Charles had lived there when he was young and perhaps returned to those places out of nostalgia. However, it was not this that excited me, but the fact that it had been months since he had been anchored in his stronghold in Seattle.

I thought that if he was going away, it should have been something extremely important at stake. I could be wrong, but my sixth sense urged me to act quickly. So, I set my organization in motion, and some of my best men began to discreetly stalk our enemies.

Charles, with his mania for grandeur, was not content to rent a normal car. He rented a black limousine. It was not difficult to stalk that car. My men followed him until he came to your home in Redlands. Unfortunately, we could not listen to what he told you, so your meeting remained a secret to us. We didn't know if you could be a key character in the whole affair or not, but we decided nothing should be left to fate. Then, one of my men hid a bug in your apartment, taking advantage of a momentary absence.

I had the feeling you must have been involved in some shady affair. This became a certainty since Charles, after leaving your home, went to a local restaurant to eat a quick lunch and then left immediately with his henchmen for Seattle. That fellow had come to Redlands to visit you for a specific reason. So, day and night, we were anxiously waiting for news.

From the phone message Lewis left on your answer machine, we knew something was boiling in the pot and that eventually, you would go to Mexico.

Then Cindy suddenly appeared, and your conversation about the operation, the itinerary and the money clarified the whole situation.

The rest is quite simple. Since the beginning of your journey Henry, you have been carefully watched. For this we used all the means at our disposal and even a couple of helicopters. In fact, it was our helicopter that followed you to the ruins of that church.

While the helicopter kept us constantly informed about your route, some of my men moved by land with jeeps, following the directions indicated. The men in the helicopter saw nothing that happened in the mission. But they realized that something had gone completely wrong when they saw fewer people get into the Toyota and leave and not you.

Meanwhile, Coco, Roberto, Luis, and Maria were stationed on a surrounding hill. Although they couldn't see what was happening inside the courtyard, they heard two gunshots and saw a jeep drive away. They arrived about half an hour later and began exploring the ruins of the monastery. They found a stolen Yamaha off-road motorcycle hidden behind bushes, which Tom Atkinson had used to arrive a few hours earlier.

Then, by chance, Coco heard calls for help. At first, it was not clear or loud enough, but then Maria also heard something—like a groan or lament—that seemed to come from the well. Coco leaned over to check and saw you, more dead than alive. A few minutes passed, and Coco and Roberto went into the well and found you unconscious in the water. You are alive by a miracle, Dawnin, and must thank your patron saint and great luck. You had two bad wounds, one on your left shoulder and the other between your chest and stomach.

Above all, you had lost a large amount of blood and even had water in your lungs. A couple of minutes more and... goodbye Henry Dawnin. Maria oversaw the ground operation and called the helicopter back while she was following the fugitives.

The helicopter landed almost immediately. Meanwhile, Roberto, who has good medical knowledge, gave the first treatment. He managed to get the water out of your lungs and began to disinfect the wounds and contain the blood. You have been taken away by helicopter to a hospital in the area and operated on urgently.

Although the operation succeeded, you went into a coma for four days. Then, the condition improved considerably. At that time, we did not know what to do with you. In fact, we were uncertain whether to hand you over to the police or keep you as a prisoner.

It was Maria who had the idea of that ruse. In fact, she was certain that it could be a satisfactory solution to find out something more about you and Charles Lewis without using stronger methods. I was hesitant enough about all this. I did not know what kind of person you could be and for this reason, I did not trust to bring you here to my home, among my loved ones. So, after long reflections, I thought of Pedro, who lives close to my home, and you know the rest of the story.

You were brought here from the hospital to Puerto Vallarta, again by helicopter and then by Pedro. Now you understand the embarrassment he had every time you asked him to go to the old church. That place is hundreds of miles from here, and Pedro does not even know where the hell it is. It was funny that he created stories about that place to satisfy your curiosity.

Maria has been exceptional in this whole affair. She did her part well, pretending to be the good wife of the shepherd and discovering a little part of your character.

Oh yes! Henry, if you are here, alive, and unspoiled, it is only for her. I could call Maria your guardian angel. She kept me informed of your health condition daily, telling me how positively impressed she was with you. She always believed that you were quite different from the rest of Charles' gang and that maybe you were not a part of it. Although you revealed nothing about what happened in the ruins of the church, Maria soon discovered that you had found something in the well.

As soon as I heard this, I went with my most trusted men to find out what was in there. And it was a success. We found three hermetically sealed crates and a briefcase. In two of the crates, there were weapons; in the remaining one, there were thirty kilos of heroin, while in the briefcase, there were five million dollars. This is thanks to you, Henry. Without your involuntary help, we would never have found this.

Finally, I managed to solve another problem that had tormented my mind all these years: what had happened to Brian Holtz. It seemed like he had vanished into thin air. But coincidentally, he was there, at the bottom of the well. The remains of his corpse were recovered along with his discolored documents. One less enemy to fight, one enemy killed by his own friends. You do not live long when you stay and work with Charles Lewis."

XI

Fuentes stopped to catch his breath and to hear the reaction of his guest.

Henry, who had followed the whole story carefully, was speechless.

He looked at Maria, who smiled at him affectionately, and he returned to stare at Fuentes, who was lighting another cigarette. Instinctively, he went to drink his margarita, but the glass was completely empty and contained only the water that had melted from the ice cubes.

Taking his pack of cigarettes, he lit a Marlboro and asked, "Can I have another margarita?"

"Of course," replied the landlord, ringing the bell.

The stocky server from before reappeared at the door.

Fuentes ordered the drinks.

Henry took a margarita, Rodrigo another gin and tonic, and Maria a coke.

"This story you have told me is incredible, truly incredible," Henry exclaimed as he began sipping the second margarita.

And he added, "Then that bastard of Charles was a CIA agent? I would never have believed that. And all your story in Central America! Gosh! Science fiction stuff."

"So, do you finally start to understand what an incredible story you are involved in? Anyone could have been fooled, not just you, believe me. You are fortunate to be still alive, but you must not throw to the wind this grace that the Lord has granted you. Try never to make the same mistakes you made in the past," Maria told him in a preaching and worried tone.

"Of course! You are right. I will be much more cautious in the future and will never again seek the path of crime to survive. I will never make the same mistakes again, I swear. But above all, I will never trust treacherous and poisonous people like Tom Atkinson, Charles Lewis, or Cindy Hyatt," Henry said in a distressed tone.

"Would you like to work for me?" Fuentes asked him seriously.

Henry did not answer the question immediately, instead looked Maria in the eyes and from what he captured in her gaze, understood that she was upset about that proposal.

He returned to stare at Fuentes, who seemed to have picked up his perplexity and said, "I'm sorry, Fuentes, I don't work for anyone."

"What does that mean? I am proposing that you work for common purposes against our enemies. Don't you understand? As long as Charles Lewis remains alive, every day, you will be in danger for your life. You will not be able to remain safe in any corner of the world. You will be anxious and scared for the rest of your life thinking about those cruel, ruthless assassins who are hunting you. Listen to me, I speak in your best interest. From reliable sources I have confirmation that Cindy Hyatt and Tom Atkinson are back together in Seattle. Do you understand this? Cindy is with Charles right now, and maybe they are in bed together, making love. After betraying Charles, Miss Hyatt came back to him, and who do you think she has accused of stealing the money? You, Dawnin. You are the thief who took the money of Charles. While Tom and Cindy consider you dead and gone, the rest of the gang are looking for Henry Dawnin in the seas, mountains, and everywhere. One day or another, they might even find you. Listen to me! There is no future for you if Charles Lewis is alive."

Henry paid close attention to Fuentes's speech, and what the man said made logical sense. For Charles, he was not dead. On the contrary, he was alive, rich, and happy.

After quickly reflecting on his situation, he decided to propose a pact to Fuentes.

"What do you mean by working for you? If you think that day and night, I will be holding a rifle at the limits of your property to defend it from offenders. Or that I will push your wheelchair around, my answer is no. Categorically not. I prefer that someone killed me in a bar while I drink a good beer, or they slit my throat on a beach while I tan and see beautiful women around. However, I can say yes if you are willing to accept my collaboration for future action plans, for risky operations and to give the final blow to

Charles's organization. In short, I am willing to work for you only if I maintain my independence, my autonomy, and I want to be paid."

Fuentes thought that Henry's behavior was arrogant and conceited. He certainly did not need him at all costs because he had many good men and so many means at his disposal. Despite this, he thought that Dawnin was useful for the organization since he could be the perfect lure to use for his plan.

So, with a falsely resigned attitude, Rodrigo finally replied, "Okay, Henry, I agree to your terms. I accept your cooperation, and I will pay for it. It is certainly not money that I lack. I will give you $15,000 dollars right away for upcoming expenses. The important thing is that you find accommodation not far away and that you can be reached by phone day and night. If you need more money, let me know. Thus, let's do the deal! You will work on a case-by-case basis. I will pay you a good amount of money for each operation or collaboration to use your term." They shook hands.

"Well now that we agree, I would like to show some slides on the organization of Charles Lewis, which I think you will find interesting. Please! Let's change rooms."

As soon as he finished saying this, Rodrigo Fuentes rang the bell three times and Coco immediately opened the door.

As they left the room, Henry asked, "I missed a detail of your story. Fuentes! Why did Charles and associates, after stealing the money in Nicaragua, hide it in that church and not spend it? What is the point of keeping money hidden in the most remote place in the world? And all this time? I wonder why. I don't get it."

"Oh no! Perhaps you misunderstood, or perhaps I have not expressed myself clearly. The money stolen in Nicaragua has gone, disappeared, vanished into thin air. Certainly, it has helped Andrew Martin, Charles Lewis, and associates to make a good life during these years. The money found in the well is much more recent. Many banknotes are from the years eighty-three, eighty-four, eighty-five, and even eighty-six. That well is like their bank. I do not have the slightest idea why they use it. Perhaps because it is far away from any cities and inhabited areas. It is the safest place in the world. This shows that these criminals have numerous illicit trafficking here in Mexico. If you think about it, it is not a bad idea. Think of a warehouse where the most different goods are stored. A secure place where you can also store illicit money. There is no need to worry that the police may find out the origin of it or that the first homeless person breaks through the door to find shelter from the rain. It was a great idea as long as it lasted."

"How could they store the suitcase with the money underwater without ruining the contents? What about drugs?" Henry asked with keen interest.

"That is a good question! See! Those scoundrels used suitcases and crates resistant to water, and in addition, they were sealed hermetically with plastic on both the outside of the bag and the interior. Money, weapons, and drugs had a double waterproofing seal inside. Not a drop of water could have entered it."

"Our guys are quite smart!" Henry exclaimed.

"Indeed!" Fuentes answered while making a signal to follow him.

They left the room, walking along a long, dark corridor with a purple carpet and paintings attached along both walls. Fuentes had the guests seated in the fourth room on the right. Coco opened the door and followed the boss. They entered a spartan room without any decoration. In the center of the room was a long rectangular table and numerous chairs. On the wall opposite the front door was a white nylon tarpaulin that served as a screen.

Fuentes, after waiting for his guests to sit down, began to introduce the topic, "What we are going to see is the result of years of work, research, stalking and stakeout. The whole of Charles's gang is photographed in these slides. This is essential for you, Henry, to know the enemies who are hunting you and what they look like. On each of them I will make a brief introduction of the character. If you have any questions, or you know some details I don't know or I didn't say, stop me anytime, okay?"

"Okay."

Coco turned on a slide projector.

At the nod of his boss, he turned off the light and began with the first slide showing an old, sick-looking man, a person whom Henry instantly recognized, Mr. Harold Lewis.

"Good! I think you know who it is," Fuentes said.

Henry responded by nodding his head.

"I wanted to start with Mr. Harold Lewis just for a matter of age. Harold Lewis, in fact, is no longer a danger to us. He died twelve years ago of natural causes. This slide was taken a few months before his death. Go ahead, Coco."

The second slide, certainly much more recent, showed a middle-aged man, impeccably dressed. The man was holding a deep brown leather briefcase in his hand and had just come out of the back door of a black Mercedes.

Coco quickly moved on to a second and then a third slide showing the same person. Now, the guy had gotten out of the car and was shaking hands with two other men.

Coco, after those slides, quickly moved on to a fourth that portrayed him in a close up.

Then, Fuentes began to describe the character.

"We are at the cream of the cream, Mr. Andrew Martin himself."

"He looks like a priest! He has such a good and honest face. I could confess my sins to this gentleman here," Henry exclaimed sarcastically.

The slide portrayed a grizzled middle-aged, handsome gentleman, of medium build and height, with blue eyes, a slight smile of happiness, and a very sharp, inquisitive look.

He wore an expensive blue jacket, a white shirt, and a blue and black patterned tie.

Fuentes resumed speaking, "Don't be impressed by the appearances. This man, who seems so respectable, is the real leader of the gang. Sorry if I dare to say this, well!... I no longer believe in God, in the Saints, in Heaven, or in Hell. However, if demons exist, Andrew Martin is one of them. He is the chief."

Fuentes's tone was agitated, tense, and frightened. It seemed that Martin's slide alone terrified him.

"The real brains of the gang, Martin inherited power upon Lewis's death. Given the friendship between the two, he was Charles's true godfather. There is a notable difference between the two. While Harold Lewis was a prudent, conservative person who reasoned carefully before taking a step forward, Martin is unscrupulous, cynical, relentless, and unstoppable. He has the finest brain in the world and never makes mistakes, at least so far. In a few words, Andrew Martin is a genius. I know I can easily defeat Charles, but I don't know if I will ever succeed with Martin."

Maria made a brief, odd nod, which Henry did not understand well and interpreted as if she meant to say, "We will talk about this subject later."

He nodded his head too and continued to watch the next set of slides on the screen.

Three of these portrayed Charles.

Fuentes didn't talk much about him, knowing that Henry knew him well. He said that young Lewis had moved with his father to Chicago a few months after he finished high school, exactly on October 5, 1968.

That date seemed to ring in Henry's brain, October 5, '68... October 5, '68, something was familiar to him on that date. Fuentes wasted even less time on the two slides depicting Tom Atkinson and the next four on Cindy Hyatt.

Then he introduced Doug. Two slides depicted the giant man training in the gym. His muscles were scary. In a third slide, Doug was portrayed lifting more than 400 pounds on the bench.

Henry hoped never to meet the man again. He was scared to death of him.

"That is Doug Harrison. He is Charles's bodyguard. Doug was born and raised in the Bronx. At the age of eighteen, he was a champion in bodybuilding. However, he is not just a huge mass of muscles; he is also a black belt in kung fu and an excellent shooter. He is a ruthless and bloodthirsty killer like his boss, but he is not the most dangerous member of the gang. Doug follows Charles as a dog follows his master. For this reason, it is unlikely he is searching for you now, since Lewis rarely leaves Seattle. It will not be him, nor Charles, hunting you down. Here is who you'll have to worry about the most in this period."

That said, he showed another slide on the screen. This portrayed the albino and the Latino that Henry had met, or rather clashed with, in Joe's bar the night old Ray Brown was killed.

Seeing that slide, Henry shouted, "Shit! I know those two fellows. Sure! They are those two guys who came to Joe's pub. I even argued and chased the dudes away, kicking them in the butt. Those two animals terrorized old Ray. I even thought they were the ones who ran him over and killed my friend on the same night."

"Well! It is probably those two who are hunting you right now. That blond who looks like an albino is Scott Johansen, and the dark one is Ramon Espinoza. Two tough guys. I must congratulate you, Henry, if you kicked those two guys out of the pub. You kick ass, my friend," Fuentes exclaimed, surprised, concluding the speech.

Henry did not want to talk further on that topic. So, Fuentes returned to stalking, introducing a second slide depicting the two guys of before with a third man, short and very thin.

"Scott Johansen and Ramon Espinoza are two ruthless, bloodthirsty, former Green Berets who have been working for some time for Charles and for those deviant CIA forces. Often, they are assisted by that man there. That little guy is Greg Murphy. Greg, despite not having the physical prowess of others, is an important man in the organization. In fact, he is a particularly good driver. He even raced for a time in the NASCAR championship races. He is also capable of piloting planes and helicopters and is a genius in electronics and computers. I heard rumors that he is an exceptional knife thrower."

Having said that, Fuentes gave a deep breath and a little disconsolate, declared, "Now let's move on to the sore points."

Coco showed a new slide, quickly followed by three more.

The first two slides showed a man photographed from behind. The man was wearing a black leather jacket, and he was totally bald. The third slide depicted him in profile, on the side of a road, smoking a cigarette. The fourth was less enigmatic than the previous ones and showed the man photographed in front. Then, a fifth was a close-up of him.

Henry, upon seeing him, expressed disgust and exclaimed, "Who is that monster?"

"That's Bruce Munro, known as the Exterminator," Fuentes replied in a worried tone.

Henry watched him closely.

He was tall, very robust, his eyes were dark, small, hollow, lifeless. His nose was long, aquiline, with a crooked tip to the right. His mouth was large with fleshy lips and yellowed teeth. The total absence of hair and a long scar on the left cheek gave this character a sinister and evil appearance.

"He worked occasionally with Charles, but he is not part of the gang. He is like a freelance helper. Charles calls him when he is in deep trouble when things get bad, and there is no other way to solve them. In addition, Lewis has another good reason to call him rarely, Munro is expensive. It takes millions of dollars to have his cooperation. He is certainly the most expensive hitman in the world. He has a reputation for never failing a mission. Few but good. This is his motto. This animal has its own code of work and honor. Once he makes a commitment, he completes it all the way. They call him the exterminator because he often kills not only his victims but also their relatives and friends. He is a worm that does not hesitate even to kill women, old people and children. If you make a contract with him, you already know it will end up in a bloodbath. I just hope we will not find him in our way for our own good."

The next two slides depicted a clown, and the third, an old homeless humped woman who was crossing the street with a shopping cart full of empty cans.

Henry thought there was a mistake and giggling exclaimed, "Hey Fuentes! What do you show me these pictures for? I am no longer a child who likes to go to the circus, you know?"

In a sarcastic tone, Rodrigo replied, "It sounds like a joke to you, doesn't it? Do you think that we made a mistake putting these slides in the wrong place? Yes! Laugh, Henry, but that being who is there killed three of my men."

"Really?" Henry exclaimed in amazement.

"Yes! You heard well that person there had killed three of my best men. We do not know who the hell he is, we don't know if he's a man or woman, we don't know anything. For us, he is the chameleon. At least, that is what we call him. The chameleon is the most dangerous of Charles's gang. He is the most dangerous because he does not have an identity. He can be anyone, even one who is trusted."

That said, Fuentes signaled to Coco to move on.

This time, the slide portrayed a woman. It was on the third slide that Henry's brain set in motion, and he was so surprised by his discovery that he screamed, "I've already seen her."

"Yes! Henry! You have seen her several times when she was in Redlands."

She was the Asian woman who followed him all over in that period.

He remembered seeing her on the edge of the highway and several times in town. The slide left no doubt that it was her, in the flesh.

The girl was incredibly beautiful, tall, with long, dark hair. He recognized that she wore the same jeans jacket, and it seemed like she was watching something or someone carefully.

This time, Henry saw her well, not like in the past when it was just a fleeting vision.

She was attractive indeed.

Fuentes, reading the amazement on his face, said, "We used a super powerful zoom to take a decent picture of this beautiful lady, professional stuff. However, before moving on to the next slide, taken at the same time, please stay calm. Do not be agitated, Henry."

Henry did not understand what Fuentes meant.

So, he took the opportunity to make a stupid joke, "Did you photograph her naked? Only in this way, am I excited and agitated, dear Fuentes."

Rodrigo did not answer and with an amused smile, signaled to Coco to move on.

Maria, in the dim light glimpsed that grin of Fuentes and clenched her fists in anger.

Something was not right for her.

On the other side, Henry had not paid attention to all this, he was still meditating on the beauty of that woman.

When the new slide was projected on the screen, he exclaimed in amazement, "Damn."

The slide showed an overview from different angles. This time he recognized the place where it was taken. It was the main street of Redlands. This was not what struck him but seeing the woman in the upper corner and recognizing himself in the lower corner of the slide while he was reading the newspaper.

Henry was reading about the death of old Ray Brown.

He was leaning on his motorcycle while the kid who sold the newspaper was leaving.

Coco switched to another slide from the same place.

This time Henry was shown when he had finished reading the article, his head was raised. The woman seemed to be about to move. A third slide showed Henry looking towards the woman who was now behind at the edge of the photo.

At this point, Fuentes began to speak, "You see, Henry! That woman has been stalking you the whole time. We discovered this by chance, and then we started to follow her and tried to discover something, but without much success. The problem is that we don't know who the hell she is. We don't know if she is part of Charles's gang or not. We don't know anything about her. It is an enigma, but I think we will be able to find out as soon as possible. We had solid information that the woman is now here in Mexico. If we find out where she is staying or something about her, I will contact you immediately. I do not see any other solution."

Fuentes made the usual signal to Coco who, promptly as always, changed slides.

This time a close-up of Henry appeared on the screen. He was in front of the door of his house, with a reefer in his mouth and a beer in his hand, and he was collecting mail from the letterbox.

A second slide portrayed him on the bike.

Henry was irritated and gave a dirty look to Fuentes, who began to speak, "Well I want to finish this photographic review with you, Henry Dawnin. Not because you are part of Charles's gang, just to see how accurate my information is. Henry Robert Dawnin was born in Arcadia, California, on March 3, 1949. His father, John William Dawnin, was a professional musician. His mother, Betty Hughes Dawnin, was a teacher at South Pasadena Elementary School. Both parents passed away years ago. He has a sister seven years younger, Jane Emma Dawnin, who married Jake Smith. After graduating from high school in Redlands in 1968, he moved to San Francisco, where he studied Philosophy and obtained a bachelor's degree. He remained in San Francisco until 1979. In 1970, Dawnin married Nathalie Dupree, his former schoolmate, and in 1972, had a daughter, Chris. In 1979, Dawnin returned with his family to Redlands. Unfortunately, the relationship between he and his wife deteriorated and they ended up divorcing in 1981. His wife moved to Santa Barbara where she remarried a wealthy lawyer in the area. At the same time, Dawnin opened a co-owned pub with a good friend, Jim White, in downtown Redlands. Business was going quite well; it was a serene and positive period. Dawnin began to hang out increasingly with Theresa Morrison, and the two started living together. Then, there was a crack in Dawnin's existence. His friend Jim White died and...."

"You have accurate information about me. Enough is enough, Fuentes. Your informants are very good, but now stop this crap. I'm not here to listen to the story of my life," Dawnin furiously interrupted.

Fuentes instantly shut up as Henry's tone was exasperated and explicitly threatening. Rodrigo had a moment of panic when he saw in Dawnin's eyes a furious beast was going to be unleashed.

To justify his behavior, Fuentes replied, "I just wanted to show that we are quite informed about you. This was just a demonstration. Why are you so upset? There is no reason to be. I didn't want to hurt or make fun of you. We must respect each other and have no secrets as we work together."

Henry became really upset. The initial good impression he had felt for Fuentes quickly turned into dislike. It did not seem right to him that Rodrigo had interfered and spied in this way in his private life. He did not like being stalked and photographed by Rodrigo's men. He also thought that Fuentes could spare the speech despite having photographs or valuable information about him.

It seemed that the man took pleasure in humiliating him. Henry began to lose trust in him. It was time to have a long discussion with Maria to understand to what extent he could really count on her. Maybe she was the only trusted friend in this damned story.

Henry had seen Maria several times making an irritated face during Fuentes' offensive monologues. He even remembered that enigmatic nod she had given him just before when Fuentes was talking about Andrew Martin. Yes, he was sure he could trust Maria.

He remembered what Maria had confided in the car: that she had been attracted to him from the first moment. Moreover, if what Fuentes had said was true, it was Maria who had pressed the organization to help Henry. Fuentes had no reason to lie about that. Yes, Maria was his guardian angel. Henry was sure that he could trust this beautiful lady with those sweet, big, dark eyes.

When Maria realized that Henry was staring at her, she smiled candidly, and in that look, he found the solution to many of his problems.

In that look, he read, "Rest assured! You are not alone and abandoned. I am on your side, and you can trust me. We will talk about it later when we're alone. For now, you are just playing the game."

Henry smiled at her and felt relieved. The silence between them was broken by Fuentes, who said, "Would you like to have lunch with us?"

XII

Four Days Earlier in Washington D.C. in The FBI Offices

It was nine o'clock in the evening.

Dick Tolone had stayed late to work in his office, spending hours on extensive computer research, but unfortunately, he had not found anything useful for his investigation.

"Just a waste of time. I could have gone home to my wife, damn it," he complained, irritated.

He was upset.

Dick Tolone was a twenty-eight-year-old FBI agent, small and thin, with short dark brown hair, an eternal teenager's face, and regular facial features. He wore sturdy glasses that gave him a bit of a mad scientist look, complemented by his sweet, endearing smile.

For some time, he had been investigating the deviant forces within the CIA, involved in trafficking weapons, narcotics, and other shady dealings. However, so far, he had had no luck. He and his colleagues always moved a moment too late, trailing behind their opponents.

Dick turned off the computer, put away the files he had just read, and got up from his chair.

He was worried about this new and further failure, so he began to think of what excuses to invent the next day to his superior, Matthew Collins.

Collins was a nasty, unfriendly person, always rude and blunt with his agents, and he never appreciated their efforts. Tolone had never liked the guy, but unfortunately had to abide by his superior now that he had a permanent position in the department.

"Collins will become furious when he learns I wasted all this time on this stupid research. Shit! How can I justify myself?" He exclaimed loudly in a concerned tone.

As he stood up and walked through part of the large room, he realized he was the only one left in the office.

Dick had just turned off the light in the whole room when he heard the phone rang.

Who the hell could it be?

He turned the light back on again and saw it was his phone that was ringing. It was probably his wife wanting to ask when he would return home.

He answered the phone, "Gosh! Is it you? Can I know where you are? You should have called me three days ago... and I am here inventing excuses for Collins."

"Do not worry about me, Dick, I know what I am doing. Don't make me waste precious time. Listen! I have a concrete trace. I think we are going in the right direction. I am here in Mexico. But tell me, what did you find on Henry Dawnin?"

"Nothing! Dawnin is clean, or almost... clean. He has no serious criminal record, except a denouncement for assaulting his boss several months ago, a couple of fines for speeding, and as a young man he was stopped a couple of times for blatantly protesting the Vietnam War. Dawnin has always called himself a nervous pacifist against the corrupt capitalist system. He does not seem to be a hardened criminal, what should I do?... Do I keep investigating him?"

"No! Dick, no! That seems to me to be a waste of time. Anyway! Now I must go. I will call you in two or three days depending on what I find out, so long."

Dick Tolone hung up the call and thoughtfully walked away from his office, cursing the moment he had begun to investigate this case.

SEATTLE, Charles Lewis's Office, the Day after the Phone Call Received from Dick Tolone

Charles had returned to the office after having lunch with a group of friends in an expensive Italian restaurant. It had been fun. He had not seen them for several months. In a group of six, they drank six bottles of Chianti red wine and ate like pigs. Feeling slightly tipsy, he thought it was the right time for a nice sniff of cocaine.

Charles was really upset with Tom. Once again, Tom had found a good excuse not to join them. For some time, he was always busy. Charles was beginning to be annoyed by Tom's behavior.

He remembered what Uncle Andrew confided to him that day, to be aware of the guy because he was treacherous and feared Tom could be having an affair with Cindy, noting the frequent little smiles and tender moments between them.

At first, Charles had not given too much importance to those words, but he knew his Uncle Andrew never spoke without having some concrete reason. Now, it was time to be cautious and ascertain the truth.

His mail had been deposited on his desk by his secretary, Sharon.

He found many business letters for his import/export firm, and then advertising coupons. He opened the envelopes listlessly, one after the other, without reading, or paying too much attention to them. He noticed among them, a white envelope without the name of the sender.

Lewis noted the letter had two Mexican stamps from Guadalajara. Curiously, he opened and read it. It was written using a typewriter:

"Thanks for the money, asshole! I will drink to your vanishing health, hoping you will die very soon. Ah! Ah! H.D."

"Henry! Ugly bastard! I will break your bones and poke your eyes out! I'll find you... even in the deepest hell, you are dead, I swear," he screamed angrily. Charles was furious.

He never expected a provocative letter from Henry. The time had come to intensify the research. Eventually, he had to find that worm, who had fled with his money.

Charles began to worry, as this was the second unwelcome letter he had received in just three days.

He opened the top drawer of the desk and picked up the letter in where it was written: "Even the worst pigs die sooner or later, so be prepared."

He was about to trash the letter when something made him stop. Seeing the alleged letter Henry had sent him, something intrigued him. How the hell could Henry know the address of his office? He had never given it to him. Maybe Cindy had involuntarily revealed his address during the trip? It was time to talk with her.

After that Charles felt depressed.

Henry's insult, coupled with the first letter bearing the Seattle stamp, had left him worried and thoughtful. Henry could only be responsible for one of them, so who was the author of the other threatening letter?

Could it be he had made a mistake? He prided himself on being the most perfect and cool man on earth, born a winner, always a step higher than anyone else.

Nervously, he snorted a huge dose of cocaine, the only thing that could help him in this sad moment. He needed energy and something to help vent his anger. It seemed as if he heard the voice of Uncle Andrew, who in the silence of the room asked him, "Charles! Charles! Are you sure of the woman you are going to marry?"

Instinctively, he grabbed the phone and dialed the house number. He just wanted to hear Cindy's voice to be reassured. The phone rang, but no one answered. This pushed Charles over the edge, and he lost control of his nerves, violently slamming the phone down so hard it bounced to the edge of the desk.

He was furious. At that moment he wanted to smash and destroy everything in front of him. Then he had an idea. A perfidious and violent idea that only a person like him could conceive with his sadistic and sick mind. He called his secretary, Sharon. The woman entered the room, pale, and uneasy as if she already knew what Charles wanted to tell her.

"Come, Sharon! Get closer," he said with a satanic grin.

The woman hesitated, stuttered, and tried to take time and not think about what she was already imagining. Sharon moved close to him and accidentally bumped into the telephone, crashing into the wall, and breaking.

"Sharon! You know you have always been my favorite secretary."

Charles sneered, grabbing her blouse, and tearing it off.

His sexual fury soon ended.

Charles had another success (depending on whose point of view).

He took one hundred dollars from his wallet and aggressively threw it in the woman's face, saying, "Buy yourself a new shirt and keep the rest, bitch, and I'll see you soon for another shot, you will not be disappointed, ha-ha."

Sharon Miller was forced to take the money in her hands like a prostitute. Quickly, with tears falling down her face, she walked out of the room and noisily closed the door. Seeing the trash can, she crumpled the banknote and threw it violently into the can. Then she went to the bathroom to clean herself up.

For almost six months she had been forced to live this life. Only fear kept her from going to the police, from quitting and calling a good lawyer. And it was a very legitimate fear.

Sharon feared for her family and for herself. She knew that when Charles told her he was going to kill her husband, he was not kidding.

Charles had shown her one day when her husband, John, returned from work savagely beaten. John explained that he had gotten into a quarrel with two thugs over a stop sign they had ignored, and other similar nonsense.

In short, stuff that could happen to anyone. The poor man could never have imagined the quarrel had a different origin.

Not even Sharon knew because she believed her husband. However, one day in the office she had resisted Charles and his sexual advances and had even threatened to denounce him.

Lewis told her what had happened to her husband had not been a simple coincidence and could happen to every person in her family if she did not... cooperate.

"I can make you and your family disappear in less than half a second if I want to," he told her.

Since then, abuse, fear and sexual violence began. Charles never beat her, but he constantly abused herLuckily, he often did not stay at the office and was very busy at other times, but when he had nothing to do, he never hesitated to put his hands on the blonde, busty secretary.

Sharon remembered all those different events.

At the beginning her job seemed an immense stroke of luck since the pay was excellent. Friends had even envied her knowing about the salary and the benefits she enjoyed, things such as medical insurance, paid holidays, and sick time.

Even to her it seemed too good to be true and, in fact, it was not.

Her boss Charles Lewis, who at the beginning had made a good impression, showed his true wicked behavior after several weeks.

At first, he simply caressed her cheeks and hair, then gradually his hand slipped lower and lower, until one day he opened her blouse.

At first Sharon was confused and did not know what to do. She had no idea how to stop the increasingly explicit advances of her boss. She was afraid of losing her job. It was not easy to find a well-paid job like she had, indeed perhaps impossible.

So, she decided not to say anything and to act as if nothing was happening. Sharon thought she wasn't the only woman being groped by an employer.

She also believed she could resist and keep the situation firmly in her hands. Even though Charles always touched her breasts, it would be okay if he limited it to that.

But she was wrong. Charles' advances had become increasingly insistent and continuous.

One day, Charles ordered her to strip naked. Sharon violently resisted his command and was about to threaten to go to the police. Charles seemed to read that thought in her mind, and advised her not to do so, for the sake of her family and for her own sake.

He knew everything about her loved ones, where they lived, what they did, he even knew her sister's address in Minneapolis. That man was a devil.

Charles told her, "If you cooperate, you can have so much money and benefits that you can't even imagine, but if you don't cooperate, it will be the end for you and your family."

Then he gave her proof of what he could do to her husband.

Another day Charles ordered her not to use a bra when she was working in the office. Sharon continued to experience a series of frustrations and humiliations.

She felt like a prostitute every time she walked into that office. She felt embarrassed when there were meetings with a lot of people, mostly men, and she came in carrying some documents or packages. It was so unnatural. It seemed to her that everyone's eyes were fixed on her large breasts. Sharon was desperate, devastated and was crying loudly while putting makeup on her face. How she hated that man.

Certainly, the time had come to react and rebel. Charles had never gone so far. This time Sharon had been raped and it could have been the first in a long chain. Why did he enjoy doing this to her? She knew there were so many other women, who were more beautiful and available than her. Why choose her when she was married and loved her husband and family?

Sharon was a cute blonde woman but not beautiful, in fact, she looked slightly chubby and overweight.

Trying to contain her outburst and wiping away tears, she took off her ruined shirt, got her bra and put it on. Then wearing the shirt, she came out of the bathroom, knocked on Charles' door and entered.

"I'm going to buy a new shirt," she said with a soft voice and lowered gaze.

Charles got up from the chair and went to meet her. Sharon was terrified and afraid, expecting another violence. Charles, sneering, opened her torn shirt and seeing the bra exclaimed, "I see you put your armor back on. Ah... ah, ah."

Then he hugged and kissed her as if nothing had happened and said, "Well Sharon! Come in tomorrow, take the rest of today off and... Excuse me, maybe I've been a bit... too violent, next time I will try to be gentler. I promise. Ah! Ah!"

Sharon walked out of the building and arrived in the street with her torn shirt, walking with her hands in front of her chest to cover it.

Suddenly a police car passed in front of her and stopped about thirty feet away. She was tempted to go to them and report what had happened, to denounce the rape she had suffered. Sharon froze for a few moments. Her brain went haywire and could not make the right decision. Part of her said to go, and another said no.

In her confusion, Sharon raised her head, and glimpsed Charles looking out the window of his office on the twelfth floor. Immediately, she looked down and sadly resumed walking on the sidewalk towards the Metro Tunnel.

From there, she was going to catch the first bus that would take her to Third and Pine, to the Bon Marche' department store, where she hoped to find a shirt like the one she had on.

Meanwhile, Charles felt at the top of the world. He was so pleased.

That secretary had always made him so satisfied. Sharon was the right person with whom to vent his power, cravings, and lust. Her appearance, so respectable and puritanical, had made him horny from the first moment. Charles had watched her from above, observing her walk away on the sidewalk until she disappeared into the crowd, her demeanor confused and indecisive. Oh yes! He couldn't have chosen better. He had set out to make Sharon a victim and his sex slave from the first day he had hired her.

And he had succeeded.

Lewis was attracted by her appearance: a good wife and mother, all home, church, and work. Yes! Despite being a bit chubby Sharon was pretty and to his taste.

He knew she was totally in his power and would never betray him, because she was too scared.

"The first of a long series of erotic adventures," he exclaimed happily while sniffing another generous amount of cocaine.

56

After the wild, horny instinct passed, Charles looked around and saw the chaos he had created.

Many sheets of paper were scattered on the floor, along with pens, the lamp, and the phone, which now was broken.

Charles began to put everything back in its place, starting with the papers, then the lamp. Finally, he approached the phone, picked it up, and remained paralyzed.

A spy bug had popped out of the broken handset.

He was stunned and frightened.

Something was seriously wrong.

Charles immediately decided to take drastic measures. There was no more time to lose; someone was spying on him. He opened the drawer, took the two letters he had received previously, and put them in his pocket. Then he closed the office and activated the alarm. He went to the phone booth down the street and phoned the man he trusted most.

"Uncle Andrew, hello! This is Charles! I must talk to you immediately, yes! Exactly. This is very important!" Charles, then stood by the side of the road and shouted, "Taxi! Taxi! Here, hurry!"

XIII

Even though Andrew Martin was busy, he found a free moment for Charles. In fact, Andrew canceled two appointments to meet with him in his office. For the occasion, Andrew selected a bottle of Glen Grant whiskey and two crystal glasses.

Ten minutes later, Judy, the elderly secretary, escorted Charles inside. Martin was tasting whiskey when he saw his nephew come in. He got up from his chair and hugged him affectionately.

"What's going on, Charles? Why are you bothering me right now when I'm very busy? I hope there are important things to discuss." Martin's tone was serious and a bit annoyed. Charles recounted the latest events carefully and finally handed the two letters to his uncle.

Andrew Martin began to scrutinize them meticulously, remaining silently absorbed in deep thought. Charles didn't have the courage to interrupt him while he was reflecting. It seemed Andrew's brain was charting the trail for the future. Deep down, he knew his uncle could find a remedy for everything.

After about five minutes, Martin broke the silence by saying, "Charles! You are really a moron! What the hell is happening to you? What the hell are you doing? I don't have time for these silly things right now. I am seriously thinking about becoming a politician. Damn! Don't you see the ground is collapsing under your feet? I can't believe it! You are an intelligent person, but what are you doing? The fact is that now you have become lazy, sloppy and use too many drugs. That is your private business. If the cocaine and other filth you use does not allow you to think anymore, this concerns me and becomes my business. I can see from your dilated pupils what you did just now. Look! Do what you want, but when you work, behave like a capable and responsible person."

Charles was surprised and intimidated by his uncle's stern tone; he had never seen him so pissed off in all the long years he had known him. He made a fearful attempt to answer him, but Martin silenced him unceremoniously.

"Shut up and listen. What is happening is very serious. It's like a red alert, or a siren that is ringing. The fault is yours because you did not take the right precautions for the micro spy. Who knows how long it had been there, and you didn't know anything about it? Now what is done is done, but don't make the same mistakes again, and now you must correct the mistakes.

First, we must find out who is behind this bug. It could be anyone, FBI, cops, or competitors. Second, increase surveillance, and then... be cautious. We must capture alive those who placed the bug, so we understand what's going on. Only in this way can we find out why they did it and what their aims are.

Regarding those letters I have doubts and suspicions. I don't know Dawnin, so I can't put my hand on the fire for him. It seems stupid to me that someone who is on the run with our money wastes time sending you some cheap letters. No! This is strange and this letter stinks to me. You should start looking around at those close to you. The last time we saw each other I told you what I think of Cindy. Now I won't tell you gently anymore.

It's time to find out if what I think is true: that Tom is having an affair with your darling Cindy. It may be that I am wrong, for sure there is only death in this world, but I have a nose for certain things. Regarding the second letter, of course, Dawnin has nothing to do with it.

Someone is spying on us in the shadows, right here, in Seattle, perhaps even in this moment. We must find out who he is and then destroy him. Charles! I see hard times," Andrew said in a concerned tone.

Martin stopped for a moment, to hear the reactions and opinions of his godson but Charles had been caught off guard and could not express any ideas at the time. Finally, after moments of silence, he exclaimed, "Uncle! What do you think if we hire the bald?"

"Who? The exterminator?"

"Yes! He is the best for these jobs."

"It's not a bad idea, but that animal will ask for a lot of money."

"Not when we promise him money that has already been stolen. At the beginning we will pay half of the contract and for the other half we will promise him a big reward, like one of the millions of dollars that Dawnin stole. You can bet that beast will search to find Henry Dawnin everywhere. We will give him a down payment to find out the person responsible for this. For the rest of the money, he must earn it by finding Dawnin."

"Ok! Proceed in this direction. I also think I have other good ideas. I strongly suggest that you go to Mexico to the old mission, to collect the rest of the money, I don't think it's appropriate to keep it hidden there anymore. In this way, you can also get an idea of what might have happened. Take Scott and Ramon with you, for protection. But by the way? Where the hell are they now?"

"They are in Mexico, on the trail of Dawnin."

"I don't think they're doing a good job. It's time for you to start coordinating men and operations. Without you, those are lost. You can leave the bald working on his own because he is used to this way and is a loner but keep an eye on the others. Scott and Ramon are two tough guys, but they are more muscle than brain. When did you go to Dawnin? Did you take a commercial plane?"

"Yes! Why?"

"It was a big mistake! In the future, only use our personal planes, is that clear? One last thing—work with the bald one to set a nice trap for our unknown friends who are spying on us. The exterminator is a genius in these matters."

Andrew Martin seemed to be finished, so Charles took the opportunity to ask him politely, "By the way, Uncle, what is this about politics that you mentioned a little while ago?"

"Dear Charles! I am seriously thinking about getting into politics. For now, I'm just weighing the pros and cons. I think this is my future."

"Awesome! Best wishes, Uncle! I hope you will have a great success in this new enterprise."

"Thank you dear! I will certainly do my best, rest assured. And remember what I told you before: stay alert, be prudent, and watch your back. Only in this way will we get out of this jam."

Having said that, Andrew accompanied Charles to the door and shaking his hand vigorously, asked him, "When are you going to Mexico?"

"As soon as possible, maximum in a week."

"Good. Try to speed things up. Quickly contact the bald and as soon as you return from your trip, give me the news. We must always be in close contact for any emergency. I also want a meeting to be organized among all of us when you return. So, tell everyone, even Tom, okay?"

"I will do whatever you told me to do. Don't worry about anything, Uncle, everything is under control, see you when I come back, bye."

Charles left his uncle's office.

Andrew closed the door and going back, told his secretary he did not want to be disturbed for any reason. Then he walked into his office and sat in front of the desk, absorbed in deep thoughts and fears.

Pouring another shot of whiskey, he exclaimed loudly, "Harold! Harold! I am starting to believe your son isn't as good as you thought."

Andrew loved Charles, always had, but he was acutely aware of his nephew's limitations. Once again, his fears were confirmed. Charles was mediocre in every field, even as a criminal.

Martin had kept an eye on him constantly, cleaning up the messes the young brat was making.

At the beginning it was not a burden for him. However, he was getting tired of this because it seemed Charles was getting sloppier and more unreliable every day. Also, Andrew knew about Charles's behavior toward women, that dark, sadistic, evil side of his nephew's personality, who was constantly roaming around searching for any female to hurt and rape.

He did not care about that and had never interfered with or confronted Charles about it.

He blamed the father Harold and himself for Charles lack of skills.

It was Harold who had always adored his son and treated him as a supreme being, creating this winning personality in him to be the best in everything.

Andrew did his part too, but not as much as the father.

Thus, Charles grew up a spoilt, useless man, who was used to having everything on a silver tray, and every problem resolved by someone else close to him.

All in one swallow Andrew drank the contents of the glass and then quickly sank back into deep contemplation.

He was very worried. Something was wrong. Shaking his head, as a sign of disapproval, Martin picked up the phone and when someone answered, said, "Hello! It's me. I need your help, it's for my nephew Charles, let's get together as soon as possible."

He put the phone back and kept shaking his head.

Charles had left his uncle's office about twenty minutes ago. He could not have imagined such a violent reaction on Andrew's part, but Charles knew that with his uncle's help he could resolve the crisis. After all, he was satisfied, and even proud, that his uncle Andrew was deciding to go into politics.

He thought the support of a powerful politician was important and helpful in all fields, and especially in his own, where the illicit was part of his daily work. Being pushed and supported by a powerful political force could change the course of many things.

His uncle was right when he said that Charles was losing the right rhythm, that he had to wake up and not make any more mistakes.

Yes! He was totally right. Reflecting on this, Charles agreed he had become lazy, had gotten worse, and was not as shrewd and intelligent as he once was. But he was born to be number one, was a winner and would continue to be.

For the third time he turned back to see if by chance he had been followed.

Everything seemed in order.

Lewis had passed two phone booths, but both were occupied. Instead of waiting, he decided to keep walking because he knew another was a few blocks away.

A red small car slowly passed close to him, while he was walking on the sidewalk. The car had attracted his attention because it had dark windows, so it was impossible to see inside. He continued to walk slowly as if nothing had happened.

Charles found an empty phone booth. He took his little agenda, from the inner pocket of his jacket, and looked for the number of Bruce Munro, the exterminator.

Munro was not at home, so he left a short message on the answering machine.

"Bruce! Hello! This is Charles... Charles Lewis. I need your help immediately. As soon as you can, get in touch with me and let's have a meeting. I have a job for you of the utmost importance. So, I hope to hear from you soon, bye."

He was disappointed. He hoped to speak directly to him but had not been lucky. Now he didn't know when Monro would contact him. Maybe he was out of town and would return after a long time.

As he was picking up his phone card, casually he saw that same red car pass again slowly near him.

Then the car parked about fifty feet from him, but no one came out. At that moment Charles caressed the outside of his revolver 357 Magnum, hidden under his jacket.

With a grin he said to himself, "Let's see if I have to send someone to the creator." The vehicle remained there, with the parking lights on and the engine off.

Charles walked more than 150 feet on the opposite side. Then he called a taxi to take him home. Ten more minutes and he could take off his shoes and relax on the couch.

Charles was reflecting on this day that had started well and then ended so badly. He remembered eating at the restaurant with friends, having fun, making jokes and then that big violent fuck with Sharon. Oh yes! That had been the pinnacle of his day.

Thinking about her big tits, gave some peace and pleasure and momentarily he was distracted, excited, and chased away all other negative thoughts.

He meditated on a whole new series of erotic games he could do with her, in the office, when he had nothing to do. It was nice to have a handy secretary, especially one like Sharon: shy, introverted, puritanical and scared to death.

The idea of dominating Sharon, of doing what he wanted with her, excited him so much. He promised to tell her to wear only semi-transparent, revealing white blouses for the future, where nothing was left to the imagination. He was already enjoying the idea, thinking of her roaming around in the office dressed in that way. Charles's perverse and erotic thoughts were interrupted by the Indian driver who said to him, "Very hot today, but they say tomorrow will be even more sultry."

He replied with a stunted "Yes."

Then Lewis asked, "Is there a small red car with dark windows behind us?"

The taxi driver looked at the rear-view mirror and replied, "No! I do not think and ... oh yes!... A moment, yes! I see it! It is two cars behind us. Is a Ford Escort, the car you are referring to?"

"Yes! Exactly. It's a red Ford Escort with dark windows."

"What should I do? I pull over?"

"No! No! Do not bother, drive as if nothing has happened, but control the car carefully keeping me constantly informed."

The taxi parked under Charles's large villa in the Magnolia neighborhood.

"Look! Sir! That car stopped at the corner of the street," the driver told him as Charles was paying the fare.

"Thank you! Good fellow! Keep the rest."

The taxi had already left when he opened the front door.

Charles had done well not to arouse suspicion, not to look back, not to do anything at all. Very soon, he would find out who was in that red car.

He walked into the living room of his house and had another surprise. Tom Atkinson was sitting in Charles's favorite armchair with a glass of his favorite brandy.

Cindy was on a couch rather far from him.

Seeing Charles coming, she got up and went to greet him, saying with a sweet and happy tone, "Hello! Sweety! Welcome home! Look who came to visit us."

At that moment Charles wanted to kick Tom in the mouth but opted not to.

So, as if nothing had happened, he approached and greeted him.

After an exchange of pleasantries, Lewis asked in an irritated tone, "Hey Tom! Can I know what the fuck you are doing in this period? You never show up, always have an excuse not to come, even today. A couple of friends asked: And Tom, how is he? What is he doing? Is he coming? In this period, you are always busy. I can no longer count on you. Don't you care what is going on?

"You're right, Charles! I have been quite busy or had other issues. This morning for example I did not feel very well, so I did not come to the restaurant. I tried to call you at the office in the afternoon, but the line was always busy. So, I decided to come and visit you guys, also because I needed to get out of the house and enjoy some fresh air."

"Do you want some fresh air? Well, let's sit outside in the garden. It's hot and humid inside the house. Head out there, and I'll grab a beer from the fridge."

Charles joined Tom and Cindy in the garden.

"How is it going? Do you have any news?" Tom asked him with little interest, only to break the ice between them.

"Everything is crap, we're in the shit." Charles answered with a most concerned and dramatic tone.

"What do you mean?" Cindy asked.

Charles concisely recounted what had happened that day.

The two were incredulous hearing the story.

"I told you to come to the garden because I don't know if there are bugs inside the house, and it's time to be alert," Charles concluded, worried.

"So, this red car followed you here? Now I'll take care of it. I'll break the bones of this bastard," Tom exclaimed with fiery ardor.

As Tom was about to go, Charles stopped him, "Don't do it, stay calm! Drink your brandy and don't move rashly. I don't want to make the people behind this whole story suspicious. We will not act against those jerks; we will keep doing nothing, so they believe we still don't know about them. I did my best not to arouse suspicion. So, I don't want you to ruin anything. What I recommend now is to use the utmost caution and pay attention to what you do. I am sure these illustrious strangers have it in for me, not you.

Why should they follow you, Tom? Anyway, when you leave, check if this red Ford Escort with dark windows is still parked in the area. I will now disassemble the phone piece by piece. On my side I will make sure I don't have any bugs in the house, and if all goes well, I will call Doug and tell him to check the surroundings and possibly catch this guy."

Charles entered the house and went directly to check the phone and the surrounding area. Finding nothing suspicious, he decided to call his trusted man.

After four rings, Doug picked up the phone. Charles explained what was happening and urged him to try to catch the spy. He alerted him to be extremely cautious. In case he thought it was impossible to capture the guy, he absolutely should do nothing and not be suspicious.

While Lewis was on the phone, Cindy asked Tom, "What is this new story? What do you think?"

"I don't have the faintest idea. But I think we must be very cautious from now on."

Tom left Charles's house after a few minutes, and passing by on the street, saw nothing suspicious.

The next day, Charles was upset with himself. He believed he had made a serious mistake by revealing the news to Cindy and Tom. In fact, he thought, this could become a boomerang against him.

"Now those two will be more careful and it will be much more difficult to find out the truth. I'm an imbecile," he kept repeating to himself.

Charles was not satisfied with what he was doing. He felt tired, insecure, and uncertain. For the first time in his life, he was truly depressed. For him, a winner, it was a serious fault. That day was especially bad for him. He did not play any erotic games with Sharon, who had left the office before five o'clock.

Charles was still there, contemplating and meditating on his misfortunes and licking his wounds. Except when he had dealt with a couple of customers for not very important matters, he had spent the rest of the day thinking, looking at the wall, not knowing where to bang his head. The money that Henry Dawnin had stolen from him was a nice slice of cake. He was angry, not so much for the loss of the money itself, but for the impossibility of capturing and punishing Henry Dawnin for what he done.

That point became his greatest concern. In addition, the cherry on the cake was that bug found on the telephone, and the red car that had stalked him everywhere the day before.

How many more misfortunes did he still have to suffer?

Charles began to curse the day he had gone to Henry Dawnin. Since he had been with him, everything seemed to have changed for the worse. Although Henry had nothing to do with the bug and the red car affair, that man was like a damnation. He was a powerful jinx from which to escape and stay away.

At least Charles believed this.

Regarding the matter of the stalking, it was almost certain it was the FBI. That's why Uncle Andrew was furious. If FBI agents were on his trail, he didn't know how he could stop them.

As Lewis thought about all this, he was looking out the window of his office. Suddenly, in the street below, he saw the same red car from the day before. From the twelfth floor he could not see in detail, but it looked just like that car.

The driver of the car put on the turn signal and approached the right side of the road, waiting for another parked car to move freeing up space.

Charles watched and observed that the vehicle was about to park under his office. Suddenly he lost control of himself. For this reason, he forgot everything he had strongly suggested to Tom, and to himself, about thinking before making rash moves. So, the desire for revenge, the anger accumulated in that period and the consequent frustrations took over.

This time the mysterious friend would pay and... with interest. Running he reached the door of the elevator in the corridor and called it repeatedly.

He was lucky, the elevator arrived after less than thirty seconds, and he went down to the road, where he saw that the car was parked. Continuing to run frantically, Charles pulled out his 357 Magnum and reaching the car, opened the door and with the revolver in his hand shouted, "This time I got you, son of a bitch! Make my day, punk! Give me an excuse to kill you."

After saying this, he understood his big mistake.

A pregnant lady got out of the car along with a child of about three years. The woman, pale and scared, began to scream like a madman, and the child cried out in fear.

This time Charles had screwed up big time.

He was about to put the weapon in his holster when he heard behind him, "Police! Throw the gun on the ground, raise your arms and do not move an inch, or I will shoot you. Is that clear?"

He instinctively obeyed and a strong, tall policeman put the handcuffs on his wrists for taking him to the police station. It was just a dreadful time for Charles Lewis.

"Let me go, or you'll regret it, are you hearing, moron." Charles shouted several times at the policeman who was driving toward the police station, together with a female colleague.

"And to you too, ugly slut! I'll make you pay; you don't know who I am." Charles continued to insult and scream without interruption.

Suddenly the sturdy policeman stopped the car, turned back, and enraged shouted, "Look! Mister, I don't know who you are, and I don't care to know. But if you don't shut up, I'll break this baton over your head. I don't want to hear a single word from you anymore, got it?"

His tone was furious, Charles was not so stupid not to understand it. So, he didn't talk anymore for the rest of the way. However, with an evil smile, he mumbled to himself, "I'm going to break your ass, jerks. You will pay for this."

His anger increased when the woman said to her colleague, "It's crazy! Now all these lunatics, drug addicts have guns too, have you seen the face of this nut?"

Those words bounced in Charles's mind like billiard balls. "How the hell could that dirty woman allow herself to talk to him like that?"

Arriving at the station, he was accompanied to the security room. There he waited for almost an hour along with thieves, prostitutes, murderers, and drug dealers. The wait unnerved him more than anything else. However, it took less than ten minutes of conversation with Captain Harris and the whole situation was clarified. The captain apologized for himself and for the entire police district. Then he called the two officers who had arrested him and ordered them to immediately apologize to this illustrious character.

The officers, perplexed, obeyed their captain but reluctantly. Charles was free and was accompanied home by a policeman.

The complaint the lady had filed against Charles remained. However, the next day the woman withdrew it. She had changed her mind after a black, big, tall, mean looking man, visited her at home and suggested to withdraw it, because the man had added, "Health is a precious gift that it is better not to lose especially when someone is pregnant."

Two relatively quiet days passed for Charles.

At half past nine in the evening, he was reading a mystery in the living room. Cindy was above in the bedroom already in a nightgown.

Suddenly someone knocked on the kitchen door.

Charles became alarmed, and taking the revolver in his hand, turned off the light and entered the room. Whoever knocked, had entered illegally by climbing over the fence.

He was ready to shoot, staying behind the wall for protection and shouted, "Who is it?"

"Charles ! It's me, Bruce... Bruce Munro." Charles recognized his voice and went to open the door.

The man sat down in the living room.

Bruce Munro was getting uglier, he looked like a monster. Charles could not help but notice that Bruce was much fatter and more swollen. Charles could not help but notice. While offering him something to drink, Charles said with a reproachful tone, "I thought you weren't coming anymore, Bruce! Luckily, I told you it was urgent."

"I've been very busy; I only heard your message last night. But tell me, what happened?"

Charles recounted parts of the events: from Henry to the red car that stalked him, to the bug. Now it was Munro's turn to speak, to ask for clarification and express his ideas.

Suddenly the sinister character froze and looked up with curiosity.

Cindy was coming down the stairs but seeing him she stopped halfway. She was dressed only in a light semi-transparent white nightgown.

Munro stared at her with his eyes wide open, almost drooling.

After a moment of uncertainty, Cindy decided to continue down to the living room and went to Charles to wish him good night. She went over to where he was sitting in the armchair and bent down to give him a kiss on the cheek. Then she coldly approached Munro, shook his hand, and quickly returned upstairs.

Bruce Munro already loved the beginning of this job. He had been hired for less than ten minutes and immediately felt a strong, unexpected, and violent emotion. That blonde lady who was with Charles Lewis was just gorgeous. Maybe it would have been even better if she had been less thin, but she was also fine as she was. Her appearance on the stairs had paralyzed Bruce. He was speechless, words could not describe his feelings toward her. Not to mention the revealing nightgown she wore.

When the woman quickly bent down to kiss Charles, Bruce was certain that he had even glimpsed a nipple. And she did not care at all.

For an old scumbag like him, peaking at a forbidden part of a beautiful girl was the most pleasant excitement in life. Only the sight of blood and the slitting of someone's throat gave him the same deep emotion, or even a little more.

Munro wondered what Cindy saw in Charles that he didn't have.

"Are you listening to me?" Charles asked aggressively, as they were walking together out into the garden.

"Of course, I am listening to you." Bruce replied, annoyed.

Charles saw Munro distracted and listless. He already regretted calling him.

That man did not seem to be what he once was. Charles had noticed it immediately, in fact, he looked out of shape. He thought Bruce must have serious problems with alcohol and drugs. He was also too old for this job. Certainly, Bruce was older than fifty years.

Charles tried to act as if nothing had happened, hoping he was wrong.

"What can I do for you, Charles?"

"This is a personal, private affair that no one should know about."

"I will be as mute as the grave; you have my word."

"Okay! ...Well!... It is ... it's Cindy. You must find out if she is betraying me with ... my old friend Tom...Tom Atkinson." Lewis said stuttering and with extreme embarrassment.

Monro said, "That's it?"

"And it seems insignificant!" Lewis replied ironically.

Munro promised to act immediately. In a couple of days, he would give Charles a clear and definitive answer.

Charles was optimistic he would soon solve the problem of the red car following him.

"Child's play," he called it.

About Cindy, it could take longer to discover something concrete, it depended on luck. He also thought that FBI agents might be at stake for the bug deal, but that did not scare him so much.

However, in the end Munro comforted Charles by telling him something essential: whoever was spying on him knew little, or very little, about him and his organization. If not, why hadn't they already arrested him? His enemies were still looking for evidence, and a solid track to follow.

Who knew if they could find any clue or not?

It was still possible to come out victorious, one just had to be cunning.

Having said that, Bruce left the house, as he had entered, climbing over the fence. Charles came back in a good mood, went up the stairs and entered the bedroom.

"Next time, put on a dressing gown when you come to the living room if there are people, especially certain kinds of people," he said to Cindy aggressively. She was reading and lying on the bed and did not care or listen to any of his words.

XIV

BETHESDA, MARYLAND, THE SAME EVENING

Dick Tolone was relaxed quietly in front of the television, without a real program to watch. In fact, he had spent more time switching channels than watching a show. Dick was sleepless, so he preferred not to follow his wife to bed.

At about 10 o'clock someone knocked on the door.

"Who the hell can it be at this hour?" He mumbled and went to open it.

"Hi Dick! Did I bother you by chance?"

"What in the world! You! But what are you doing here? Weren't you in Mexico?" He exclaimed in amazement.

"I'm back as you see, can I sit down?"

JULIE SUE sat in the living room.

Julie seemed tired and fatigued. Before sitting on the couch, she took off her jeans jacket, shoes, and collapsed heavily on the couch.

"What happened to you, Julie? You look haggard," Tolone asked anxiously.

"I'm incredibly tired. I can't wait to take a nice shower and go to sleep for thirty-six hours straight. I returned a little while ago from Mexico and decided to come and visit to let you know the latest news. I'm more comfortable here than in the office, there are too many distractions there."

"Probably you have a lot of news to tell, since you have been on the road. On the other hand, I stayed here and had the same monotonous life."

"Don't make me think about it, please! Everything went so wrong. This trip was a disaster, a waste of time and nothing else" Julie complained annoyed.

"On the phone you told me you had a trace, something concrete. What happened next?" Tolone asked perplexed.

Julie asked Dick for a drink before starting her story.

Then when she had a cold orange juice, she began to narrate the events: "I thought that I had a trace of something concrete, however I was wrong. At first everything was fine. I stalked Dawnin without any problems. I even took pictures of him, and other people he knows. But in the end things got tangled. I followed Dawnin to Mexico, but after I lost track of him. And there's more. Do you see this man talking to Dawnin?" Julie said while showing the first of a series of photographs she had pulled out of a bag.

The photo was of Henry and the old Ray Brown.

"Yes! What's special about it?" Dick asked with keen interest.

"This fellow a few hours after being photographed, lost his life, in a hit and run. I don't believe it was a traffic accident, and the driver left in fear. Not a chance. He was deliberately murdered; I am sure of this" Julie said with a dramatic tone."

"Maybe it was Dawnin?" Dick asked with little conviction.

"No! Dawnin had nothing to do with it. He is innocent. I saw Dawnin leave on his motorcycle a few minutes before the accident. Do you know what the curious thing is?"

"No," replied Dick.

"The curious thing is that I saw who killed that man."

"What! Why didn't you go to the police to report him, or you could have arrested him? You are an FBI agent, aren't you?" Dick exclaimed surprised, shaking his body in the armchair he was sitting in.

"Calm down, don't get agitated, I probably didn't express myself well, I said I saw, but maybe I didn't see anything."

"Julie! You're making me crazy. What did you see? Have you seen it or not? Are you drunk?"

Julie concisely told the story.

She had noticed Henry and Ray entering a pub. Knowing that Dawnin was there and was not running away anywhere, she had just passed by a couple of times to check what he was doing. Julie had given up going there, because it would have been too obvious, she wanted to stay in the shadows as much as possible. She was walking down the street, looking at shop windows to kill time. During her wanderings, she saw an old Buick, blue in color, parked on the sides of the road. Then she observed that two big guys got out of the car, one so blond as to look albino, the other the opposite, dark, Latino.

The two walked to the pub.

"I was really intrigued by them, from the beginning and had the distinct feeling I had seen them somewhere, but I could not remember where. I was certain those two were not going to the bar to drink and chat with friends. My gut feeling was telling me this, those lads were there to cause trouble. I approached the door of the pub to check. It had only been a few minutes safter they entered that a quarrel started. Guess with whom?"

"Don't tell me. With Dawnin and that other guy?" Dick replied.

"Correct, but it was not Dawnin or the other man who started, but those two scoundrels. Dawnin was attacked and fell on the ground, badly beaten, poor man. It was the other person, Dawnin's friend, who impressed me the most. At the end of the fight, he seemed to have gone mad.

Those two bullies walked away, insulting, and threatening Dawnin, still lying exhausted on the ground. Dawnin's friend suddenly ran away from the pub shouting nonsense phrases, the only thing I caught was that damn night ... that night… that night.

I was stunned, the quarrel had lasted for such a short time and had been so raw and violent. I had moved away from the threshold of the room to the edge of the road. After a few minutes, Dawnin left the pub, quickly got on his Honda and left. I had the impression that he noticed me while he was driving full throttle on his bike.

Everything seemed calm, but it was not true. After about ten minutes I was returning to the hotel, when I saw, that friend of Dawnin, what is his name... Brown, Ray Brown, walking at a brisk pace. Suddenly, before my eyes a car arrived at high speed and hit him without slowing down. It was not an accident; there was deliberate no doubt about it.

I can swear. I was too far away to see exactly who it was, but the car that hit Brown was blue, and it was a Buick like those two guys drove. I'm ready to bet it was them."

"What did you do next?"

"What could I do? I ran as fast as I could towards that poor guy. When I reached him, he was already dead, I could not do anything, unfortunately. Then before people or the police came along, I disappeared. Returning to the hotel, I tried to remember where I had seen those faces, and suddenly I remembered them. Those two are part of Lewis's gang. We had seen their photos in the dossiers we reviewed together.

Now you understand why I did not do anything in order not to compromise the whole operation. If I reported those bastards to the police, it would screw everything. Think of going to testify at a trial against those two individuals, it means announcing to Charles Lewis that we are investigating his organization. To trap those two, we would have given up the whole gang. It is Lewis we must incriminate, frame him, and all the small fish will come to the hook. Finally, I was too far away, I could never swear in a court that it was just them. I cannot go to a trial accusing someone without firm evidence. My own credibility was at stake."

Reflecting on the whole story Dick Tolone agreed with Julie.

In fact, he understood that she had behaved like a real professional.

Suddenly he asked, "Do you think Dawnin is not involved in this matter? What opinion do you have of him?"

"Do you want my honest opinion?"

"Of course, Julie! You are talking to me, not Matthew Collins or some other asshole at the department who wants to brainwash you."

"To me, Dawnin is just a poor guy who happened to get involved in this whole thing. I don't know what he did, but he doesn't look like a criminal. Surely, he is an eccentric, half-hippy, and stoned dude. But he is not part of the gang of those criminals. If you want to know the whole truth about him, I think he's a handsome man, damn! He is beautiful. Too bad!... That it is on the... wrong track."

Dick Tolone was surprised by Julie's confidence. It seemed to him that she had an infatuation with a man she did not even know, and a possible criminal.

Therefore, he didn't hold back to make a joke, "Hey Julie! Did you fall in love with that scoundrel?"

"What do you say, Dick, don't be witty. I only said Dawnin is not ugly at all, and that he is probably not as evil as the others. What is strange is that I don't even know him. He could be a gentleman as well as a delinquent. You revealed to me that you found out nothing about him. His criminal record is almost completely clean, excluding the assault on his boss, a couple of unpaid fines, and being stopped for protests during the Vietnam War at a time when thousands of people were protesting. When did the last infraction happen?"

"I do not remember the date precisely, but they are quite recent. I am sure of that,"

"So, for a good part of his life Dawnin had no criminal record."

"Yes! That is right."

"What did you find out about his economic status, private life and his bank account?"

Dick briefly summarized what he had found Dawnin, his private life, friendships, and occupations. Then he shared the present condition of Henry, unemployed and broke.

"Henry Dawnin has no money and several debts to settle. In his bank account right now, he has 19 dollars and 17 cents. I don't think he swims in gold, this fellow."

"Bingo! It is perfectly clear, and I was right. Henry Dawnin is a man adrift. A desperate man who agrees to work with Lewis to survive is not a hardened criminal. After all, we don't even know if he committed anything illegal. Don't you understand? Dawnin is our track. We absolutely must find him; he can be the ace up our sleeve. If he knows something important about Charles Lewis and associates, he may be a valuable witness. We must ascertain what he knows, and if it's as I believe, we can finally frame Lewis."

Despite Dick did not have any crucial news to reveal, he believed there were key facts to discuss. The first concerned the bug, illegally installed in Charles Lewis's phone in the office, which no longer worked."

Knowing this, Julie asked, "Do you think Lewis discovered that bug?"

"I don't know, I hope not, I wish it has been defective. I hope with all my heart, because if Lewis discovers the bug, we are in trouble. We were already before, when, without any permission, we installed it, wondering if Collins knew what we had done. This morning, I was in front of my desk when Collins came in, so I immediately followed him to the office. He was more unpleasant, grumpy, and aggressive than usual. He ordered me to close the door, and then began to ask several questions. For example, who we are investigating, what other leads we are following and if we have discovered anything. I had spoken to him a couple of days before and promised that at the first concrete lead, I would clarify the whole situation and...."

"Did you tell him about Dawnin?" Julie interrupted upset.

"No! Not about him, but I told him about Lewis."

"What! Have you gone crazy? Why did you tell him about Charles Lewis? It's too early and we don't have anything concrete."

"You're right, Julie, I regretted it bitterly, yet you don't know how Collins pressed me, he would kick me in the butt if I didn't tell him something. I swear to you! It was all very frustrating, I didn't know what to say to him, so in the end I made up that name to have some breathing space," Tolone answered ashamed.

"Did you tell him about the bug?"

"No! Absolutely not! I was a moron, but not up to that point. At the end of our meeting, Collins introduced me to a new agent, I did not know, saying: this is your new partner for the operation."

"Are you kidding me?"

"No! Julie, I am not kidding. He introduced me to this guy... Jeff... Jeff... I don't remember the last name, a new guy, never seen before."

"What was your first opinion of him?"

67

"Well! I have not much to report on him, I do not know how to describe him, about 30-32 years old, Caucasian, average build, short brown hair, clean shaven, a man with an ordinary appearance. The only thing that struck me about him are his eyes, cold and inscrutable.

You know that I always stare people in the eye when I greet them. Shit! The eyes of this chap are strange, they have something false, perverse, but I may also have been wrong. Of course, it was just my fleeting first impression. For the rest he seems introverted, quiet, perhaps Jeff was negatively impressed by Collins' bad temper."

"I can't understand why Collins wants to give us a stranger for this investigation. You understand! This is our investigation. If we manage to frame Lewis, promotion is guaranteed, and we will be a great success. Think about how many untouchable people will go down with him. Think of the headlines in the newspapers: defeated deviant CIA forces, arrested illustrious personalities for illicit trafficking, murders ... etcetera, etcetera."

Dick, looking at Julie, replied in solidarity, "Julie, maybe I shouldn't even tell you, but watch your back. I heard a rumor that Collins wants to suspend you from service."

"What?" Julie exclaimed, surprised.

"I don't know what he is going to do, I guess he's going to suspend you, and unfortunately this Jeff will be your replacement. Maybe I should not have told you this, but I think it's better that you're prepared for the worst. Anyway! I will always be on your side as usual and we will finish this investigation together, whatever the cost, and fuck the bureaucracy, and assholes like Matthew Collins."

Julie had left her friend's house ten minutes ago. Now she was heading home in her car.

Dick had asked if she wanted to sleep on the sofa in his living room, but politely she refused. In fact, her apartment, in Georgetown, was not far from there.

She felt really depressed, and that was the real reason for her refusal.

That secret Dick revealed, regarding a probable suspension, had given the final coup de grace to her frustrations.

On the other hand, even in her gloomy mood, Julie felt lucky and happy to have a partner like Dick. They had worked together for a while, and it was good from the start. The two of them had always been in harmony and never had a problem. Furthermore, building a solid relationship at work, they also become good friends in life. They even attended parties together.

Julie was constantly invited to Tolone's house for events such as lunches, dinners, special celebrations. Occasionally, she even looked after his kids when Dick and his wife had things to do. Julie Sue was the new kid on the block when she arrived in the FBI department. She was a young promising agent, very sharp, but with no experience. And it was Dick Tolone, who guided and protected Julie and made her feel at home in the office. Not only that, but Dick had also been a fiery opponent against Collins and his abuses toward Julie.

Matthew Collins hated Julie from the beginning.

He was nasty, angry, and unfriendly to everybody, but with Julie was even worse.

The man always put Julie down on every occasion he could, mocking, insulting her. Dick confronted Collins many times about his poor treatment of Julie. They had quarrels about this; however Matthew was his superior and Dick knew it.

Julie arrived home at midnight, opened the door and pulled her suitcase inside with difficulty. Suddenly the suitcase, losing its balance, fell noisily to the ground.

"Who is it? Who is it?"

Lisa Barnes, the friend with whom she shared the house, shouted, frightened. Lisa was a twenty-five-year-old, blonde, thin, medium in height, with green eyes, and rather delicate facial features.

"It's me, Julie."

Lisa, in pajamas, opened the door of her room and met Julie in the living room.

"Hello, Julie! You scared me to death; I wasn't expecting you right now."

"I apologize, you're right, it's a bit late to come back. Why didn't you put the chain on?"

"I always forget to put it, you know."

Lisa helped her friend by taking the suitcase to her room.

"How are you? Anything exciting to tell me?" Lisa asked smiling.

"Oh! If you only knew, I have nothing nice to tell and I feel so tired, so depressed."

Lisa, realizing that Julie didn't really want to talk about her latest experiences, affectionately hugged her and told her to go to sleep. Before leaving the room, Julie asked her, "What time are you going to work tomorrow?"

"At nine o'clock, why?"

"Please wake me up as soon as you get up, so we can have breakfast together."

Remaining alone in the room Julie took off her clothes and without taking the coveted shower, desired for the entire day, went straight to bed. She turned off the lamp, crawled into bed, and began to cry. Eventually she fell asleep.

At half past seven Lisa came into Julie's room and woke her up. "Wake up, sleepyhead, it's late, and be ready for a hot, muggy day."

Julie had slept heavily but despite this, she had not fully recovered and struggled to wake up. Finally, with difficulty, she got out of bed and, taking clean clothes, went to the bathroom to take a shower. While she was in the shower, several negative thoughts flowed into her mind, almost overlapping with each other. Julie thought about what excuse to invent for being late and tried to guess what reaction that asshole, Collins, would have after listening her story. She only hoped he did not suspend her.

She tried to imagine what kind of person this new agent Jeff was, and if he could be a valuable help for the investigation, or not.

Finally, she recalled the most absurd and far-fetched story that could exist remembering parts of the dream she had the previous night.

It had been a strange dream, a bit disturbing and meaningless.

She was with Henry Dawnin, and it seemed as if they had been friends forever. They had played tennis together, and now the dude was taking her away on his motorcycle, leaving Redlands for the ocean. The ocean was different, more like a tropical sea. In fact, the beach was deserted and was composed of white coral sand, with several coconut palms reaching as far as the shoreline.

They parked the bike under a tree and ran to the water. They took off their clothes and dived naked into the calm, warm sea. After swimming for a while, they returned to shore and lying on the shoreline began to kiss romantically.

They began to walk along the shoreline and here was the strangest and most singular part of the dream. Henry told her about the Runners, a sect that practiced voodoo, considered immortal, who were from Haiti and had spread all over the world with members of every race and color. Henry had met the first Runner while standing with his uncle on the edge of a crossroads between two dusty country roads. They were sitting on boulders of white limestone; his uncle was reading a newspaper, and Henry was quietly smoking a cigarette.

Suddenly a dirty beggar had arrived, with a bandage on his left eye, asking for money. Henry refused and, before leaving, the man had cursed him for life. Since then, the Runners had hunted Dawnin in every place where he had gone and tried to kill him several times. However, one day he found a way to destroy a Runner. Simply pouring cold beer on their head and the head melted as if it had been corroded by sulfuric acid.

"Julie! Breakfast is ready. Be quick as it is quite late," Lisa warned as she knocked on the door. Hearing Lisa's call, she woke up with remnants of the dream in her thoughts.

After answering Lisa, she got back in the shower. Glancing at the clock she discovered she had been more than half an hour underwater. She quickly dressed, wearing a pair of shorts and a wide sleeveless white cotton t-shirt. After that she went straight to the kitchen, still with damp hair.

Lisa was sitting at the table and ready to go to work.

"I hope you are not going to the office dressed like that. Your colleagues will think you are going to the beach, ha-ha," Lisa told her amused.

"Why? Don't you like how I am dressed? Don't worry! I will certainly not go in this way. But you instead, why are you particularly elegant?"

"Today I have a case in court, it's not the usual office day."

During breakfast Julie recounted parts of what had happened recently, without giving either names or too many explanations, which were all strictly confidential. She told her about the time wasted in California and Mexico, and then she told her what Dick had said, that she might be suspended.

"Now you understand how I feel, I've wasted precious time and that's it. Not only that, now I'm afraid that asshole of Collins will give me a tough time. He will be so angry. That is why I'm taking it easy, at this time, I should already be in the office, I think I'll go there late in the morning."

"Be brave! Julie, you must face Collins sooner or later. Try to go there unbiased, perhaps he will just give you a rebuke, a small reproach. Your best friend is telling you this, you'll see that things will work out." Lisa said with a supportive tone, trying to cheer her up. She gave Julie a warm hug and left home before nine o'clock, saying she would be back late.

Julie, after finishing reading the newspaper, went to the large terrace of the apartment to get a breath of fresh air.

The day was splendid, there was not a cloud in the sky, and it was already hot. She would have liked to stay there, sunbathing, relaxing a bit, reading an enjoyable book, with a good drink in her hand, but unfortunately, she had to go to the office. She saw those soft mats where Lisa and she used to lay, when they were sunbathing, and saw the inflatable small pool they had bought to get wet when it was too hot.

Oh yes! Everything was so comfortable and inviting.

Julie loved the penthouse apartment where she lived, and loved that terrace, private and away from prying eyes. In fact, all the buildings around the complex were lower and no one could peek at them. Thus, often she had taken the opportunity to sunbathe topless. Resisting the temptation to lie in the sun and take a nap, she decided it was time to take "the bull by the horns," the horns of Collins. For this reason, she went to her room, changed clothes, and drove to the office.

She entered the FBI building, and had just called the elevator when a bloke, never seen before, stood next to her. The elevator arrived and the man signaled her to enter first.

"Which floor are you going to?" The man asked.

"To the third, thank you."

"Oh, coincidentally! I'm going there too."

"Do you work here?" she asked him.

"Yes, for a couple of days, please let me introduce myself. I am Jeff Wilson."

Julie shook hands, introducing herself in turn.

Dick Tolone, saw Julie coming, stood up to greet her and seeing she was in the company of Jeff exclaimed politely, "I see that you have already met, Jeff! This is Julie, the colleague I told you about."

The man grimaced and walked away.

"You are suspended indefinitely." Matthew Collins said dryly during their meeting.

"Indefinite time means that when I want and feel it will be appropriate, I can call you to resume work. It can be in a week, a month, or six months. Feel lucky that I will not confiscate your badge and fire you, kicking you in the butt. Today is your lucky day, given I am in a good mood, and I will not make any drastic decision. If I were a referee in soccer, I would give you a yellow card, a caution alert, instead of giving the red one, so you are out." Collins said in the meanest tone possible.

"But … I … I... I had a... lead a...."

"Shut up! You went away for more than a week, without me knowing anything. Looking for what, glory and adventure? There are specific rules to respect, we are not at the amusement park.

Above all, I demand that everyone who works here keeps me constantly informed of what they are doing and where they go. I am the one who decides if one thing is good, and another is not. None of my staff have ever allowed themselves to contradict my rules. You are the exception." Collins shouted angrily, abruptly interrupting Julie's umpteenth attempt to apologize.

"Then what is this story you are investigating about Charles Lewis? Don't you know who Charles Lewis is? He is one of the most eminent businessmen in the nation. His father Harold was one of the top figures at the CIA, and his son was part of the same organization for many years. Now he has turned to business. What do you have against him?"

"I think he's involved in illicit trafficking, drugs, weapons, and murder."

"Do you have any definite and tangible evidence about this?" Collins asked irritated.

"No! But I think...."

"Do not think. Don't think anymore, do you understand? Unfortunately, if Charles Lewis finds out that the FBI are investigating him, for no obvious reason, I will get fired, but you before me. Lewis has powerful and influential friendships that would make me lose my job in less than 24 hours." Collins shouted, interrupting her again and slamming his fists violently on the table.

"Thus, because he is a powerful, rich man, he can do what he wants to do, breaking every rule, and killing people?" Julies replied dryly.

"How do you know? Before you said you have nothing on him. You want that I arrest Lewis by saying, you know, a twenty-five-year-old rookie agent, who has been working for me for less than a year, thinks you are a murderer and an arms dealer. We have no evidence against you, only her intuition. You are crazy. Forget about Charles Lewis, that is an order."

"We have dossiers that clearly involve certain rogue CIA forces in illicit trafficking. Give us a week and you will see that Dick and I will not disappoint you, in fact we will bring you unequivocal and solid evidence of his guilt."

Collins paused for a moment to reflect on what Julie had just told him, and in the end, he seemed to have made a drastic decision. However, he didn't answer but picked up the phone and called Dick.

"Are you busy? No! Good! Then come to my office immediately and bring Jeff here as well."

A few moments later the two men showed up.

Collins, after making them sit down, began to speak in a very authoritarian tone, "I have decided, for the good of this department and everyone involved, that the illegal inquiry into Charles Lewis initiated by Dick Tolone and Julie Sue is officially over, terminated, suspended, and concluded. From now on, any case originating from this office will be ordered and followed by me in person. For this act, which I consider to be insubordination, Dick Tolone is officially removed from the investigation of the corruption in the CIA and will begin to work on different cases. While Julie Sue is also removed from the case and is suspended until further notice, it will be Jeff Wilson who will continue this investigation and determine if there is anything positive and concrete, or just a handful of ridiculous nonsense."

Collins stunned both Dick and Julie with his speech. Unfortunately, Julie was too upset to reply and barely held back her tears.

Earlier, when Matthew called Tolone, Julie had hoped, for a moment, that Collins might change his mind and let her continue the case. But she was wrong and now did not find the energy necessary to say a single syllable, defending herself.

It was Dick who was furious and tried to confront his superior.

"I do not understand you Collins! Can you explain why you have this negative attitude towards us? Why are you shutting down the Charles Lewis case, while letting Jeff Wilson manage the corruption investigation at the CIA? Don't you understand that we are doing a good job, let us proceed."

"I know what I'm doing," Collins replied nervously.

"Matthew! What in the world! What are you doing? The Charles Lewis case is crucial—for the good of the entire country. You have known me for how long, for six years? Or more? You know I am not a person who wastes time on nonsense. I concretely believe we can frame Lewis if you give us time and resources. Also, you were too strict with Julie, after all, she acted in good faith, hoping to be able to discover something useful. Why are you suspending her? This is unfair, very unfair. Julie is a good agent, very professional and sharp. Not only that, I can also state she is the best partner I ever had. You are simply wrong." A feisty Dick Tolone spoke with vehemence and passion.

"Dick! I do not want to talk about it anymore and thank God that I'm not suspending you too, but I will, if you continue to bother me." Collins replied aggressively.

"And Jeff! Are you able to continue this investigation and achieve something positive?" he asked dryly.

The man, who had not opened his mouth the whole time, sarcastically replied, "I think you made a good choice, Collins, you won't regret it. I know how to work."

71

Then, he arrogantly asked Tolone, "I need all the documentation, so I can start to work. Can you give it to me now? You know! I don't waste time when I work."

Having said that, without waiting for an answer, Jeff left, with a slight amused air.

Julie had a great desire to go home, as she felt tired and depressed, and had no desire to socialize, but Dick had insisted on going for something to drink.

Finally, she agreed. They headed to a pub near the office, where they often spent time together.

Dick had ordered a draft beer, while Julie had a coke. They got a small table overlooking the street in the uncrowded local.

They were venting to each other when by pure chance Jeff Wilson, seeing them in the pub, entered and walked towards them.

"You talk about the devil and the devil comes out," Dick whispered annoyed in a low voice.

Jeff came up and said, "Hey guys! Why do you have those sad faces? Come on! It did not go that badly. There are so many investigations and so many crimes in the world, Dick, you can start a new case, can't you? And you, beautiful girl! You are suspended, not fired. What more do you want? Now you have time to run errands, to chat with friends, to flirt with your boyfriend and to think about the hypothesis of searching for a new job. A real job for women, you know? You must have the balls for this job, and you don't have it, ah! ah!"

Feeling insulted, Julie got up from her chair and threw the contents of the glass in his face. Then she ran from the restaurant to the parking lot where she had left her car.

In the car, she suddenly burst out laughing hysterically.

She thought about what Henry Dawnin had told her about the "Runners," in the strange dream, she had the previous night and, laughing, said to herself, "Damn! If I had a glass of cold beer instead of coke, I could have seen if that bastard was a Runner, and if he was, I would have melted his face. But patience, that will be for the next time."

XV

SEATTLE, WASHINGTON

Charles was in a great mood the morning after hiring Munro. In fact, he believed he had a solid organization, made up of serious professionals, who could be trusted blindly. The exterminator was his flagship, and the one who would make the difference.

After taking a long shower, he shaved and whistled at low volume, so as not to disturb Cindy who was still asleep. He wore an elegant suit and tie and was ready to go to the office.

He walked out of the bedroom, when he heard Cindy calling to ask where he was going.

"I'm going to the office, I have work to do, and what are you doing today?"

"I don't know! I plan to stay at home this morning and go on errands this afternoon, and even tomorrow."

Continuing to whistle blissfully, Charles went to the garage, got his BMW 635 convertible, and came out, closing the door with the remote control. Driving down the street he suddenly noticed the red Ford Escort about sixty feet from his house parked among other cars. His dark glasses prevented him from seeing if there was anyone in the car.

He did not blink and passed quietly, without paying attention, saying to himself, "You will see the trick that I will do to you my friend" and continued to drive downtown. Arriving at the office, he noticed he had not been followed.

After parking the car, he went to a nearby phone booth and called Munro. After several rings, Munro's unfriendly voice replied, "Who is breaking my balls at this hour?"

"It is me, Charles! Look, it is almost nine o'clock. It's time to get to work."

"Charles! What do you want?" Munro asked annoyed.

"The red Ford Escort has been parked near my house this morning; I have nothing more to add."

"Don't worry. I will take care of it, just relax, stay serene, and enjoy the day. Also, regarding the other question concerning Cindy, rest assured, I am working on it. I'll call you in a couple of days, bye."

Without waiting for Charles to reply Munro hung up the handset.

Charles went to a coffee shop near the phone booth and ordered a cup of latte to take away, then went to the office. Sharon had not yet arrived.

She arrived after about fifteen minutes, a little embarrassed by the delay, "Excuse me Mr. Lewis... Charles... unfortunately this morning I missed the bus, that's why I'm late."

"It doesn't matter, don't worry about it. Soon a guy, Tim Boyle should arrive. When he is here, show him right away to my office."

After a few minutes Tim Boyle was in Charles's office.

"Tim! I want you to scrupulously check this office inch by inch, and all the other attached rooms. I do not want any other bugs or similar filth."

The man immediately started to work, turning things upside down, moving furniture, paintings, chairs. After a while he came back saying, "I am done. Everything is fine, I did not find anything. The phones are also clear, you can rest easy Mr. Lewis."

It had been a particularly intense and fruitful day for Charles.

After having the office checked, he had five clients with whom he had done good business. Also, he organized a trip to go to the old mission. His goal was to go quickly and come back soon. He had no time to waste. For this trip he would have brought with him the trusty Doug and Greg Murphy, and would have met Scott and Ramon in Mexico, where, without success, they had remained in search of Henry. They would have gone the next day.

Finally, he had news that had calmed him and that he would have revealed to the men very soon. Oh yes! Now he was much more relaxed. It seemed things were slowly coming together.

While Charles was enjoying the fruits of his temporary triumphs in his office, Bruce Munro was also getting busy.

In fact, after receiving Charles's phone call, he had organized his own plan of action. He had given himself two days to capture the man, or men, in the red Ford Escort and make them confess. The important thing was to catch one alive. Bruce was overly excited because he hadn't tortured anyone in some time.

His second move was to hire Tom Chong, an old acquaintance to stalk Cindy.

Tom was an excellent photographer and had also participated in several private detective courses. Moreover, with his almost insignificant appearance, small, thin, with thick glasses, a nerdy look, he was the right man to stalk Cindy.

Tom looked like the classic Asian tourist going around the city taking photographs.

He knew that if Cindy Hyatt showed even the smallest affection with Tom Atkinson, even a short one, Chong would capture it with a nice, explicit photo.

The next morning at seven o'clock, Charles had not yet left the house, and no light was on inside his home. However, the red Ford was there, lurking, parked in the same place as the previous day, in the deserted and silent street.

Suddenly as fast as a lightning bolt and silent as a bird of prey, Bruce Munro appeared as if out of nowhere, armed with a gun equipped with a silencer. Munro approached the driver's window, and taking a quick glance inside, through the window that was open about three inches, he noticed two men inside. Unable to open the locked door, he shoved his gun through the window and pointed it at the driver's temple. At the same time, he shouted, ordering "Open the door or I will blow your head off."

The man, surprised by the appearance of the exterminator, opened the door but stupidly tried to remove the gun from his hand.

Munro was not surprised and as quick as a rattlesnake shot him twice in the head, killing him instantly.

In the bloodbath, the man's body collapsed heavily on the steering wheel causing the horn to sound. Entering the vehicle Bruce moved the dead man away from the steering wheel, and without waiting for the other man to react, violently hit him in the head with the gun. Then, taking the man by the nape, slammed his head a couple of times into the windshield, stunning him completely. Once the chap was knocked out, Bruce put on handcuffs, lifted him up and threw him into the back seat.

After making sure the doors were closed, he put his seat belt on, like a good citizen, turned on the care and drove away. The whole thing took place in less than two minutes.

Munro was humming "Nessun Dorma," with the dead man at his side and the hostage in the back and, headed to a safe place, to have a chat with his mysterious friend.

He was particularly happy because he had kept his promise to himself: he had captured the men in the red Ford Escort in less than two days.

Bruce took the prisoner to the predetermined place and along the way got rid of the corpse and the car. He knew the man had been beaten violently and could be stunned for several hours. To pass the time he had decided to call Charles to tell him the good news. Unfortunately, he could not talk to him, because Lewis had gone out of town. A little disappointed by this, Munro went for a walk, waiting for the right moment to interrogate the prisoner.

After about three hours Munro returned to the base and found his prisoner awake. The poor man was tied to a chair, and gagged in a dusty, dirty, and empty warehouse.

With a big smile the wicked bald man approached his prey, like a vulture, and removed his gag saying, "I think you have so many things to tell me, is that not true my love."

The man stared straight into his eyes but did not answer.

Changing his approach, the grim character started to speak, "Maybe I was not very clear, maybe we didn't understand each other. I want you to tell me everything, to spill the beans. I want to know who you are. Are you an FBI agent? What do you know about Charles Lewis? Who are your accomplices? Do you understand? If you do not talk soon, it will be worse for you, because in one way or another I will make you spit out the truth.

"Son of a bitch!" The prisoner replied in Spanish.

Feeling insulted, Munro gave him a hard slap, then approaching his face, shouted, "Look at this guy, he even knows Spanish. Are you a cultured person? Bastard! Speak! I am losing my patience, buddy." Having said that, he slapped the prisoner again.

"I won't tell you anything, son of a bitch, scumbag, do you understand?" The prisoner replied.

Hearing this, Munro was quite surprised. He was not surprised by what the prisoner had just said, because most of the people he interrogated always tried to resist him but was surprised by the accent. In fact, that man did not seem to be American.

"I will set you free if you cooperate and talk. Tell me why you and your partner stalked Charles Lewis? Tell me only this and you will be released, I give you my word."

The man, looking at him with contempt, replied, "I know who you are, you are Bruce Munro, a butcher, a treacherous being. We know everything about you, and I know you're lying. I know I'm doomed, even if I speak, I wouldn't get away with it. I'm not going to tell you a single syllable and go fuck yourself."

Munro was amazed.

That man knew about him, knew his name. By now it was more than certain he did not belong to the FBI. His accent was quite marked, the man was a foreigner. Rummaging through his trouser pockets Bruce took out his wallet, but found no identity documents, nothing that could reveal his name.

Seeing two hundred dollars in the wallet, he put the cash in his pocket, saying, "We are rich! Ah! Dear friend, apparently business is good, but you no longer need this."

That said, he punched the prisoner violently in the nose.

The man was in a bad shape. His face was bloody, he had broken ribs, as well as his nasal septum, and moreover he had fainted several times, wasting precious time for his tormentor.

Munro began to worry slightly, in fact, no one had ever resisted him. After many hours of intense interrogation, the man had not revealed anything important. So, he decided to change his method. Violence and cruelty did not seem to have any effect on the mysterious stalker.

Quite disappointed by the lackluster result, he decided to use a method that was not usual for him, to use drugs on the prisoner. But he could not do it at that moment as the hostage had lost consciousness. Seeing it was also quite late, Bruce decided to resume the interrogation the next day.

Punctually the next day Munro returned with the right tools.

He injected drugs into the veins of the man, who was more dead than alive, and then began to interrogate in his own way.

Many of the things the man said made no sense, in fact he mumbled, did not pronounce words clearly and mixed Spanish with English. Eventually, Munro grasped he was Mexican, and his name was Pepe Gomez. Apparently, he was in close contact with a certain Carlos Gonzales. Finally, the guy had repeated the word organization several times but had not revealed any information about it.

It seemed that Gonzales often hung around in a Mexican restaurant called "El Toro." However, when Munro asked more about this individual, the prisoner had once again fainted, cutting off the stunted conversation.

Bruce, nervous, sat on the floor, waiting for Pepe to wake up. After waiting a long time, he checked his wrist and realized Gomez was dead.

"Shit!" Munro screamed angrily.

Bruce was not satisfied at all with his work. He thought he had made a resounding mistake in tactics. If he had used the drug from the beginning, he could have gotten more useful information. He should have understood that Gomez was a tough guy, and it was useless to use strong methods with him.

It was too late. In any case, he had a vague idea of what was happening.

First, there was an organization, a gang, or something similar, that was on Charles's trail. He had no idea who they were or why they were hunting Charles, but he had the vague impression it was something related to his trade and business.

Second, it must have been a Mexican organization or affiliated with Mexicans.

Third, that Carlos Gonzales was the organizer of the stalking and was wondering if Charles knew who he was.

Fourth, the FBI was not involved in these stalking.

Fifth, (his greatest concern), this organization knew about him.

The trouble arose because the matter became personal, and it was his task to find out who was hiding in the shade. What drove Munro crazy was that neither the police nor the FBI had ever discovered his existence as a ruthless hitman.

Incredibly, now he discovered that a filthy organization of Mexican idiots knew of his exploits as a murderer.

Bruce Munro had remained with no criminal record for all those years and was considered a model citizen. He had never been charged with a crime or had never run a red traffic light and those few times he had been fined for parking, or some other small irregularity, he had always paid the fine immediately.

The fellow with more than 150 murders behind him, had always gotten away with it in the eyes of justice and the system. The dude that with his skill had become probably the most expensive killer in the whole hemisphere, now had to fear a dirty gang of Mexican impostors.

He could not allow this. After getting rid of Gomez' corpse, Bruce hastily went to a phone booth and dialed Charles's office number. After a couple of rings, the secretary answered the phone, "Oh! Sorry, Mr. Lewis is still out of town, no! I do not know where he went, but he told me he will come back soon. If you want to leave a message, please, go ahead. What is your name, mister...?"

"No! Okay, I do not have any message to leave, or any time to waste. I will call back later," Bruce said, and abruptly ended the call.

On the other side, Sharon, with the handset still in the hand, exclaimed, "How rude!"

XV

Puerto Vallarta, Mexico

Henry had enjoyed the succulent lunch Fuentes's cooks had prepared for him.

At the table he had met Mrs. Fuentes, a beautiful but not very talkative woman, who after greeting him had not spoken and her daughter Luisa.

Fuentes's wife, Carmen, was a dark-haired, Latino-looking, thin, tall woman with sad eyes. He had noticed this detail from the beginning. While Carmen did not speak and kept her eyes down, eating slowly, Rodrigo had acted the host of the table with grace and delicacy. The conversation had been pleasant, varied and not a word had been said about work or Charles.

After lunch, they smoked cigarettes in the huge garden, with Fuentes opting for a cigar, having momentarily abandoned his Gitanes. They had coffee, and then the host, pushing the wheelchair to his office, took $15,000 in hundred bills from a safe and handed them to Henry.

Dawnin at the sight of all that money was on the verge of fainting. For someone who had not seen a cent in a long time, that amount felt like a mystical experience.

Then they returned to the terrace, where Maria and Carmen were. When the time arrived to leave, Rodrigo accompanied his guests to the car, bidding them a warm farewell.

Before getting into the car, Henry suddenly froze and worried asked, "Don't you think Charles will go to the mission to get the rest of his loot relatively soon?"

To this question Fuentes nodded his head and replied amused, "It is possible. I would like to see the face he will make when he discovers all his money is no longer there, ah... ah."

"Well! I am certain that bastard will suffer a heart attack when he verifies it. When are you going to act against him? So far, I have seen only skirmishes?" Dawnin asked.

"Soon, very soon. I have some great ideas I would like to implement soon. You must know I have men in Seattle who watch over him day and night. I am also thinking of playing a trick on him, but we will talk about that later." That said, Fuentes said good-bye.

Maria drove the car toward home. Henry would be a guest in her apartment.

At one point, Henry staring at her intensely asking with concern, "I would just like to clarify one important thing. I do not want more lies subterfuge, or deceit of this kind between us. Can I trust you, or can't I?"

"Deal done, no more lies between us," Maria replied, smiling.

"That is not enough for me. You must promise me, understood? I already have too many problems and too many enemies to keep at bay, I would not want you to become another concern. In fact, I hope you are a faithful friend and companion, and no longer... a ... Concita."

"Yes! Okay! I promise! I will never fool you again. Concita is dead and buried. Is that enough for you? Or must I add romantic words of love, to make you forgive me for what I did to you in the remote past." She replied, teasing him.

"That is enough for me! Don't add anything else. I believe you. I just hope it will be true."

The conversation seemed to have ended there, when suddenly Dawnin asked, "I did not understand what kind of person Fuentes is. It is strange! I don't know how to judge him. At first, I liked him, but not in the end. If you want to know the truth, I don't trust Fuentes at all."

"You are right not to trust that guy, just remember that Fuentes was an associate and a colleague of people like Charles Lewis and Tom Atkinson, and I say it all. Anyway! I don't want to talk about it now. Soon, I will tell you something interesting about him."

"Why, before I met him, you told me not to worry, to be serene, because I was among true friends and now you tell me the opposite?"

"Believe it or not, you are among friends, I am your friend, and you can trust me. I told you this, so you had no preconceptions about him. Only in this way, could you form your own ideas about Fuentes. You know! It was not easy to convince him to help and take you to Pedro's farm to heal you. What he said is only half correct. It is true that I was the one who had the idea of helping and finding out as much as possible about you, but Fuentes made more fuss than you think. I tried to talk as little possible about him at his house, because I had the impression Fuentes had ears everywhere. I would not be surprised if he had hidden bugs in his office, so he could hear what his guests and business associates say to each other or think about him. Nor would I be surprised if Fuentes had bugs installed even in my car and is listening to us right now. That dude is capable of anything."

"Ah yes! Do you really think our beloved friend is listening to our conversation now? Well! So, I want to give him a warm greeting, because he deserves it. Hey Fuentes! Fuentes! If you are listening, go away, got it? Fuck you, idiot."

Maria laughed after Henry's affectionate greeting to Fuentes made with such spontaneity.

He had also joked about it, but after a first moment of joy, sadly said, "You know Maria, I think we should go away, leave this country and all these vultures around us. We could start a new life, abroad, without anyone bothering us. I am fed up with this whole affair. I would like to call Charles Lewis to tell him he is a cuckold, that his girlfriend cheats on him and even steals his money, and that I have nothing to do with it, so let me go."

"We can think seriously about the idea of leaving together, running away from our troubles. I am annoyed too with this whole story. And I am also tired of working for the Secret Service. I believe it is now time to make a new turn in my life. Anyway! Let's think about the present. Do you know that my apartment is on the ocean?"

"No! You didn't tell me that. Fantastic! What is the beach like?"

"Frankly, I don't know. I only recently rented this house, and I have not yet had time to go there. From a distance it looks beautiful. This is the fourth residence I have changed in less than four months."

"Why all these moves?" Henry asked with curiosity.

"For safety," replied the woman without adding anything else.

After an hour Maria parked the car under the house.

The apartment was on the third floor in a large building located on the waterfront. Henry entered the house and opened the curtains and windows to let in light and to ventilate the room. He saw a spacious terrace overlooking the ocean. Intrigued, he went out and walked to the railing to admire the fantastic panorama, enjoying the warm sea breeze blowing on him.

Many people crowded the beach, even though it was late afternoon.

He saw children playing in the sand. Some who built castles, others who sprayed water, or threw algae on themselves.

At the sight of this beautiful beach and inviting ocean, he wanted to stay there, in peace and have a long and beautiful period of vacation. Touching his wallet, full of money, he thought the idea could be concretely realized.

"What are you thinking?" Maria asked as approached.

"Are you busy tomorrow morning?"

"Not really why?"

"I want to stay on the beach or rent a motorboat and go around a bit. If you are free, we can wander around together, what do you think?"

"Of course! Very gladly I have no commitments for tomorrow. If you feel like it, now we can take a stroll on the beach, and explore, what do you say?"

"With immense pleasure."

"Good! Let's go now, however when we come back, I need your help," Maria exclaimed.

"For what?"

"Do you see those big cardboard boxes in the corner? They are full of knick-knacks, frames, and more stuff. So far, I haven't had time to get them out, so if you help me, I can finally finish my move."

Having said that, she went to the bedroom to change clothes.

She returned dressed for the beach, wearing tight jean shorts cut a couple of inches below her groin, a light pink cotton t-shirt, and beach sandals.

Henry was paralyzed looking at her. Maria was gorgeous.

They walked about a mile on the shoreline, hand in hand like two lovers. Henry felt good, that Maria was giving him peace, tranquility, and joy. It was something he had not experienced for a very long time.

He was happy to stay with her and did not want to screw up this opportunity to be with her. Henry could not let her slip away.

Maria gave him balance, new fresh energy to keep going on, and a purpose in life. The stretch of beach where they stopped, had a mixture of sand and rocks, and there were only a few people far away. Henry was hot and had a great desire to go for a swim. Not resisting he took off his clothes and in his underwear, prepared to dive into the ocean.

"You should take more care of your look, my grandfather used that underwear before the war," Maria teased.

"I know! I need to buy a swimsuit for tomorrow."

There are several shops around here. We can stop by before returning home."

"Very well," he replied.

"Why don't you swim with me? The water is fantastic."

"I can't, I don't have a swimming suit."

"Just do like me, there's no one around."

Henry quickly took off his underwear and started swimming.

Maria remained on the shoreline, undecided whether to go into the water.

Henry was continuing to swim with strong strokes.

After moving away from the shore, he returned, shouting: "It's fantastic! Come in the water."

In the end, Maria decided to join him, it was such a beautiful day, she could not lose the opportunity, so she took off her clothes, and just in underpants jumped in.

"If they fine me for obscenity, you will pay the fine," she said jokingly.

Henry was positively surprised because he did not imagine such an act of courage from her and replied, "Finally, you did it. Is the water great or what?"

They spent time playing in the water. At a certain point, Henry approached Maria and romantically kissed her on the lips. The two made love with passion, immersed in the heavenly tropical scene.

At the climax of his orgasm Henry literally shouted, "aahhh!" In such a noisy way it could be heard miles away.

Coming out of the water, Maria asked in a mocking way, while giggling, "My God! You really enjoyed our passionate love, didn't you? I feel like a sex machine. Wuhu! You shouted like a madman."

"Enjoyed and sex machine? Damm! I stepped on a sea urchin. Shit! It is hurting bad. It was attached to a rock." Henry said in pain, showing his right foot which was full of the long thorns of a tropical sea urchin on the bottom of his foot.

Maria, after getting dressed, helped to remove the thorns stuck in his foot. In the end she had removed twelve of them and another five or six were threaded so deeply they had to be removed with hot oil and a needle.

"Let us go home so I can disinfect your wounds. Does your foot hurt?"

"Yes! But luckily, I can walk. Damn these tennis shoes! They are so tight."

Slowly they headed home.

On the way back, they stopped in one of the shops for beach items. Dawnin took the opportunity to buy three swimming suits and a pair of sandals, which he immediately wore to give relief to his poor battered foot.

"Start going home, Maria, I will join you shortly."

"Can't I stay with you?"

"I prefer not. Come on! Go home."

"Why? What are these mysteries?"

Maria asked, puzzled.

"No mystery, just do what I tell you. Please! In ten minutes, I will be back." Henry said with a big smile. Maria walked away confused.

Finally, Henry was alone and was able to implement the plan he had carefully prepared since he arrived in the small town.

He had promised to amaze his partner, to give unexpected gifts to show her his infinite gratitude. So as a first step he went to a florist, where he bought twenty-four red roses.

Then he walked into a small supermarket and bought the most expensive bottle of Merlot, a bottle of champagne, veal steaks, two boxes of fries and tomatoes and lettuce for a salad. Not yet content he visited some small local jewelers, and in the end, after taking a careful look around, he opted for a golden bracelet and a necklace. Feeling satisfied, limping slightly, he returned home.

Maria was pleasantly surprised when, after opening the door, she saw the roses and hugged and kissed him.

Dawnin put the champagne and steaks in the fridge, opened the bottle of wine to breathe, and decided to give the necklace and bracelet to her during dinner.

"Henry, you didn't have to! You didn't have to! Thank you very much. These roses are beautiful." Maria exclaimed, as she put them into a crystal vase with water.

"For what! For this! You deserve much more."

"Well! Now do not exaggerate. What have I done so extraordinary?"

"You have done so much for me. Remember that I am infinitely grateful for the help you have given me. You saved my life." Dawnin replied affectionately.

About twenty minutes later he opened the champagne, and they went to drink it on the terrace.

When they finished, he asked, "Are you hungry?"

"Yes! But first I would like to unpack these boxes. Would you like to give me a hand? It will not take more than half an hour."

"Of course! No problem."

They opened the first of the two crates and arranged the items where Maria wanted them.

At one point Henry took a frame and looking at the photograph, recognized the same girl he had seen in the medallion some time ago. The photo, a close-up, enhanced the beauty and smile of the young woman.

He placed the frame on the table and then took another larger one, with four different photographs inside. (In the first picture there was a gentleman and lady both middle-aged, the same people were in the second, in the company of Maria, in the third photo it was Maria and the mysterious girl, in the fourth only the girl).

"Who are the people in these photos?" Henry asked intrigued.

"They are my parents and that girl ... near me…is my sister Luisa." Maria replied as if she was struggling to talk about it.

"Your sister is beautiful, man! She is gorgeous!"

"Yes! It is true, she is gorgeous, indeed, actually… she was." Maria stopped after saying those words, her expression became sad, suffering.

Henry, realizing something bad must have happened to Luisa, and in a concerned tone asked, "What happened to her?"

Barely restraining herself from crying, Maria began the story. "My sister has been in a coma for four weeks, after a car accident and currently is still in the hospital. She was in the car with her boyfriend, Armando, who was driving, and they were on their way to work. Suddenly a truck with a trailer lost control and from the opposite lane crashed into their car. The impact was frontal. Luisa's boyfriend lost his life on the spot, while she went into a coma and hasn't come back. At first, we were confident that she would wake up and, come out of it one day. However now, after all this time our confidence is fading away. Even my father, who was the most optimistic, has given up hope, and now he is desperate. Luisa... is a great girl... exceptional... my most dear... friend."

"I am sorry! Maria! Sorry I asked you this, I didn't want to."

"What are you apologizing for, it is certainly not your fault. See! My sister is close to me, although she is a few years younger. Every time I think of her, tears come to my eyes. She was supposed to get married two weeks ago, but bad luck struck. You cannot imagine how excited she was about her wedding. Luisa wanted a traditional wedding in a white dress, with many guests, relatives, and friends."

"Isn't there a chance she can come out of the coma?"

"I do not know, maybe but nothing is improving. Everything is in stasis. And the doctors are now quite skeptical. Luisa is in a private clinic using a ventilator, a special machine that keeps her alive. My family is wealthy and can afford to keep her there indefinitely. Unfortunately, hope is fading in each of us, especially in me. The last time I visited her, about a week ago, I was shocked. You cannot imagine the sorrow I felt when I saw her so pale and unhealthy. She is shrinking like a ... larva... a skeletal larva," Maria said in a very emotional tone.

"I hope Luisa recovers as soon as possible, I really hope so with all my heart," Henry exclaimed sadly as he lit a cigarette.

"We all hope so."

Henry finished grilling the steaks. When he brought them to the table, he took the opportunity to hide the two small boxes containing the bracelet and necklace, under Maria's napkin.

Once this was done, he went to call her. Maria was lying on a beach chair on the terrace.

"It's ready, you can come and eat." She sat down at the table and when she opened the napkin, the two boxes fell into her lap.

"What are these packages?" She asked surprised.

"Open them and you'll see."

Maria opened them with trepidation and after seeing the contents, exclaimed with joy, "They are beautiful! Why all these gifts? There is no reason!"

"Why do you say there is no reason? The reason exists. You saved my life. Without you who knows where I would be now, in jail, or even six feet underground. You did what no other person would ever do. You gave me peace, love, serenity and, above all, you treated me from the beginning with dignity, making me feel like a human being. And you have had complete faith in me. In fact, I could be a hardened criminal who, after being saved from death, could have slit your throat. Instead, you have decided to take a risk and not think about this eventuality. Finally, my main reason is that I love you."

"Do you really love me?" Maria asked, smiling.

"Yes, I do, I really love you. It is so strange; everything is happening with such speed. I certainly do not hate you," he replied, winking at her.

The next morning after breakfast they decided to rent a motorboat for the day. Maria knew a small marina not far, where they rented motorboats for the full day. They wanted to rent a small motorboat, or dinghy equipped with a twenty-five-horsepower engine.

Henry was excited at the idea.

Even the smallest motorboat was fine with him, as long as he did not have to row or make any physical effort. Humming happily, he wore his flamboyant new Hawaiian-style shorts, with coconut palms depicted on both sides, and looked in the mirror with admiration. The admiration disappeared instantly when he saw a thread of belly and the pale complexion of his skin.

"Maria, do you have sunscreen?"

"No, we have to buy it," she replied from the shower.

A few minutes later she came out of the bathroom wearing a tiny black bikini.

"This time, I will not be unprepared like yesterday. Do you like my new bikini?" She asked proudly.

"I liked more what you were wearing yesterday." He answered laughing.

"How! I did not have any."

"Exactly, that is the style I love most," Henry said jokingly.

"Shut up! I feel more comfortable this way than naked. We are in Mexico not Saint Tropez. For your information, here we are quite "conservative", as you are in the United States. I understand, in fact, that you are puritanical there, aren't you?"

"Okay! All right! I give up, you are right! I withdraw what I just said. I was kidding. Now, come on, let's go as it is getting late."

After leaving the apartment, they headed to a supermarket to buy sunscreen, and then directly to rent the boat. They were lucky because they arrived just in time to rent the last of the small motorboats with a twenty-five hp engine. Henry paid in advance, asking for two extra tanks of gasoline.

Maria gave her license as a pledge to the owner of the company.

"Sir! Come back by 6.30 when we close, okay?" The bearded owner told him before letting him go.

"Don't worry. I will be back by then, goodbye."

"This is life!" Henry exclaimed, as he drove at full speed, quickly moving away from the marina. "I haven't been on a boat for at least four years, dear Maria. It looks so beautiful to me, it's like I'm dreaming. How wonderful! What a fantastic day. I think we should celebrate; don't you? Pass me a bottle of beer please?"

They anchored in a small, deserted bay, about fifty feet from the shore. After diving into the water, Maria returned to the boat to get sun, while Henry continued to swim to the shore.

Returning on board he found her asleep.

She woke up when he got into the boat.

"Could you put sunscreen on my back please? I will be grateful to you for life." Henry asked smiling. As Maria gently smeared on the sunscreen, he asked, "I would like to know more about Fuentes and his organization. Would you like to talk about it?"

"What do you want to know?"

"Well! Tell me something more about him and your views of him. I had the impression you do not like him too much. I still remember the face you made when he was introducing Andrew Martin, you looked disgusted."

"No! I was not disgusted, Fuentes is fixated with Martin, surely mine was an expression of annoyance, more than anything else. See! Rodrigo is a strange guy, sick, obsessed with the thirst for revenge. I do not remember how many times he told me about Andrew Martin, repeating the same things to me over and over. He really fears him, unlike Charles, or the others in the gang, who he thinks are just dirty brainless, idiot, killers. He is probably right, Martin is smart, nothing is in his name. His criminal record is totally clean. If you want to know the whole truth, you must swear to me not to say anything to anyone, okay?"

"Of course, I want to know the truth. What in the world! Maria! You know that you can trust me, come on tell me."

"I'm investigating Fuentes, not Charles Lewis."

"What?"

"You got it right. Fuentes is my goal."

"Christ! What! What does this mean? Are you not interested in sending that scumbag, cuckold, thief of Charles Lewis to jail until the end of his life? Do you want to send a nice bouquet of roses, complimenting Charles on his epic exploits as a criminal?" Henry asked quite upset.

"Do not misunderstand Henry, that is not what I meant. Of course, I would like to arrest Charles Lewis and send him to jail. Unfortunately, we don't have any proof, not even a tiny, stupid, little fact about him. You understand! Lewis is as pure and immaculate as a virgin. I know he sells weapons, drugs and who knows what else, but how can we act against him if we have nothing? His organization is diabolical, never a mistake, never an imperfection. Now we have your testimony, not against Charles but against Tom Atkinson, yet he was not our goal.

If you want, you might try sending Atkinson to jail for attempted murder. But do you really want to face a trial? You can turn yourself into the FBI, ask for their protection, and be a witness. However, don't you think someone as powerful as Charles Lewis would find you in the end?

Do you think you can survive the entire process? Even if you change residence and your identity you would always remain in danger. You also would not be able to trust anyone, you would have to depend on the decisions of influential and often unscrupulous people. This is the raw reality of the facts; in case you want to appeal to justice.

I repeat that Charles Lewis and Andrew Martin are our real targets. Once they fall, even their minions will fall like skittles. I think if we are cunning, in the end, we could defeat those criminals, just the two of us together, without the help of Fuentes, or others like him."

"You're absolutely right, Maria, what you said makes total sense to me, but you still haven't told me anything about Fuentes, and why you want to frame him."

"Give me time and I will tell you, don't be impatient. You asked me about his organization, now briefly, I will tell you how it works. The Fuentes organization is divided into four distinct levels or sectors. Think of a pyramid, it is a geometrical shape, this is a fitting analogy. At the top is the head, Fuentes. One and only master, arbitrator, and judge of the various disputes. He has the decision-making power for everything. Then there is the second sector, what I personally call the *4 G.,* or the four generals: Coco, Roberto, Luis and Tonio. They work closely with him and are his advisors, especially Coco who we can say is number two.

The 4 G. work and are in contact with a bunch of other people, let's also call them lieutenants for this occasion, to use a military terminology. There are many lieutenants, I do not know how many exactly, nor do I know who they are. In turn, these lieutenants work with the fourth sector, let's call them the soldiers. Again, I have no idea how many soldiers work for the organization, I am sure Fuentes keeps dossiers carefully catalogued in his safe, with all the names of those who are part of his clique. Returning to the soldiers, they are the ones who stalk, spy, take photographs and act. For example, you were photographed in Redlands by one, or more, and I, despite being part of the operations at that time, have no idea who it is."

"Therefore, Fuentes created a para-military organization, divided into levels or sectors, a bit like organized crime, like mafia. The boss at the top and various levels of sub-command if I understand correctly."

"Yes! That is right, but with a substantial difference. In fact, I think anyone who works for a gangster knows they work for him. Let me explain: if you enter the lowest level of a mafia organization, let's make you the shoeshine boy on duty, you know you work for this guy or another shady individual. Sure, you do not take his orders personally, you will probably never talk to him, but you know he is the head of the organization, the big man, the boss. In the organization of Fuentes this does not happen.

The soldiers who work for him do not know at all about his existence, they are in contact only with lieutenants. I suspect, not even the lieutenants know anything about Fuentes, because they dialogue with the 4 G. Fuentes has organized his gang in this way, because if a soldier is caught in an operation and he speaks, the chain would be broken only up to the second level. Do you understand? For instance, someone is stalking, you catch him, you can torture the guy, but he will never talk about Fuentes, or the 4G, because he knows nothing about their existence. And that is why we are investigating him."

"What do you mean? I do not understand."

"You see! Several of the men who worked for Fuentes as lieutenants disappeared into thin air, without wives, and family members knowing anything about it. Fuentes has eliminated certain of his men in the past to prevent opponents from finding out. We are sure of it; we only lack solid evidence. Do you remember that photograph of the person dressed as a clown that Fuentes showed when you were at his house?"

"Of course, I remember it, he called him the chameleon if I'm not mistaken."

"You remember very well. The chameleon appeared during an operation that Fuentes, let us say sloppily, had tried to organize against Andrew Martin. The operation was a failure, several of his soldiers were killed or taken prisoner, but the lieutenant of the operation, a certain Pablo Senora, although never captured by enemies, disappeared into thin air. I personally believe that Fuentes punishes his men by killing them when they do not carry out an assigned operation."

"My God! Do you think he is really that ruthless?"

"Yes, Henry, I really believe that and so does my direct superior."

"Aren't you afraid that is too dangerous? Fuentes has influential friendships that can play in his favor. Aren't you afraid for your life? If one day you succeed in incriminating him, your life will not be worth even half a cent."

"You are right! Fuentes has many powerful friends. He knows politicians, judges, heads of the secret service, police, and others. That is why I don't feel protected and safe."

"Maria! We talked about it yesterday, I repeat it to you once again: let's go away, let 's flee from all these reptiles around us, before it's too late."

"I am seriously thinking about it, but I believe it is not the right time. We must wait to see how things turn out. If we give up everything now, that is not to our advantage. I do not want to take refuge in a remote place forgotten by God and fear that one day or another some henchman of Charles Lewis or Rodrigo Fuentes will come to cut my throat."

"I think you are exaggerating. Why would Fuentes send his hitmen to look for you? Once you have abandoned the investigation, what purpose would he have in killing you? On the contrary, you are doing a big favor for him. As for Charles Lewis, unfortunately, that is a different story! If you stay with me, you could be in serious danger."

"Henry! We must work together, studying a realistic plan of action, and then implement it. We cannot stay sitting ducks." Maria said concerned.

"For me it is fine, No problem. I have a couple of questions to ask you. First, why don't we contact the FBI right away? Don't you think they could help us?"

"We have discovered there is a mole in the FBI. If we contacted them, Charles Lewis would immediately find out about us, and the investigations into him. No! Contacting FBI agents without knowing who you are dealing with, could be a boomerang that instead of helping would complicate our lives."

"Ok! I get it. The second question is: Why don't we go to Seattle to the lion's den? I have been thinking about it for a while. We could finally start taking action instead of waiting for someone else to act for us. Think what a surprise it would be for dear Charles and the beautiful Cindy if they found me in their living room, with a gun in my hand pointed at their temples. Finally, the showdown could begin. What do you say?"

"I think it is not a bad idea, risky yes, but not a bad one, indeed. I could get you valid documents, a Mexican passport with visa authenticated by the American embassy, an identity card, and an international driving license. Of course! Why not! Tonight, we must toast to a new Mexican citizen. How about Jose' Vargas? And I could be Maria Vargas, your wife."

"Hey! Do not run so fast, my dear! We are not married yet. However! Long life to the Vargas," Henry replied jokingly.

XVI

SEATTLE

Tom Chong was extremely excited. In fact, Munro had promised him $1,000 for the photographs to be taken of Cindy Hyatt, plus another $1,000 if he did so quickly and professionally.

Tom was confident he would earn the extra $1,000, considering himself a genius, an artist of photography, and Munro knew it well. He thought that if luck assisted him, even on a single day of work, he could pocket his lavish compensation.

Throughout his career, Tom had taken hundreds of embarrassing photos—wives cheating on husbands, or vice versa. Chong had probably destroyed more marriages than anyone else in town, if not the whole state. His profession as an action photographer, or paparazzo when needed, had always been rewarding, making him abandon his dream of becoming a private detective.

However, the main reasons for his renunciation of that career were undoubtedly the terror of firearms, the sight of blood, and his small, thin, and poorly performing body. He always felt comfortable spying and taking photographs of people at a distance, using various and powerful telephoto lenses, but he never dreamed of holding a gun and breaking through a door to save someone.

He was loading his Nikon camera with a roll of thirty-six film in his home office when the phone rang a couple of times. He couldn't get to the call because the youngest of his three daughters had already answered it in the living room.

Only a few moments passed, and little Connie entered the office, scared, saying, "Daddy! There is a man on the phone, an ugly person with a spooky voice, who wants to talk to you."

"Thank you! Honey," Tom replied puzzled, as picked up the handset.

"Tom! It's me, Munro. Listen! I have another assignment for you. You must find me a certain Gonzales, Carlos Gonzales, I know that he hangs around in a restaurant called El Toro. Unfortunately, I do not know where this place is and above all I have no time to waste. Find me this dude and I'll give you another 500 dollars, actually let's make it a $1000, if you are fast."

"Well!... Munro... well!... You know that ... I don't … like to go looking for people ... who have disappeared, it's not my style...." Tom stuttered very undecidedly.

"Two thousand dollars, I'll give you two thousand dollars just do it quickly, and don't keep making a fuss, or bug me anymore. We are not negotiating in a farm market, ok?" Munro interrupted loudly, getting irritated.

"Okay! Bruce! Let's see what I can do. I'll give you some news when......" Tom stopped talking and put the handset of the phone back, because Munro had already hung up.

"Well! Another 2000 dollars, Munro seems in the mood to pay a lot in this period. Gosh! I can make $4,000 in a couple of days, or at least I hope," Chong thought smugly.

Thinking back to what his daughter Connie had told him, about an ugly man with a spooky voice on the phone, no kidding! Sometimes children seem to have a sixth sense. He wondered how the little girl had guessed that Munro was ugly and mean. Well! Who cares about it? That ugly man soon will have paid him a lot of money.

He immediately started to work. Taking the phone book, he discovered there were five El Toro restaurants in the city. That was a complication. Who knows which of those five restaurants the man was hanging around in.

He visited three of the five restaurants, with no luck. Nobody knew that guy. Arriving at the fourth restaurant near Greenwood, Chong had the feeling it was the right place. The restaurant was closed to the public. It would open an hour later, but from the windows he could see that people were cleaning the room.

85

He knocked on the door.

"Come back in an hour, don't you see that we are closed," a boy of about fourteen years replied with a slightly agitated voice.

This did not stop Tom, who knocked again and again.

"This fellow must be deaf or stupid," the boy exclaimed to a sturdy lady in her fifties who was washing the floor. The young man went to open the door and shouted, "Hey mister! We are closed, don't you see? Check the schedule. We are going to open in an hour, and now we are cleaning. Ok! Bye."

Tom could finally open his mouth, "I know you're closed, I didn't come here to bother you, but I'm looking for an old, dear, friend of mine, Carlos Gonzales. They told me he comes here often, that this is his stomping ground, do you know him by chance?"

"Who?"

"Carlos... Carlos Gonzales."

"Who is the... nut? Carlos the nut? Yes of course it is him. Carlos Gonzales! The weird guy. The one with those the big mustache and hair full of glitter, that's who you're looking for, isn't it?"

"Of course! Yes, it's him," Tom replied, lying with his best poker face.

"We call him the nut because he has that funny face and that crazy air and looks like a cartoon character. Your friend is also rich, he often comes here to eat with his friends and spares no expense."

"Don't you know where I can find him?" Chong asked anxiously.

"Of course! He lives there," the boy answered confidently, pointing his finger toward the street.

"Where?" Chong exclaimed, looking in that direction.

"There, you can see his house one block away. Do you see that short brown house with the damaged fence?" Tom, paying attention to where the boy was pointing his finger, saw a small, modest, old house in terrible condition.

"The nut does not care at all about the appearance of his dwelling, not to mention the garden is a disaster. The grass is tall and dry, he never waters the lawn, I don't know why! Say hello for me if you meet him. Ok! Now I must go."

"Thank you very much, you have been very helpful, and this is for you." Chong gave five dollars to the lad, who thanked him and happily entered the restaurant to resume his work. Tom slowly walked to the small house.

Meanwhile, the boy said to the woman, "The madman's friends are as rich, and generous as he is. Look! That guy gave me five dollars, lucky us."

Chong arrived at the outer gate and could personally see what the boy had told him. Gonzales's house was badly maintained. The dry weeds were so high they looked like heavy thickets and an old rusty rocking chair was upside down in the middle of the garden. Beer and coke cans were scattered here and there. He wondered what kind of person Gonzales was, and especially what Munro had to do with him.

It seemed no one was at home. Tom entered the garden and walked to the door. He rang the bell a couple of times, but no answer. He rang again, nothing. So, he instinctively grabbed the handle and to his surprise the door opened.

Tom was rather hesitant; he did not know whether to enter the house, or not. After a moment, he called out loud, "Hello! Hello! Is someone home? Hey! Can I come in?"

No answer. Waiting for endless seconds Chong called again, and again. No one answered. Suddenly his love for the investigation prevailed over his fear of the unknown and almost, with a jump, entered the house.

The door led to a poorly furnished living room. A dusty old yellow sofa, quite faded, was placed in the center of the room in front of an old television.

Between the television and the sofa was a low wooden coffee table, with an ashtray full of butts, two bottles of Budweiser, and an empty and crumpled pack of cigarettes. There were also a couple of white plastic chairs around the table. In one corner of the room was placed a large brown trunk built of wood with metal frames. The floor was covered with a smelly brownish carpet.

Looking around, Chong felt thrilled in his hunt for clues.

Now he was becoming a real detective, so approaching the table, he picked up the ashtray and observed there were three types of cigarette butts, Merit, Marlboro and Camel. Then he went to the trunk and opened it, but the trunk was empty.

Tom was disappointed because he expected to find clues of some kind. He went into the kitchen, opened the refrigerator, and saw that it was empty. Rummaging through the various drawers he found nothing but a couple of pots, plates, plastic cups, paper napkins, and a couple of cans of tuna.

He began to believe this place had been abandoned for some time.

As a last wish, he hoped to find some remarkable clues in the next rooms.

Then, he walked down the narrow, dark, short corridor with one door at the end and another on the left. The left door was slightly open, it was the bathroom.

Instinctively he decided to move on, into the bedroom.

Upon entering, he turned on the light and saw an unmade mattress on the floor, a chair with clothes thrown haphazardly, and a pile of pornographic magazines. There was nothing else.

Tom thought back to what the young boy had told him, about this Carlos Gonzales, was a rich and generous person, but everything he had seen so far indicated the opposite. Chong started to believe it was not the right house and that he was undoubtedly wasting time.

Without conviction he approached the smelly bed, observed it, then timidly took one of the pornographic magazines, with the title on the cover: "Warm Wet Virgins Pregnant with Lust," glanced through a couple of pages and threw it back into the pile. As he was turning back, looking, he saw a large stain on the carpet. He bent down to check it carefully and realized that it was blood. Looking around, he saw other smaller spots, both on the carpet and even on the wall in front. A chill ran down his spine. The sight of blood and the unsettling atmosphere made him feel queasy.

Tom hadn't expected this and his passion for being a detective was rapidly fading.

He repeated to himself that this meant absolutely nothing, everything could be fine. Maybe it was red paint, or maybe the owner had cut himself badly. Apprehensively, Tom left the room. As he walked away, passing through the corridor, he saw the semi-open door of the bathroom and instinctively stopped for a moment. Then he slowly opened it and turned on the light. The bathroom was empty, and there didn't seem to be anything suspicious. Looking around, he saw that the curtain of the bathtub was closed, Tom opened the curtain and leaning over to look was petrified. The corpse of a man was lying at the bottom of the tub.

Chong felt faint. The sight of that body made him dizzy. The man had been slaughtered like a beast, some of his blood was sprinkled on his body and part in the empty tub. The man had his eyes and mouth open, a big moustache, and was in his underwear. Tom covered his eyes in horror.

Suddenly, he felt something touching his shoulders. He turned back and glimpsed a human silhouette, so in a deep panic he screamed as loud as he could and fainted.

Munro unceremoniously threw a bucket of cold water on Chong's face. Tom woke up as the exterminator was carrying the trunk from the living room into the bathroom.

"What... what happened?" Chong exclaimed still dazed.

"Come on! Fast! Get to work, we have no time to waste, hurry up." Bruce shouted at him with his usual unfriendly, rude tone.

"Munro what are you doing here?" Chong asked totally confused.

"I'm saving your ass, that's what I'm doing."

"What do you think? That I killed him?"

"Certainly not! But that kid at the Mexican restaurant saw you go here; do you want to be indicted for this murder?"

"No! Certainly not! How do you know about the young boy?"

"I'll tell you later. Now help me to put this corpse in the trunk, I will personally take care of making it disappear. See! They will never find it. I also need you to help load it into my van."

Tom helped Munro without any joy. The exterminator disappeared as quickly as he had arrived. He had given Tom an appointment two hours later at a downtown bar.

The little photographer was cursing the moment he had agreed to work for Munro.

The two men were sitting at a table in the bar. While they were drinking a strong espresso, Munro, seeing Chong as pale as a white sheet, tried to cheer him up.

"I'm sorry! Unfortunately, these are the risky aspects of the job. I didn't think this could happen, I thought that if you were lucky, you would find out where the man lived, so I could contact him. If I had known the corpse was there, I would not have involved you in this affair. I know you don't like the sight of blood. I was sure they didn't know you, while I am sure that anyone involved with this Gonzales knows my identity. I didn't feel like going to that restaurant personally and asking about him. I followed you, and from a distance I saw that you were talking to that young boy, then I saw you enter the house. Believing that I could act personally I decided to come and join you. And it was good for you, Tom. Think, where would you have been now, if I hadn't made the body disappear? Well! Probably in a police station. I am satisfied with your work, I will pay you now one thousand, actually, two thousand dollars as I promised you. For the future, rest assured because your new assignment is part of your ordinary job. I don't think you'll find any corpses stalking Cindy Hyatt, and I assure you this chick is simple smoking, just gorgeous. If you had seen her as I did it..." The exterminator stopped in the middle of the sentence, involuntarily, creating suspense.

"Why? What happened with her? What did you see?" Chong asked intrigued.

"Well! I don't talk about it... well! Ok! Why not! I will confide in you a secret. That woman has a soft spot for me. If I want to, I could snap my fingers, and she would immediately come to me." Munro said with a pleased tone, trying his best to be convincing.

Tom Chong left the bar and, after a few minutes, got into his car. He was reflecting on two facts.

First, Munro had repeated twice that he had saved Tom's ass regarding the dead body, and Chong didn't understand where Munro was going with it. Why would the police suspect and arrest him? How could they even find out? How could that kid give an accurate description of his looks when there were hundreds of Chinese men like him? No, the police would never catch him, he was sure. The bald man was just trying to exaggerate his merits.

Second, he didn't understand how a beautiful woman like Cindy could have a soft spot for Munro. That didn't make any sense at all.

"Well! Life is full of surprises," he exclaimed at the end, still puzzled.

Anyway! Tom was happy. He could finally return to his usual routine of stalking, stakeouts, and taking photographs, and he couldn't wait to get started. He decided to begin the next morning.

Meanwhile Bruce Munro, walking in the street near the bar, was very thoughtful. In fact, he kept repeating to himself, "Goodbye Gonzales, and now what should I do? Damn."

He was eager to talk to Charles and update him on the latest events. To curb his anxiety, he decided to call him immediately, hoping Charles had returned from his trip.

Nobody was at Charles's office, and he did not leave a message on the answering machine. Munro was about to call his home when a sudden idea flashed in his mind. Why not go directly to him? That could also be the perfect excuse to try to see that beautiful woman he liked so much.

Munro arrived at Charles's house and rang the bell and in the meantime fantasized about Cindy, how she would be dressed, or if she was alone at home. He thought of that body of hers, a little thin for his taste, but beautiful. He thought of the joy of being able to spend time together with her, the two of them alone, romantically. But all he had left were his thoughts. After ringing a couple more times, he eventually walked away disappointed he hadn't found anyone at home, and... especially Cindy.

MEANWHILE IN WASHINGTON D.C.

Julie was very depressed about the suspension.

That whole situation was damaging her health. Her mind was in a total state of confusion, sadness, and shock. She struggled not to think about anything, to do nothing. Ever since she had returned from the office—or rather from the pub where she had quarreled with the newcomer, the cordially unwelcome Jeff—she had locked herself at home and had not gone out once, not even to go to the courtyard.

The whole world seemed to have fallen on her. Her hopes of glory, of doing her job well and of promotion were miserably wrecked.

Julie was seriously considering giving up everything, quitting, and starting a new career in a different field. Her eyes were dry, having shed all her tears, and her lips were cracked. Her hair was disheveled, and her face looked tired. In these days, she hadn't even bothered to get dressed, staying in a nightgown or, worse, in her underwear.

Now she made the effort to put on the bikini bottoms of the swimsuit and lay in the sun reading a book. She had read a large pile of books in but didn't remember a single title. Suddenly, she had an irrepressible desire for something to drink, so she went to prepare a cocktail in the kitchen. Julie was not used to drinking. She usually drank moderately and only on special occasions. But at this time moderation could go to hell. Thus, she poured half a glass of tequila into the margarita she had just prepared.

After that she returned to the terrace and began to sip the cocktail.

She had laid down and resumed reading the book, and had almost finished drinking a second margarita, when she heard someone trying to open the door, without succeeding, since there was the chain.

"Julie, could you open the door, please?" Lisa asked and Julie went to open it.

Lisa noticed how depressed Julie was and began to worry. Not because she had opened the door half naked, they were used to being free in their privacy, but because of her sickly appearance, haggard face, and with her hair in disarray.

Julie, after greeting her, returned to the terrace.

"Give me time to change and in five minutes I will come to you," Lisa said while going to her room. Lisa put on her swimsuit, and decided it was time to talk to her best friend, to help and support her. Shortly, she reached Julie on the terrace, took the rubber mat, and lay down next to her.

"How long have you been in the sun? Your shoulders are slightly reddened." "Oh! I have no idea... probably for a couple of hours," Julie replied listlessly.

"Put this protective cream on, it will prevent more sunburn." Lisa smeared the lotion on Julie's shoulders and back, providing some protection to her parched skin.

"I see you've bought some sunscreen," exclaimed Julie, seeing a couple of different bottles.

"Of course! My darling! Haven't you heard about the ozone hole? If you're not careful, your skin will shrivel up," she replied jokingly.

"What is that little bottle? Wow! Forty-five skin protection, with this you will never tan." Julie said critically.

"It's for the face and the delicate parts of the body, and since you tan your tits all day long, you should use it constantly." Lisa teased while giggling.

She smeared the lotion on Lisa's body, then Julie returned the favor by rubbing the cream on her back. Doing so, she unhooked the top piece of Lisa's bikini and suddenly took it off.

"Hey, what the hell are you doing?" Lisa shouted, surprised and amused.

"Lisa! You have a horrible white line on your back. Do you really want to keep that pale swimming suit sign all summer? Do like me, stay without your top."

"No! No give it back to me, come on, please," Lisa continued to shout and laugh, turning around, and covering her breasts with her hands.

"Come and get it," Julie replied giggling, while walking, staggering towards the living room window. When she got there, she threw the bikini top as far as possible into the room, laughing hysterically.

Lisa stood up, covering herself with her hands, and walking at a brisk pace, she approached the window. Julie, laughing, went to catch her. Both girls ended up falling into the inflatable plastic pool, which contained hot water.

Julie, very tipsy, kept saying, "Do you want to compete against me? I beat you; I screwed you!!"

Lisa capitulated and laughing too, replied, "Okay! I give up, I give up."

Lisa was no longer covering herself. Seeing this, Julie said, "Don't you see I was right? Watch! You have the mark of the swimming suit in front, so you must also tan that area."

As Julie said this, her hand began to slide over Lisa's upper chest and then slowly until she reached and caressed her breasts.

At first Lisa was incredibly uptight and in obvious embarrassment.

She blocked Julie's hand, but her friend leaned toward her mouth.

"What are you doing Julie?"

"Nothing, nothing."

"No! Enough! No! Please! No."

"Come on! Just let me caress you for a second, please come on!"

"No! I don't feel eh...."

Julie resting her lips on her friend's cut the speech in half. Now she was kissing Lisa passionately.

Lisa, after timidly resisting, began to reciprocate. She had given up stopping Julie's hand, which returned to caressing her, and now it was Lisa, who was touching Julie.

After some time, the fumes of alcohol vanished from Julie, and she felt slightly ashamed of what she had done. She remained lying under the sun umbrella and was reflecting, while Lisa continued to sunbathe.

So, keeping her eyes down, Julie approached her friend and sat next to her. "I'm sorry for what I did, I'm sorry. I don't know, I could not control myself," she exclaimed seriously .

"Don't apologize for anything, Julie, I'm an adult and able to reason and choose. I am responsible too for what has happened. If you want to know the truth, it was nice for me. Have you ever had experience with other women?" Lisa asked curiously.

"A few times in high school, however I won't tell you the names, because they were our classmates, and you know these girls very well. I'm basically bisexual, I like girls too, and you?"

"For me it was the first and probably the last time. I'm glad I did it with you," Lisa said smiling.

"Have you ever believed in platonic love, Lisa?"

"What do you mean? Certainly, in my life I have had infatuations with this or that boy, like everyone else. For example, as a child, I was platonically in love with a friend of my father. I ran away to my room every time he came to visit us and wouldn't answer him when he spoke to me. My mother believed that I hated him."

"That's not what I mean. Believe... in the sense of ... oh damn! I don't know how to express myself. Imagine seeing a person on the street whom you are attracted to and fantasize that he could be the man of your life. When a part of you says, shit! Why can't I t meet this person, why am I here, and he is there, and why can't we ever meet or talk to each other."

"I understand what you mean, or at least, I think I do. When you see a person who attracts you, but you know you will never meet them. This could happen anywhere. For example, on the bus seeing a stranger nearby, with whom you don't exchange a single word, but you feel damn attracted to him, or going to a pub, to the beach, to a concert. Am I right or am I wrong?"

"No! You are not wrong at all, on the contrary. I have felt this emotion, for a guy we were investigating, a certain Henry Dawnin."

"What in the world! Did you fall in love with a criminal?" Lisa asked, astonished.

"I didn't fall in love with him, and I don't even know if he's a criminal. Anyway, this man fascinates me," Julie answered with a defensive tone.

"I'm wondering, who is this handsome dude?"

"Wait a minute."

Julie went inside and got the photographs she had taken of Henry.

90

"This is Henry Dawnin."

"Oh! Yes! He's a good-looking man, there's no doubt about that, but he's not my type. His hair is too long. Now that you've started, tell me more about him."

Julie talked about Henry and her investigation, giving more details than she should have.

But she believed the investigation was over, and it was stupid to keep Lisa in the dark, her best friend.

Lisa, after hearing the story, said firmly, "If I were in your place, I would not care about all these chains of command, superiors, and so on. I would continue the investigation on my own."

"Are you talking seriously?"

"Of course! I'm serious! If you really believe this is a essential investigation for your career, I advise you to go all the way. You must assess whether it is worth it or not. Undoubtedly you could get into big trouble but think about it. After all, it is not just the FBI that exists. If you do not feel protected by them, you can turn to the mass media. Think of the headlines in the newspaper, or the television, corrupt CIA agents accused of smuggling drugs, weapons, murders."

"That might be an idea, although I think after that, my life wouldn't be worth even a cent. Surely Charles Lewis would make me pay." Julie said pessimistically.

"Everything is possible. If you decide to proceed, you must be sure to have solid evidence against Charles Lewis's dirty affairs. Once this is done, consider whether it is worth continuing the investigation or not. And look for support, for allies, someone you can trust."

"I could go to Seattle. That's where Lewis lives." Lisa said with satisfaction, thinking she had somehow awakened Julie from idleness and depression.

"Very well! Go to Seattle and start investigating your suspects."

As the two friends were continuing to talk, the phone started ringing.

"I'm getting it," Julie replied.

Coming back, she said, "Hey! Lisa! My colleague Dick is coming, we can talk to him about this plan."

"Very well! I know Dick is a good friend of yours. He can help you make the right decision."

"I'm going to put on a t-shirt, and will be back," Julie said, going inside.

Dick Tolone had left the office early and being close to Julie's house, decided to visit her. Dick had been anxious and worried about her. Recently, he hadn't heard from her, and for this reason, decided to find out what was going on. Unfortunately, he had to report bad news.

So, he went up to the top of the building where Julie lived and rang the bell. Julie opened the door and let Dick come in.

"Have you been to the beach?" he asked, after greeting her.

"No! I sunbathed on the terrace, but no beach."

"You look good," Tolone exclaimed with little conviction.

"Dick! Did you come here to say bullshit?" Julie answered annoyed.

"Why?"

"How can you find me looking good if I haven't slept for two days, am not wearing makeup, haven't combed my hair, nor...."

"Ok! Ok! I tried to be courteous. You're right. I was lying. Let's change the subject. Do you want to know the latest news?" Dick interrupted.

"Of course! Let's move outside to the terrace. I want my friend Lisa to take part in the discussion."

Dick followed Julie to the terrace, where she saw Lisa lying on her stomach.

"You two know each other, don't you? Lisa this is Dick, Dick, Lisa."

"Yes! We met once. How are you?" Tolone said, as he shook Lisa's hand vigorously.

Julie offered a beer to Dick, who began to talk between sips, "Well! Julie! Unfortunately, the investigation into Charles Lewis and the corrupt CIA is officially concluded."

"We already knew about Charles Lewis, but why has the whole investigation been concluded? Why? It's so strange and ...fishy." Julie yelled in rage.

"Exactly! I agree! The other morning, I gave Jeff the information we had. That bastard wrote a dossier reporting there is not a single piece of evidence to prove the existence of any corrupt CIA agents. Gladly, Collins took this as an opportunity to terminate the entire investigation."

"A cover-up," Lisa exclaimed.

"I believe so, a big cover-up." Dick said sadly.

"I think Jeff was paid by Charles Lewis to cover up the investigation, and Collins, being afraid of encountering problems in the future, happily facilitated the cover up," Julie said nervously.

"It's very possible. I don't trust or like Jeff Wilson. However, I don't think Collins is part of the conspiracy. I believe that if we had overwhelming evidence, he would reopen the case. Collins is the most obnoxious and unfriendly person in the world, but I'm sure he's not corrupt" he said with confidence.

"We must find a way to frame Wilson. If he is a corrupt agent, we must stop him," Julie exclaimed angrily.

"We will Julie. But let's not be hasty. I will try to find clues to prove his guilt. Unfortunately, you can't help me while you are suspended, so I will investigate on my own. Because of this piece of crap, all our efforts have been in vain. Don't worry, together we will prevail against them." He said, trying to relieve Julie's bad mood.

"Dick! I have decided to go to Seattle, to the wolf's den, to Charles Lewis."

"Look, it could be seriously dangerous."

"I know! But I don't feel like staying idle here, this is the most important investigation of our lives. Can I count on you?"

"Of course! When will you leave?"

"As soon as possible, I want to get out of here."

Dick said good-bye to the two ladies and before leaving asked Julie, "Please call frequently and tell me what's going on. I will do the same for you, hoping to find something useful. Be very careful, don't take any risk and watch your back." Tolone then left the apartment.

"I feel so happy to have a partner like Dick. I really love the guy, and I am confident he will be helpful in the investigation," Julie exclaimed happily.

"You are lucky, Julie. It's not easy to find a good work partner. I had so many bad experiences. However, I am worried about this Jeff Wilson. If he is a scumbag, you must be very careful."

"I know this. The scary part is that now we cannot stop him. That is the reality." Julie said pessimistically.

"I am confident that you and Dick Tolone in the end will be victorious," Lisa exclaimed, smiling.

SEATTLE

Early the next morning, Tom Chong parked his car near Charles's house, waiting for Cindy to leave.

The curtains of the house were still closed, and the porch light was still on. It looked like Cindy was still sleeping. After spending a good half hour inside the car to kill time, he decided to inspect the other side of the villa.

Munro had told him on that side there was a crack in the fence large enough to see inside and monitor the living room. Additionally, the bedroom was visible from the street since it was on the first floor.

Tom slowly approached the fence until he found the break.

After a few minutes, he saw the curtains in the bedroom open, and noticed a slender, blonde woman in a white nightgown. Returning to the main entrance he heard the door open and watched the same girl come out, pick up the newspaper and go back inside. He recognized it was Cindy. In fact, Munro had given him a photograph of her.

Slowly he returned to his car, quite satisfied. His day was about to begin.

More than an hour passed since she had taken the newspaper, and nothing had happened. Suddenly, Tom saw the garage gate open, and a white Volvo 740 sped out. He barely had time to check that the gate had closed automatically before Cindy, pressing the accelerator pedal, quickly entered the street.

This caught Chong a bit unprepared, forcing him to make a quick U-turn to follow her. However, he was fortunate enough to find the white Volvo stopped in front of him at a red light.

Cindy ignored speed limits, driving above sixty miles per hour on roads where the maximum limit was twenty-five. Tom, in his grey Toyota Corolla, had to keep up with her without drawing attention to himself, while ensuring he maintained a safe distance while keeping her in sight. Throughout the chase, he hoped the police would not stop him.

Meanwhile, she crossed the city to take the highway. Then she took the Evergreen Bridge over Lake Washington, and arrived at the Bellevue mall, where she parked in front of the Nordstrom store.

"Don't tell me she's going to run errands," Tom mumbled, not happy at all. He always invented all kinds of excuses, even pretending to feel sick, to avoid going shopping with his wife. This time it was different, he had to tolerate it. Tom hated department stores and shopping of all kinds. It was the worst torture he could endure.

Taking courage, he took the camera and put it on his shoulder, as well as the bag with all the spare parts and lenses.

"Maybe I'm lucky and she's going to meet someone," Chong murmured, trying to raise his morale. Therefore, following her, at a distance, Tom could not fail to notice her beautiful and tall figure. Cindy dressed casually, a pair of tight jeans that enhanced her beautiful hips and a white t-shirt.

He still could not understand how Cindy could have a soft spot for Munro. He began to question what he had already suspected. Munro had told him a bunch of lies. A beautiful woman like her could never have a soft spot for a monster like Bruce, perhaps even uglier than Frankenstein himself.

Cindy entered the building. After passing the cosmetics and jewelry counters, she stopped in the shoe department. She began to try on several, yet it seemed none suited her. She continued shopping, going to the clothes department, and seeing a blue suit she liked, disappeared into the dressing room.

More than two hours passed. Cindy had tried on more than fifteen dresses, toured the entire mall, store by store and continued to try and compare clothes. She bought three dresses, two T-shirts, three pairs of pants and two swimsuits.

"This lady is tireless," Chong murmured, sitting in an armchair to give some relief to his sore feet.

He had just sat down when he saw her walking at a brisk pace, toward the long corridor where the smaller shops, fast-food restaurants, ice cream parlors and other establishments were located.

Tom resumed the chase rolling his eyes and cursing, "Damn! Maybe I would have preferred a day like yesterday, even if there was that corpse. At least there was some action. This woman is driving me crazy."

Suddenly he felt a strong emotion, it seemed the coveted moment had arrived.

Cindy met a man, who was sitting at a table, Chong could not recognize him because he was facing away. He photographed the whole scene. But nothing happened, Cindy simply kissed the man on the cheek as she would kiss any friend and sat down next to him.

Chong was intrigued. Passing by without looking, he entered the first store on his left, the Disney store. Pretending to look at the goods displayed in and near the window, he slowly turned, until he saw and recognized Tom Atkinson. Munro had given several photos of Atkinson, so Tom was sure of his identity.

The two were arguing animatedly. Chong took a couple more photographs of them. Then he thought, "Why not try to hear what they are saying." Quietly he walked out of the store.

Passing behind the couple Tom sat at the edge of a small fountain not far from them. It was the best location available as all the chairs and tables adjacent to the couple were occupied. Unfortunately, because of the sound of the water in the fountain, and the buzz of the people, he could only catch small fragments of conversation between the two.

He heard the phrase: where did you put the money? And after: I don't know where he went, nor when he will come back.

Chong was disappointed because he could not hear more and continued to follow the two. Then he saw them say good-bye with a kiss on the cheek and leave separately.

He followed her home. Cindy parked the car in the garage and went inside the house. Tom was hungry, so decided to grab a bite at a nearby McDonald's. After finishing his lunch, he returned to his observation post. Everything seemed to be quiet, and she was still at home.

Tom decided to stretch his legs walking around the block. Then he went to check on her, looking through the crack in the fence. He tried to understand what she was doing in the living room. He could see Cindy sitting on a sofa reading a magazine.

Tom took a couple of photos. He had taken a third photo when he saw Cindy get up and disappear quickly. Only a few moments passed before she briefly returned to the living room in the company of Tom Atkinson. Then she disappeared again.

Chong took shelter about a hundred feet from the house, covered by the large trunk of a tree. A perfect location with a great view of the first floor. He had mounted a 1000 lens with which he could shoot the two in detail.

His sixth sense told him that the climax of the day was coming soon and from the first floor, the bedroom area. Several minutes passed but nothing had happened yet.

The two seemed to have disappeared into the thin air.

Suddenly, as Cindy was about to lower the shade in the bedroom window, Tom Atkinson came up behind her and gently slowed her action by hugging her. Cindy turned to him and the two kissed passionately. The kiss lasted a few seconds then the curtain was closed.

Chong had finished his work. The scene of the romantic kiss between Cindy Hyatt and Tom Atkinson had been photographed in different poses.

Tom was incredibly satisfied. He was happy, thinking about all the money he was going to get. Now he could return home triumphant in his fantastic success. Munro would have appreciated the speed and accuracy of his work.

Arriving home, he went directly to his darkroom to develop the photographs. And in the end, he complimented himself, because the photos had come out very well. Those photos left no doubt: they were damn explicit.

"Another future divorce in Seattle," he said jokingly. He phoned Munro. Not finding him, left a short message urging him to come to collect the photos.

At half past eight, Tom was having dinner with his family when the intercom rang.

"Who could that be at this hour!" his wife exclaimed.

"I'm going to answer," said little Connie, jumping up from the chair and returned with a frown on her face.

"Dad! There's that ugly man, with that ugly voice downstairs, talking on the intercom. Should I tell him to leave?"

"Don't tell him anything and go back to the table to eat. I'm on it. This ugly man is bringing so much money to Dad that you can't even imagine."

Bruce Munro sat in Tom Chong's office. There the little Chinese man, with a triumphant air, showed the photographs.

Bruce, visibly satisfied, warmly congratulated the photographer. Then after shaking his hand, gave him five thousand dollars.

Tom was amazed because it was more than agreed. Munro, with a sinister smile, reading the amazement in his face said, "You have been excellent, Tom! I'm giving you 1000 dollars more as a bonus, because you really deserved it. Congratulations."

Munro was about to leave Tom's house, when little Connie saw him on the doorstep and began to cry loudly and ran away. He was much uglier than she ever imagined.

Returning home, Munro thought Charles was right to believe he was being betrayed by his girlfriend. Those photos were unequivocal. Bruce also thought about the reaction Charles would have on seeing them

Despite being a born and hardened criminal, something held him back at the thought that a misfortune might befall the pretty woman, Cindy, with whom he had fallen madly in love.

However, he was a serious professional and had to do his job scrupulously.

Munro knew he had already earned the compensation, but he had decided not to show Charles those photographs right away. He would show them when he thought the time was right. And he did not believe that the matter was essential at this time.

It was necessary to find out who was hiding behind that gang in the red Ford Escort.

"Charles is a cuckold and will remain a cuckold, nothing can change for him. I will give him the information later," Munro exclaimed with sarcasm.

The real reason was he hoped to see that beautiful woman again soon, and maybe talk to her for a while, without Cindy being upset, scared, or beaten to death.

XVII

Charles had just returned home very angry.

The expedition in Mexico had turned out to be a disaster, in the truest sense of the word.

All the loot painstakingly saved and ready to be invested at the appropriate time, had vanished into thin air, or rather had been stolen. Charles didn't know whether to cry or throw himself out the window and had no idea what was happening.

He wondered if there was a conspiracy against him, a nasty plot by his enemies to destroy him. Lewis started to believe even in ghosts because it was probable ghosts who stole his money.

The only person who knew about that money had not existed for a long time.

He personally had killed Brian Holtz and then thrown his dead body into the well, and Brian died immediately no doubt about it. So, since no one else knew about that money, who the hell had robbed him? That was the riddle. Charles had not revealed where he had hidden the loot to any of his most trusted collaborators.

Not even to Doug who was the most loyal of them. When he had given Cindy directions to take some money, he had revealed only one part, the one hidden in a tomb. The story he knew was that Dawnin stole the money, but even he, as a thief, could never have known where the rest of the loot was hidden.

"No! Henry has nothing to do with the theft. I would bet on it," he murmured nervously.

He went into his bedroom and remained there in total solitude, trying to find a solution to the dilemma, but none came. He sat on the green armchair near the bed, holding his head with both hands, thinking and cursing. After a while, he ended up falling asleep.

Waking up and looking at the clock, he saw it was four o'clock in the afternoon. Cindy hadn't returned home yet, and he had no desire to continue lazing around. On the contrary, now he wanted to find out the truth.

Charles had a great curiosity to know the latest news from Munro. But before that, he wanted to talk to Uncle Andrew, tell him the bad news and discover what his uncle thought about the situation.
He phoned Martin's office. The secretary told him that Andrew was in a meeting and could not be disturbed and advised him to call back in an hour.

A little disappointed, Charles called Bruce Munro, but he was not at home, so he left a short message telling him to show up as soon as possible.

After exactly an hour he again called to Andrew Martin's office and this time was lucky. His uncle had just finished his business meeting. Martin replied in an affectionate tone.

"Charles how are you?"

"I'm fine Uncle! I would like to speak to you as soon as possible, privately," Charles said in a gloomy tone.

"I hope you don't have other bad news to give me, son."

"Well! Uncle... it depends on your point of view," he replied with embarrassment.

"Okay! Understood. Why don't you come to dinner at my house tonight? Alone, if it is possible, am I clear?" Andrew said with a stern tone.

"Ok! All right! Uncle! So, see you tonight."

"At 7:30, be punctual, bye." Andrew Martin ended the phone call before Charles could even say goodbye to him.

That phrase: "Alone if it is possible am I clear?" It was still rambling in his mind.

He was increasingly convinced that Uncle Andrew could not stand Cindy.

How come? After all, she was a lovely girl, nice, beautiful, intelligent, and loyal. Yes! Why not? Cindy, until proven otherwise, was loyal. So far, all the rumors about her affair with Tom Atkinson were false. There was no evidence and certainly Munro would have discovered she was not guilty. He was extremely disappointed that Uncle Andrew didn't invite her.

"By the way, why hasn't she returned home yet?" he wondered.

Meanwhile, Cindy was getting dressed, after spending a lovely long afternoon in Tom Atkinson's bed. Taking advantage of Charles's absence, Tom and she had dated more than normal in these few days. They had done everything discreetly and prudently, at least that's what they believed.

"Do you think he might be back?" Tom asked.

"Maybe. If he has not already returned, he will return very soon, I can guarantee you. When he uses his small suitcase, it means that he will stay away just a couple of days, three at most. I know him well by now."

"Too bad! End of fun," Tom replied disappointed.

"Why? Even when he's here, we see each other often, don't we?"

"Yes! But we have often taken risks, and you know this."

"Why? Don't you get excited by the risk?"

"Yes, it excites me! And above all what excites me most is to make Charles a cuckold. You cannot imagine how much I enjoy it," Atkinson said loudly with hatred.

"What do you mean? Don't you feel anything for me? Do you do it just to take revenge on him?" Cindy exclaimed, irritated.

"No! Cindy! You know that I love you. However, being able to take revenge on Charles and hurt him is the thing I adore the most."

"I don't understand. Isn't Charles your friend?"

"Friend... friend... friend damn! You have no idea how I hate him, Charles is not my best friend, but my worst enemy. You probably don't realize what it means to be always number two, the spare wheel. We grew up together and he was always the boss, the strongest, the richest, the coolest and I have always been his servant. He orders, and I execute, he talks, I listen, he decides something stupid, I must shut up, abide, and follow his bullshit, this for a lifetime."

"Do you hate him for that?"

"I hate him because Charles has had everything in life, and I, who have the same abilities, have always been a step below him. It's frustrating to know you're better than your boss, but you can't take his place because he's untouchable."

"However, you took advantage of his friendship to arrive where you are now. You have a beautiful house, a car, a rich bank account, and a nice standard of living, and you can't deny this. So why are you complaining?" Cindy rebuked.

"Well! What does it mean? I have worked super hard to get where I am now, and I earned it, nothing comes for free in life. Now it's time for me to prove I am number one, not number two. Do you get what I mean?"

"You're starting to worry me, Tom. I don't like this anymore. We could be in the Bahamas, in the Maldives, we could start a new life in a tropical place with all the money we have, and instead you insist on staying here in Seattle. When are we going to leave?"

"Cindy! Going now means getting into trouble. Disappearing into thin air is like signing a death sentence for ourselves. I don't want to spend the rest of my life hiding, waiting for someone to find and kill me. Instead, I'm thinking of some remedy that can get us out of trouble. You don't know I have insurance."

"Insurance! What do you mean?" Cindy asked puzzled.

"It's the most powerful weapon I have against Charles Lewis. Do you know if I wanted to, I could send him in jail for the rest of his life?"

"Of course! I know, with all the shady business you've done with him over the years, but you'd end up there too, don't you know?"

"No! I am talking about something totally unrelated to our business. Something I have protected well and preserved. I call it my insurance and you can't imagine how much it would harm Charles."

"Tell me what it is? Why are you being so mysterious?"

"No! The time has not yet come."

97

At exactly seven thirty, Charles parked his BMW in the large parking lot in front of Andrew Martin's villa. Then he was accompanied by the butler, in livery, to the luxurious living room, where the grizzled businessman was personally preparing special cocktails.

"Hey Charles! I just poured you something to drink. Please take a seat."

Charles affectionately embraced his uncle and sat in a comfortable armchair.

After talking a little bit, at a certain point Andrew Martin pressed on the sore button.

"So! Tell me! How was your trip to Mexico?"

Charles shared the latest news, and to his surprise, Martin did not explode with anger.

On the contrary with a certain demeanor Andrew turned to him saying, "What can I say, Charles? I am as surprised as you are. This shows you we are dealing with well-organized people who are doing their best to destroy us. That is why now more than ever we must be careful. The enemy is lurking, and we must be ready to annihilate him," Andrew said with a serious tone.

"What do you think we can do, Uncle?" Charles asked like a child would ask someone older and more experienced than him.

"First, arrange a meeting with all our men in your office, so we can clearly chart the way forward and the procedures to follow. Let's see, I am free tomorrow at five o'clock. Call Munro and the others for that hour; I'd like to see what he pulls out of thin air. And let Cindy come," Andrew ordered severely.

"Of course! Uncle! Okay! At five o'clock they will all be there. Who do you think could be our enemy? I am confused. What can we do?" Charles asked again with the same childish and uncertain attitude.

"Well! I have no idea. However, I am confident we will find out soon or later. One last thing... do you have pictures of Henry Dawnin?"

"Yes! I have several pictures of him, from my school days to some recent ones."

"Very good! Bring those along as well, so I can see them."

Charles enjoyed a succulent dinner offered by his uncle and cooked especially for him by the Italian chef Sebastiano, who had been working for Andrew Martin for a while.

Sebastiano had prepared for the occasion bruschetta as an appetizer, trenette with pesto as the first course, sweet and sour wild rabbit as a second course, oven potatoes with rosemary and a salad as a side dish and apple pie for dessert. And a nice bottle of vintage Merlot red wine completed the meal.

After the succulent dinner, Charles, satiated and satisfied, said, "Uncle! You must invite me more often to eat at your house, this dinner was fantastic, indeed."

"Eh! Yes! Sebastiano is great. Now I eat real Italian food every day. What do you think about that? Authentic and genuine food, not that filth served in many restaurants here in the United States that pretend to be Italian and serve food not even good for dogs. When you order a second course, they bring you overcooked pastina as a side dish. Sebastiano instructed me perfectly. I can go to Italy and compete with the best local gourmets. By now I know the difference between a first and a second course, and I no longer dare to eat pasta and salad at the same time. In Italian cuisine the salad is a side dish for the second course."

"No! I always eat the salad together with the pasta, or with what I have in front of me."

"And that's wrong. Anyway! I think you are not the only one. If you want to eat a good meal with me, let me know a little earlier and come. Remember! You are always welcome here in my home." These were Andrew's last words.

Charles, after thanking his uncle, left the villa before ten. Back home, he found Cindy reading in bed.

"Charles! That Munro called an hour ago."

"Oh! Well! What did he say?"

"He wants to talk to you soon, call him back. It's strange. This ugly fellow Munro tried to be gallant on the phone, do you believe it?" Cindy said with a hint of bitterness.

"Gallant? What do you mean?" Charles asked, amazed.

"It gave me the impression he was striving to be kind and nice, that ugly monster."

"Ah! Ah! Gallant Munro! This is great! The ugliest and coldest man on earth. Well! Maybe he likes you," Charles laughed.

"I don't like it, that man gives me the creeps." Cindy replied disgustedly.

Charles called Munro and told him to come half an hour before the meeting, so they could talk in private and not be disturbed. After, he phoned all his men and ordered them to come to the meeting the next day.

At half past four, Bruce Munro, the exterminator, sat in Charles's office and told him the latest news about the red Ford Escort gang, but refrained from revealing the compromising photographs of Cindy and Tom.

Charles denied having ever seen or known this Carlos Gonzales, thus Munro's few hopes were miserably shipwrecked. He had to start over again from the beginning.

"Why didn't you leave your hostage alive until I could interrogate him? Why this hurry, shit." Lewis asked very angrily.

"Look! What he knew, he revealed to me. Do you want to teach me how to do my job? I have interrogated hundreds of people in my career, and some have been much tougher than him," the bald Bruce counterattacked, getting irritated, and lying.

"No! I don't want to teach you how to do anything. But now we're behind, don't you understand?" Charles said still irate.

"I know what you feel, I can't do anything about it, and anyway now we know enough. Let's see what winning strategy we can pull out of this meeting," The exterminator spoke in a more placating tone, trying to be positive and especially to change the subject.

At five o'clock, the whole gang sat around a long, antique, rectangular table in Charles's office. Tom, Cindy, Doug, Munro, Scott Johansen the albino, Ramon Espinoza, and Greg Murphy, the pilot, were ready to start the meeting.

Only one was missing, the man himself, Mister Andrew Martin. After about ten minutes, the middle-aged, good-looking man walked in, accompanied by Sharon who closed the door and left. As usual Andrew Martin was impeccably dressed in one of his countless Armani suits. He was well groomed, hair combed, shaved, and had a dazzling thirty-two carat smile.

All those present, seeing Andrew arrive, stood up to pay homage like small rubber puppets moved by the expert hands of the master.

"At ease! Boys! Sit please and excuse me for the delay, but there was a lot of traffic."

Martin sat at the head of the table. After a moment of silence, in which the distinguished gentleman got comfortable in his chair and began to scrutinize those present, Charles began the meeting.

They concluded that a mysterious organization was threatening them. An organization of which nothing was known, and which had also seized their money hidden in the mission in Mexico.

At one point Charles said, "Not only is this mysterious organization trying to harm us, but even FBI agents are on our trail. Happily, now I can tell you they will no longer bother us, everything has been arranged for the best."

"Were they the ones who put the bug in your phone?" Tom asked.

"Yes! It was them! But I repeat everything has been fixed. It was just a couple of young agents, who, to advance their careers, started a rogue investigation on their own, without respecting either procedures or superiors. Now the investigation is officially closed. I already know their identity, it's a man and a woman, a certain Dick Tolone, and a Julie... Sue, if I'm not mistaken. In the coming days, I will also receive their photos, so we have the complete picture of the situation. My Uncle Andrew asked me about photos of Henry Dawnin, the last time we met. So, I brought some of them. I think the only people who haven't met him are Uncle Andrew, Bruce, and Greg."

Andrew Martin looked closely at Henry's photos and was attracted by his blue eyes and gaze. He got his own idea of the man. Andrew thought he was a shrewd and fearsome adversary, but not the source of their current problems.

Martin began speaking for the first time since the beginning of the meeting. "So, is this the man who stole the money, Cindy?"

"Yes! It's him. He is a rattlesnake, Uncle," she replied.

The meeting ended after a few minutes, however nothing important was established. They had decided to stay alert and wait to counteract the enemy's next move. In fact, they knew nothing about them, nor about Henry Dawnin who seemed to have disappeared from the face of the earth.

Charles had ordered his men to stay in the vicinity of Seattle. No more searching for Henry, as the man could be anywhere, and he had neither the time nor money to waste. In any case, Charles was extremely disappointed with the meeting, especially with Uncle Andrew. He had expected some brilliant ideas from him, some of his skillful insights, but got nothing. The elderly gentleman had been listening the entire time and, except for a brief question to Cindy, had remained silent.

As the meeting concluded and the others left the room, except for Cindy, Charles approached his uncle. "Uncle are you feeling well?" he asked, concern evident in his voice.

"Of course! Charles! Why?" Andrew answered, surprised at the question.

"You were silent almost all the time. I honestly expected your opinions and more input from you," Charles said with a disappointed tone.

"About what? When I have nothing to say, I don't waste my breath unnecessarily. I've been listening and that's it. I don't think there is anything to do, at least until we have some news. I think Munro has done a very mediocre job. He acted quickly, but it was a mistake to eliminate that prisoner. Unfortunately, people like him have neither finesse nor grace. They are just ruthless, violent, and gross. From this moment on, keep me informed, understood? Even something you think isn't important."

"Of course! Uncle, you can count on it."

The next morning, Charles still had not fully understood his uncle's attitude and was shaken and disappointed by the unsatisfactory meeting the previous day. At noon he was alone in the office and had just finished talking on the phone when after a few seconds it rang again.

"Yes! Hello! It's Charles Lewis speaking."

"Go check your mailbox," someone whispered on the other end.

"Hello! Who is speaking?"

"I told you to go check the mailbox, there's something for you."

"Who are you?"

"Go and come back quickly. In exactly fifteen minutes I'll call you back." The mysterious person ended the phone call.

"Oh! Oh! I bet my balls this is someone from that organization who loves me so much. What do they want?" He murmured worried.

He decided to send Sharon to collect it, as he fearing there would be a bomb, or other explosives of sorts in the mailbox. Therefore, he went to the other room, where she was having a quick lunch, and he ordered her, "Sharon! Go check the mailbox, there should be something for me. Come back immediately. I am waiting for a phone call from a customer in a few minutes, and I must give him an answer. And another thing, bring me the open envelope without removing the contents, understood?"

"Okay, I'll go right away," she replied in her usual submissive tone.

Sharon didn't understand why she had to open the envelope for Charles, she had never done it before, but by now she was used to his quirks and had learned to argue as little as possible. So, she went downstairs and opened the mailbox. Sharon found a rectangular yellow envelope. The envelope was without an address or return address. Whoever had delivered the letter had done it in person.

In the elevator she opened the envelope and driven by a strong curiosity looked at the contents. Sharon saw five photographs of the same man, a person in his 35s or 40s good looking, with long hair and blue eyes. That guy seemed to be a bit like a hippy, and he was one of those eccentric dudes she would never have dated.

A whole other lifestyle from hers, yet despite this Sharon was very attracted to him.

"Why are these photographs so important to Charles?" She wondered. She entered Charles's office and handed the envelope to him.

"Can I know why you took all this time?" Charles screamed, unnerved.

"What do you mean? I went and came back as fast I could," she replied a little annoyed.

"Okay! All right! Now get off my balls as I'm busy, and don't bug me for any reason. Am I clear?" Charles said in an unpleasant tone.

Sharon quickly disappeared from the room, while the anxious man pulled the contents out of the open envelope murmuring satisfied in a low voice, "Good! At least it's not a bomb, otherwise if it was, my beautiful busty secretary would have exploded into..."

Charles almost choked and finished talking to himself, after seeing the contents of the envelope. Five photos of Henry were scattered on his coffee table. Three were of close-ups, while two others showed Dawnin in the company of a beautiful, brunette, Latino woman.

Charles was confused, agitated, and excited. Something was finally moving in this very slow period.

"Is Henry involved in all this?" Charles wondered.

"No! I don't believe so. Why would he risk his life for this? No! It's not Henry, he's not that stupid. Probably that organization knew about him and is using the dude. But why? What is their reason?" He murmured worriedly.

He had just finished saying this, and the phone rang. Taking a quick look at his watch, Charles realized exactly fifteen minutes had passed.

"Yes! Hello! It's Charles Lewis speaking," he answered in a serious tone.

"Have you checked your mailbox?"

"Yes."

"Good! Did you see the contents of the envelope?"

"Of course."

"Your friend Henry Dawnin is in Puerto Vallarta right now."

"How do you know and who the hell are you?" Charles asked, irate.

"I repeat to you! Henry Dawnin is in Puerto Vallarta, and he has a lot of money that belongs to you."

"Tell me who the hell you are and...."

"Go to Puerto Vallarta to look for Dawnin and get your money back."

"Fuck! Tell me who you are, you ugly son of...."

Charles curbed his surge of anger when he heard that the mysterious person had already hung up. That phone call had paralyzed him. For more than ten minutes he had been stuck looking at the wall in front of him, motionless, while his mind formulated numerous hypotheses. Checking the photographs carefully in the light he noticed there were other fingerprints.

In an angry tone he exclaimed, "Sharon! Sharon! You are becoming too curious for my taste. You know! I have the magical cure for you, my dear! Soon I will punish you like I do."

After another five minutes Charles hurried out of his office and, passing by his secretary's room, told her, "Cancel every appointment I have for the next three hours, I have to go urgently to see my uncle Andrew."

He got into his BMW and quickly headed to Martin's office, without warning him of his arrival.

Andrew was surprised when he saw him arrive so suddenly.

Luckily Andrew had some free time to talk to him.

"Hello! Charles! What's going on? I find you quite euphoric and excited."

"I am! Uncle! Also, I am very upset and confused! I have some important news to tell you."

He recounted in detail what had happened that morning including the phone call received.

Finally, he showed the photographs he had received.

Andrew remained silent. He looked closely at the five photos, thinking about the situation.

"It's a trap." He solemnly pronounced, not saying anything more for a few seconds. "Don't go there because it's a dirty trap," he later added with resolute confidence.

"That's what I believe too, Uncle! I hadn't planned to go to Puerto Vallarta at all." Charles answered with a confident tone.

"These people are using Dawnin as bait, hoping you'll go there so they can capture you. They want your head, my dear! However, after all, I'm happy for this news." Andrew said with a smile at the end of the sentence.

"What do you mean? Uncle."

"It's simple dear Charles! I think Puerto Vallarta will be the solution to our problems. Don't you understand? Why would these mysterious folks have given you this location? Because there, they feel safe and at home, while you would be a foreigner, a stranger. However, for me, they made a huge mistake Andrew talked with confidence."

"Do you really think so?"

"Yes! I think we finally have something in our hands. If we were playing poker, I could say that we have a nice full hand of aces, while we do not know if the opponents have a poker of kings, or if they are just bluffing. And when I have a full hand of aces, I always go to the end, and I don't care if I lose by chance."

"But Uncle! A full hand of aces can be easily beaten by a poker, color, or royal flush, don't you think?"

"Yes! It's true! When you have the balls, even if you're going to lose, before capitulating, you make your opponent spit blood, and that's exactly what we're going to do."

"I finally understand you, Uncle." Charles shouted in triumphant.

Andrew didn't like that joke very much. Despite this, he continued to talk. "Don't go personally but send some of our guys. Some of those that, even if they are eliminated, could easily be replaced. I'm referring to Scott, Ramon, and Greg. If they are lucky, they will find something useful for us, even if I fear, probably, they will not discover anything and will be killed. Well! In that case. Three fewer morons on the face of the earth," Andrew exclaimed cynically.

"Do you think they will be eliminated?"

"Yes! I think so and I believe it. Anyone who has organized this trap is ready to start the game. We can bet what you want, that we will not see our men come back. However it is worth the risk, and I have an idea, an excellent idea that will certainly get us out of all the trouble." Andrew said satisfied, showing one of his 24 carat smile.

"What's your idea, Uncle?" Charles asked curiously.

"I won't tell you this now, but have confidence, you know you can trust me."

"How about sending Munro with them as well? After all, we pay him a lot of money."

"No! Munro may be more useful here, not because if he dies, I will start crying, but because he could be the man who makes a difference. I don't want to lose him stupidly. No! Just send those three idiots, give them lots of money and promise more money, when they come back, so they will work zealously and let's see what will happen."

"I will do as you said, Uncle, do not doubt."

Charles hugged his uncle affectionately before leaving and returned to his office, feeling good. The meeting had been positive, and he was especially pleased with how Uncle Andrew had behaved. It seemed like Andrew was back to his old self, and when he was at his best, the whole organization benefited.

Now, Charles was ready to follow Andrew's suggestions. He would call his three men the next morning and send them to Mexico within two days at the latest.

Meanwhile, Andrew Martin, left alone in his office, sat in the comfortable armchair in front of the desk and lit a nice Havana cigar. He felt particularly good. Finally, what he had hoped for was happening.

This time, he could toast with champagne. The mysterious enemy, who had always remained in the shadows, had made a huge mistake. It was up to him to take the reins on all operations and fix the matter once and for all. So, after taking a couple of deep puffs, Andrew picked up the phone and dialed a number.

When someone answered the phone, he simply said, "It's me. Come immediately, I need your help, it will be very easy, you can be sure. I'm waiting for you in the office, bye."

Martin was ready to play the game and use his full hand of aces.

XVIII

SEATAC Airport, SEATTLE, In the Morning of Two Days Later

Scott Johansen, Ramon Espinoza, and Greg Murphy seemed like real tourists, ready to go on a great vacation in Puerto Vallarta. All three were dressed casually.

Scott wore a Chicago Bulls shirt, Ramon a blue one without any writing, and the most colorful was Greg who wore a red and blue Hawaiian shirt. All three were in jeans and wore sunglasses. Not only was Greg the most colorful, but also the most cheerful and excited. Certainly, the three whiskies and sodas he had drunk in the airport bar, while waiting for the flight, had helped to make it so.

Now they were standing in front of the boarding gate, waiting their turn to go inside the plane. Greg, red in the face and drunk, was talking loudly, rudely, without stopping, on every topic including his sexual adventures, "So, I picked up this chick in a pub, guys! You can't imagine what a slut, with two boobs and a fantastic ass! I took her to the car and told ...."

Observing that his two friends suddenly looked serious, Greg looked behind him and saw that an austere priest was listening to his rant with a disgusted face. He instantly stopped his red-light tale.

The priest stared into his eyes for a few seconds with contempt, before leaving.

"Fuck all the priests in the world! You always find these folks everywhere. You can't joke, laugh, and have a good time. Did you see how the priest looked at me? He electrocuted me with his eyes, damn him! What the fuck is a priest going to do in Puerto Vallarta? They have the best life, these people and then complain and even preach poverty!" Greg cursed furiously.

"Come on! Greg, Calm down! Now, he's gone, and you will not see him again for the whole journey," Ramon exclaimed laughing.

Unfortunately, Ramon was wrong. Greg found the priest sitting behind him for the duration of the trip.

His presence made Greg restless and in a bad mood. "How long will it take to arrive?" He asked Scott with trepidation, after a few hours of flight.

"Another couple of hours at least." "Damn," Greg replied.

Meanwhile in Mexico

At this time Henry was really having fun.

After the boat trip and numerous other hours of idleness and rest, and having money in his pocket, he had bought a motorcycle, a second-hand Kawasaki GPZ 900.

Thus, he had spent time driving, to gain some confidence with the new vehicle. However, despite being a good centaur, he needed a couple of days before he figured out how the bike should be handled.

In the end he rejected his old Honda 450, that he had loved so much, because this new bike gave him chills and emotions he had never experienced.

That morning, he had taken Maria for a long ride, while Henry was driving slowly, his speed was over 55 miles, and for this reason she was not amused at all.

Arriving at home, they started arguing.

"Why don't you drive more cautiously when you're on a motorcycle? Especially when I am with you. The other time it was the same story, and I told you this as well. And we had the same quarrel. In the end you promised me to go slower. Which you didn't do at all even today." Maria yelled, irritated.

"Sorry! Maria! When I'm on the bike I get carried away and can't do anything about it, it's my nature," he replied simplistically.

Maria was about to answer when she noticed the answer machine was flashing and went to check the new messages. There was only one, from Fuentes.

"Dear ones! Everything is fine here, nothing new. I would love to hear from you, so when you have a free moment, call me. To conclude I would like to know how Henry is doing, and if he is always around. Thank you! Bye."

"This idiot of Fuentes where does he think I can go during this time? Why does he ask about me? Has he fallen in love with me?" Dawnin exclaimed sarcastically, hearing the message.

"Now I will call him," Maria said.

She spoke to him briefly. At the end of the conversation, Maria turned to Henry, slightly thoughtful.

"You know! This is the first time Fuentes has called me without a real reason. He asked me about you twice. What you are doing, if you are having fun? All this is strange, very strange."

"That Fuentes is a noble soul," Henry joked.

"I don't think so, not him. Who knows what he is plotting against us?" Maria answered concerned.

"Well! We just must wait to find out." Yes! Let's wait, to see how it will end," she said skeptically.

After less than two minutes the phone rang. Maria answered and exclaimed, "Mom! Hi how are you?"

Then after a moment of silence her face lit up with happiness as tears gushed out of her eyes.

"No! I can't believe it! Are you kidding me? Oh God! I can't believe it. It's great! Tell me I'm not dreaming. When did it happen? This morning, and how is she? Well! It's wonderful. Thank you, God, I thank you. So tomorrow morning I will leave, and do you mind if I bring a friend? All right! Then we'll see you tomorrow. Kisses to you and Dad, bye."

Henry did not understand, but from the expression of joy he saw in Maria's face, he had grasped that something wonderful must have happened to her.

After the phone call, Maria was incredibly cheerful and satisfied.

"What happened that is so wonderful?" Dawnin asked with curiosity.

"The miracle. A miracle happened. Oh God! ... Henry! My sister... my sister Luisa... she came out of the coma. She is... alive." Maria replied, crying with emotion.

"Awesome! I'm happy," he exclaimed.

"Tomorrow morning, I will leave for Guadalajara. You are not obliged to come with me, but your presence would please me very much. It could be the right opportunity to meet my family."

"You can count on it! Of course, I will come with you."

"Good! I'm happy."

"What do you think? We could go on my bike, and...."

"You can forget that. We'll go in my car, and I'll be the one to drive," Maria interrupted decisively.

"Ok! It was just an idea."

The next morning, they left early for Guadalajara. After hours of traveling, they arrived at the clinic, where Luisa had been hospitalized.

Henry was quite surprised to find the clinic was almost deserted.

They went up to the first floor to room nineteen. Maria knocked and after a few seconds a sturdy woman opened the door.

"Mom! How are you?"

"Maria! What a pleasure to see you."

"This is my friend Henry... Henry Dawnin."

"Nice to meet you, ma'am," Henry kindly said, shaking hands with the smiling lady.

"Maria! How are you? My dear."

"Hello Dad! Are you well?"

"I was born again yesterday morning, my love!"

They entered Luisa's room.

"She's sleeping," Mr. Sanchez said after shaking Henry's hand."

She slept part of the morning and afternoon. It seems like she has not slept for centuries," Maria's mother added.

Henry looked at the girl he had seen in the photograph some time ago. Immediately he noticed that despite being pale and thin, the young woman had retained some of her beauty.

Quickly, Maria approached her sister and kissed her on the cheeks, mouth, and forehead, with watery eyes.

"This is a miracle, a real miracle. This time Our Lady Madonna listened to and helped us." Mrs. Sanchez exclaimed in a solemn tone.

"How is Luisa?" Maria asked.

"She's fine! She recognized me instantly, and we talked in general. We didn't tell her she has been in a coma for weeks," her father replied concerned.

"Does she know Armando is dead?" Maria asked.

"No! She doesn't know this yet. We believe it is not the right time to tell her about the tragedy."

"When will you take her home?"

"Even right away if we could. Unfortunately, the doctors want to keep her here for a few more days as a precaution. I can't wait for Luisa to come back, to walk again, to start living her life again. My poor daughter has sores on her back and buttocks. Can you believe it?" Mrs. Sanchez exclaimed, almost crying.

After three hours, Luisa continued to sleep, and it was time to leave the clinic.

So, while Mrs. Sanchez stayed there with her, Mr. Sanchez accompanied Maria and Henry home.

Following her father's car, Maria entered the villa, where she had spent her childhood and youth.

Henry saw a large property, of which he memorized just the number twenty-five of the building, but not the name of the street. An old iron gate painted gray automatically opened with the remote control.

They entered a long, straight street about half a mile long, with tall eucalyptus and pine trees at the edge of the road. About every five feet, large pots of red and white geranium covered the edges of the street. They parked in front of a luxurious large villa, with a tennis court in front of the main door, and a pine grove nearby.

"This is my home, actually to better specify, the home of my parents."

"This place is fabulous! Maria."

"Yes! It is... but it's even more fabulous... stay away from it."

"What do you mean?"

"Nothing! Nothing! I'm just saying nonsense," she replied bitterly.

Henry did not ask anything else, noticing pain and frustration in her answer. Mr. Sanchez called a butler to take the guests' suitcases to the bedrooms.

"Are we not sleeping together tonight?" Henry asked surprised.

"Are you crazy? Here? At my house? My mother would be very pissed off if she knew. You must know my parents are... old-fashioned."

"That's fine with me! As long as my room has a soft bed."

"Don't worry you will get a nice comfortable bed. Anyway, don't lock the door tonight because you'll easily have visitors."

"Who your mother?" Henry said kidding.

"Are you trying to be funny?"

"No! I am not trying to be funny. But you didn't specify," he said laughing.

"But go to fu..." Maria was interrupted by her father who called,

"In about twenty minutes, dinner will be served, so if you want to refresh yourselves, go ahead."

The next morning, they got up early and had a hearty breakfast. Henry had slept well enough until Maria had laid down beside him. After that his night was sleepless and uncomfortable as the small single bed didn't offer enough space for two.

After walking around in the gardens of the villa, at about half past ten they left the house to return to the clinic. Entering Louise's room, Maria started to cry when her sister looked at her and smiled, and ran to hug her affectionately, as big tears gushed out of her eyes.

"How are you this morning, honey?" She asked Luisa, wiping away her tears with a tissue.

105

"Not so good. I feel tired and exhausted. I struggle even to move my hands."

"This is natural, doctors said it will take a few weeks, or maybe a couple of months, to return to the way you were before. Slowly you will succeed, you can count on it," Mrs. Sanchez replied.

"I hope it's true! Where is Armando? Why didn't he come to see me? Why isn't he here with you?"

No one in the room wanted to answer that question. A moment of silence, embarrassment, and mutual glances followed among those present.

Luisa, having understood that something was wrong, repeated the question, with more drama.

"Why don't you answer me, Mom? Is he wounded? Is he sick because of the accident?"

"Well!... Armando... well!... In short... he is... come... how to explain." Mrs. Sanchez did not know what to answer.

Henry watched the whole scene, but he didn't risk intruding and moved away.

It was Maria who came to the aid of her mother, saying, "Mom! I think it's time to tell her how things are, don't you think?"

Mrs. Sanchez replied with a timid nod of the head, because she did not really know what else to do. Maria began to narrate the events.

"Luisa! You must know the accident you had was incredibly serious. You still don't know, but you've been in a coma for four weeks. You must thank Mom and Dad who continued to hope for your recovery and continued to keep you on the ventilator. Even the doctors were almost giving up hope that you would wake up. For them you were clinically dead, you know? Dad and Mom even argued... with them. And in the end, they reached an agreement to keep you here, at least until your heart stopped beating. And they were right."

Luisa turned pale, even more appalled by what her sister revealed to her.

"Oh my God! Oh God! I'm here for four weeks?"

"Yes! We will take you home as soon as the doctors will agree." Mrs. Sanchez replied.

"You did not answer me yet. Where is Armando, how is he?" Luisa asked with a worried tone.

"Armando... well... he wasn't so lucky... he died," Maria answered embarrassed.

Five days passed and Luisa returned to her parents' house.

Maria had insisted on staying there for a while, and Henry had adapted well, to the small single bed, and to the comforts offered by the luxurious villa. He had played tennis many times with Mr. Sanchez, with Maria, and once they played a doubles match, he and Mrs. Sanchez against Maria and her father. And they even won 6-4, 7-5.

He had spent a lot of time sunbathing, and swimming in the large pool, on the terrace of the villa. In short, it was not bad at all.

Luisa recovered slowly. After the first several days walking with crutches, she began to recover muscle tone, and her appetite, but she was still depressed for the death of her beloved boyfriend.

One morning, Louisa was picking roses, walking along a narrow path in the garden. Henry noticed her from afar and approached her.

Although Luisa was still thin and pale, she had put makeup on, and her appearance had greatly improved. She wore a long and loose light turquoise summer dress, and a pair of sandals.

"How are you?" Henry asked.

"Better!" she replied smiling.

They talked for a long time. That was the first time Henry had been alone with Luisa. Until then, the two had not had the opportunity to socialize.

He was as attracted to her as when he had seen her picture inside Maria's medallion.

Talking together, he found a lot of interests in common, as she did too.

Suddenly, Henry spontaneously said to her, "Don't think badly of me, Luisa! And let this remain between us. The first time I saw a photograph of you I was... I was enchanted by your beauty."

She was stunned and asked him, "Why are you telling me this? Aren't you in love with Maria?"

"Yes! I am. However, I repeat to you when I saw your photograph the first time, inside a medallion of your sister, I was struck by your beauty."

"You know you're a little... crazy," Luisa exclaimed, smiling.

"Why? I'm talking about a platonic love, an infatuation. You are one of the most beautiful women I have met in my entire life, and you are very intelligent. I know you had a traumatic experience. Don't be crucified by painful memories. Turn the page and start a new life because you deserve it. You can be happy and make every man on earth happy because you are beautiful."

Luisa was deeply touched by what Henry told her. Staring into his eyes, seeing a sincere and honest look, she understood why Maria was in love with him. Impulsively she kissed him on the mouth for a few seconds, then moving her lips away from him, said, "My sister is lucky to have someone like you. You are different from everyone else."

Luisa walked away smiling, turning around a couple of times to see if he was following her. Henry was paralyzed by that brief kiss of fire. He didn't expect such a reaction, so affectionate on Luisa's part, but it had been wonderful.

He couldn't let her go that way, so he ran after her and reached her quickly.

"Do you have something to tell me? Henry," she exclaimed gently when he arrived.

"Thank you! For the kiss," Henry replied timidly, smiling at her.

A couple of days later, Maria and Henry left the villa to return home.

Henry had a great vacation.

PUERTO VALLARTA

Meanwhile, the three hunting dogs that Charles had sent to Puerto Vallarta were disappointed because they could not find the slightest trace of Henry Dawnin. Ramon phoned Charles to alert him to the situation. He received the order to return shortly.

"Stay a maximum of two more days. But if you do not find anything concrete, come back. I don't have time, nor money to throw away," Lewis said angrily.

The next day was also unsuccessful, so in the end they decided not to look for Dawnin anymore, instead to enjoy and appreciate the local beauties.

At Greg's suggestion, on the morning of the last day of their Mexican stay, they went to a trendy restaurant on the coast, called El Sombrero. An outdoor place, where people could drink sitting at tables, under umbrellas, where tourists flocked and there were many beautiful girls.

The same morning Henry asked Maria if she wanted to take a motorcycle ride.

"Not at all," she replied bothered.

"Come on! Don't do that! I promise you I will drive slowly and will respect the road signs. In fact, if you want, I'll let you drive the bike."

"I don't want to drive it, but if you promise to go slowly, I'll come." Finally, Maria capitulated.

"I promise you. Come on! What are you afraid of? I crave something to drink. We could go to one of those restaurants by the sea, there are some nice ones. Let's spend a couple of hours together and watch people. I'm tired of being indoors. And don't worry! I can't drive downtown at full throttle."

Maria got on the bike a little reluctantly. However, Dawnin, kept his promise and drove at a slow pace.

Someone told me they make good cocktails at that place." Maria said.

"Which restaurant are you referring to?"

"El Sombrero, do you see it?"

"That's fine with me! Let's go there." Henry parked the bike, and they went inside.

It was very crowded.

"Try to get a table outside, while I go to the bathroom," he told Maria. Before he reached the door, an austere priest stopped him and said, "Do you have a minute to spare, son?"

"What is it about? Father! I'm in a hurry," Henry replied, dancing lightly because of his imminent... need.

"Just a minute! Son! I'll just steal a minute from you."

"Then hurry up, Father! Or tell me after I've gone to the bathroom."

"We're organizing a mission trip Amazonia to spread the word of God to the local population. That's why we're raising money. Could you contribute?"

Without a word, Henry quickly took a $20 bill from his wallet and handed it over to the priest.

"Thank you very much! Son, thank you! What's your name?"

"My name is Henry, Father."

"Thanks again! Henry! May God bless you," the priest replied friendly, shaking his hand energetically for a long time and then let him go. Finally, Henry went to the bathroom.

He found Maria on the terrace; on the way he saw the priest sitting at one of the tables with umbrellas about 30 feet away. Maria had found one of the few tables available.

Approaching the priest Henry exclaimed, "I hope you don't spend all the money on beer and sandwiches, Father."

The man replied, "Son! What can I say? We priests have a stomach too, but I only spend my money, not the donations."

"I was just kidding, good morning."

"Good morning to you Henry." The priest greeted him with a smile, while shaking Henry's hand vigorously for several seconds, as he had done before.

Scott, Greg, and Ramon had been lucky enough to find one of the few tables available at El Sombrero. They sat down, and a lovely waitress brought the menus. They were reading the menu, when Scott started to tease Greg.

"Hey Greg! Isn't that your priest friend sitting at the table there?"

"Of course, it's him. Look at him, how he eats and drinks," Ramon added.

"This worm seems to be following me everywhere I go. What the hell is he doing here?" Greg roared nervously.

"He's doing what you are doing. He came to eat, drink and maybe to pick up girls, ah! Aha! Ah!" Ramon laughed wildly.

Meanwhile, Henry sat next to Maria and was reading the menu when he confided to his partner, "You know! I met a priest on my way to the bathroom and he started talking to me non-stop, while I was almost peeing in my pants. Do you believe it?"

"What did he want?"

"Money! For a mission in Amazonia. At least that's what he told me."

"And did you give him money?"

"I gave him twenty dollars, but I would have given even a hundred, if he left me alone at that crucial moment. I was going crazy, and he was clinging to me, like a leach, or crazy glue. It's funny! He gave me the longest, sweatiest handshake I ever received in all my life. The dude seemed so happy for my charity. You can see the priest, he's sitting there."

"Where?"

"There at that table."

"Ah yes! I see him. It seems he is having a good time." Maria commented.

Suddenly, Henry noticed, at a table about forty feet from the missionary, Charles's three men, who were joking, and laughing and having a great time.

"Hey Maria! Look at that table there. The one near the railing, on the left of the priest, do you see those three men?" he said scared.

"Christ! Those guys are part of Charles Lewis's gang," Maria answered worried.

"Exactly! What do we do now? It seems they haven't seen us yet."

"I don't know. Here they can do nothing because there are too many people, too many witnesses, and I'm armed."

"Why don't we leave before they see us?" Henry asked confused.

"It might be a good idea, but to get out of the room we must go down those damn stairs. Don't you think they would notice us?" Maria said concerned.

"It's a risk we must take. Once on the bike I challenge anyone, even that great pilot there, to catch me."

Quickly, Henry and Maria went down the stairs to reach the ground floor and the exit of the restaurant.

At the same time Scott and Ramon were continuing to tease Greg about the priest's story and were laughing loudly.

Suddenly Greg, who was the tensest, interrupted their laughter by saying, hey guys! But isn't that Henry Dawnin the one who's going down the stairs there? At least he looks like him, I've never seen him in person."

"Shit! You're right Greg. It's him, bravo! Nice job," Ramon complimented.

"He's getting away. We must stop him! Immediately, guys let's rock, damn." Scott shouted as he stood up, followed closely by his companions.

Henry and Maria had finished descending the stairs when she instinctively turned back and saw their enemies had risen from the table to follow them.

"We're in deep trouble, Henry! Those criminals have discovered us and are coming here," Maria exclaimed, frightened.

"Ah yes! All right! Get your gun and be ready," he replied.

Maria did not understand what he meant but automatically grabbed the gun in her purse.

Suddenly, Henry turned back, and instead of continuing to run toward the exit, at a brisk pace advanced toward the three criminals who remained literally stunned by his movement.

Maria was also incredibly surprised, but after a moment of hesitation she followed him, keeping her hand on the gun in her bag.

The three thugs slowed down, seeing Henry coming like a fury towards them.

"Looking for me," Henry shouted, attracting the attention of everyone in the room.

The three were speechless.

"So! Tough guys, are you looking for me or not? Do you want to kill me like you did old Ray Brown," Dawnin screamed.

The scene took place right in front of the table where the priest was sitting.

Taking advantage of the surprise, before the three men had any reaction, Henry gave a violent kick to Scott's lower abdomen, causing him to bend over. Then he gave him a powerful blow to the back of the neck that made him fall heavily to the floor.

Maria, with great courage and determination, pulled the gun out of her bag before the other two had time to react and shouted, "Stop, or I'll blow your head off."

She continued, "I am a federal agent, call the police immediately. These three men are dangerous murderers."

The whole scene took place within a matter of seconds.

Ramon had almost pulled out his revolver but Maria, was faster and fired three shots, killing him.

Scott, still half groggy and tottering from the beating he had received, attacked Henry with a dagger like an enraged bull.

Dawnin managed to dodge the blow and grabbed the hand with the dagger. A fierce hand-to-hand combat ensued. Eventually, Henry stuck the dagger in Scott's belly and he died instantly.

Taking advantage of the confusion, Greg Murphy, intelligently, managed to escape among the frightened people still fleeing the room.

Henry asked Maria, "Damn! Did you see where the third man went?"

"Unfortunately, not! Shit! He managed to escape."

"Well! However, it could have been worse. Look! We scared even the priest, who ran out as well." Henry exclaimed, pointing a finger at the empty table.

Maria bent over the two men lying on the ground and, touching their wrists, said, "They are both dead."

"This was not what we wanted. Gosh! It's incredible! Still, we can't have a single witness against Charles."

"The police are coming," one of the waiters told Maria.

"Even the police now, great," Henry commented nervously.

"Don't worry, I'll take care of them." Maria answered confidently.

Meanwhile Greg Murphy ran like a man desperate to escape capture.

"That man and woman are really two unleashed tigers." Greg murmured in terror. He would never have imagined a stunt like that. During his escape, Greg thought about what they had told him about the operation. An elementary and risk-free affair. Find a poor idiot, a failed hippy, unable to do anything. They were totally wrong, Henry was very dangerous, not harmless.

Finally, Greg saw the rental car they had parked five blocks away, on a side street. Greg already felt better at the sight of his Golf GTI.

He turned back several times to make sure no one was following him. At the end he was convinced everything had gone well, so he opened the door and quickly entered the car. He started the engine and was ready to go, when he was violently grabbed by someone who was hidden behind him.

Then he felt a stabbing pain in his neck and in the last foggy seconds of his life, he recognized the man who had just slit his throat, looking back at him from the rearview mirror. Yet he did not have time to hear the whole phrase the assassin was whispering to him maliciously, a few inches from his ear.

The sentence was: "We cannot afford to keep idiots in the organization, who can get us into trouble. That is why it is better to slit the throat of an imbecile than to keep him alive."

The police arrived after a long time. Maria showed her badge to the inspector in charge of the investigation. She explained the facts and the danger of those criminals.

"Everything possible will be done to capture Greg Murphy, Ms. Sanchez, you can bet on it. From now on all airports, ports and borders will be guarded 24 hours a day to find him. We have a good identikit of the bloke, and I am confident he will not run away from us for very long."

"Inspector! I can give you a picture of him by tonight if that will help you."

"Of course! Please give me your phone number so if I have any news, I can call you."

Maria gave him her phone number and left.

As they were walking away from the bar, Maria turned to Henry and furiously shouted at him, "Have you gone crazy? Damn idiot."

"For what?" Dawnin answered confused.

"For what? We are alive by a miracle. These animals could have killed us or committed a massacre in the restaurant. How did you get the crazy idea to go and confront them?"

"For two reasons. The first reason is because I'm tired of running. That's enough! It is time for me to act. I can't always behave like a fearful moron. The second and most important, it is that by surprising those bastards in that way, we could have benefited. I was sure that by attracting the attention of everyone present at the bar, those criminals would not dare to do anything against us. Unfortunately, I did not think the situation would deteriorate so fast. I was hoping to create some confusion so we could escape safely. It did not work but maybe it's better in this way. Do you understand? If we had gotten away, we would probably have been doomed, because when there were no witnesses around, they would have tried to kill us. Instead, they couldn't do that in the restaurant."

Maria seemed to understand and calmed down. "It wasn't difficult to fix everything with the police, did you see?" She said relieved, as they were going to get the bike.

"Lucky you! If I had been alone, I would be rotting in some remote Mexican jail. Anyway! Do you know what is bugging me right now?"

"What is it?"

"I wonder how these men knew I was here in Puerto Vallarta?"

"Can't you imagine?"

"Fuentes! That son of a bitch. Sure! It was he who organized this trap, using me as bait. Only he could play such a ruse on me, I'm more than sure," Henry exclaimed indignantly.

"I think so. Unfortunately, what I feared happened. That was his real purpose, to keep you around, checking that you were staying here. Finally, do you realize what kind of scumbag Fuentes is?" Maria said disgusted.

"Let's visit him. I want to have a nice chat with Rodrigo Fuentes," Henry yelled furiously.

"I agree! I think the time has come. Do not lose your temper and behave decently. Remember that you are in the wolf's den. And drive slowly, if not I will take a bus."

Although very irritated, Henry kept his promise and drove at a slow pace to Fuentes's mansion. During the journey he had not noticed an old red Volkswagen van following him at a distance benefiting from his relatively slow speed.

When Henry stopped in front of the gate to ring the intercom, the van passed by on the road, and from inside the car the driver gladly exclaimed, "Bingo! Here we go! Fantastic! Everything went as planned." The vehicle disappeared on the horizon.

The mere sight of that villa made Dawnin angry. Maria did not have the remote control with her. So, after someone opened the door, he drove furiously along the stretch of road uphill that separated the gate from the house.

"Now I'm breaking the legs of that big son of bitch," Henry exclaimed, while parking the bike.

"Christ! Calm down Henry! After all, you still don't know if he has betrayed you. You have no proof. Don't lose control of your temper and try to behave civilly." Maria said.

"Who do you think it was? Santa Claus! Of course, it was him," he shouted angrily.

Dawnin had just finished cursing when he heard Fuentes's unmistakable deep low voice.

"Good morning, Henry! How are you?"

"Good morning! Ugly son of a bitch! It's time to stop this bullshit, your stupid tricks, and your false respectability," Henry replied angrily.

What Maria had feared happened. Henry had lost total control of his anger and was literally pouncing on Fuentes. Rodrigo was in the doorstep, sitting in his wheelchair and escorted by his four most trusted men.

"Oh Heavens! The 4G! There must be something big at stake," Maria murmured with apprehension.

Meanwhile, Henry had come close to Fuentes, who in a gentle and mocking voice, at the same time, asked him, "But what's wrong? Henry! You seem irritated. What happened?"

"Are you still taking me as a fool, Fuentes? Finish once and for all with this crap and tell me why you have betrayed me. Do you understand?" Henry shouted in disgust.

"What are you saying? Are you crazy?" Rodrigo replied with a sarcastic smile, and an unpleasant tone of voice.

"Ugly son of a bitch! I'll break you...."

Henry froze, before he could grab Fuentes, when he saw the four men with him were pulling out their guns.

For the first time he looked at them carefully and recognized two of them, Coco, and Roberto. While he had never met the remaining two, he was deeply impressed by one of them, the one who seemed jittery slimy and the most evil. He had a stocky build, with a round face, dark hair, full of gel with a part on the side, and only one eye.

That man was staring at him with hatred and treachery and seemed ready to use his revolver to kill him.

To see his reaction Henry turned to Fuentes and said, "Bravo Fuentes! It's easy to dictate the rules when you have four flunkies behind you. Why don't you tell your servants to lay down their weapons and act like true men."

"What do you want me to do, Mister Fuentes? Do I shoot this moron in the mouth?" The little stocky man asked excitedly to his master.

"No! Stay calm! Tonio! Stay calm. Mr. Dawnin is a friend. Are you not a buddy, Henry?"

Maria approached the group and intruded into the discussion.

"Come on! Stop arguing! All of you. And Fuentes! Tell your men to lay down their arms. Let's reason as civilized people."

"You heard the lady! Lower your arms lads." Fuentes ordered his men, who obeyed instantly.

"Why did you betray me?" It was the first question Henry asked Rodrigo in the luxurious living room of the villa.

Fuentes seemed to hesitate, while smoking a Gitanes cigarette, and did not answer.

Therefore, Henry repeated the question again with more vehemence and aggression.

"I know it was you, Fuentes! Don't you pretend to be innocent. Good heavens! They tried to kill me this morning. Do you know, or do you care?"

"Anyway! You are still alive and well," Fuentes replied sarcastically once again, with a wicked grin.

"Not because of you, dear friend."

"Please, Fuentes, just tell us the truth without all these subterfuges. I think we're on the same side, aren't we?" Maria asked politically.

"Okay! Okay! You have won, I will tell you the truth. I do not know whether the word betrayal you used a moment ago is very appropriate for the occasion. Henry! No one has betrayed you. Let's say we used you for a specific purpose."

"Then I was right! You did it, ugly bastard," Henry roared enraged.

"Calm down and moderate your words in my presence. I will no longer tolerate insolence on your part. Since you arrived, you have been doing nothing but insulting me. Enough is enough! Is that okay?"

Then he added, "Let me finish! Dawnin! For all the saints! I did not betray, nor sell you out, you were just used. You work for me after all, don't you? I gave you fifteen thousand dollars, if you remember well, with which you bought a nice bike and you went off to have fun everywhere. Why do you think I gave you that big sum, for your handsome face? Or because I like you? Absolutely not. You are my employee, so like it or not, you must work for me. I consider acting as bait to be part of your job."

"But at least! Why didn't you warn me what you were planning?" Henry asked, trying to understand.

"The reason is my business. I do not have to give you any explanation. We revealed to Charles Lewis that you were here because we hoped he would come in person, so I could settle the old score once and for all. Unfortunately, it did not go as we hoped. Our friend did not fall into the trap, and only sent part of his troop. We weren't lucky at all." Fuentes said disappointed.

"You did not realize that those hitmen could pose a serious danger to us?" Henry asked animatedly, looking at Maria to ask for her support.

"We were hoping to have much more success, instead it did not work. When you bluff, you must be ready to take risks. It was, however, a failure. But what are you complaining about? Dawnin. You are still alive with a lot of my money in your pocket." Fuentes replied without showing respect.

"Fuentes! Go fuck off, you and all your dirty villains." Henry yelled loudly, heading for the door followed by Maria.

It was she who before leaving, turning to Rodrigo, said, "Fuentes! You disappointed me deeply and literally disgust me. I don't see why it is necessary to work with you. You are worse than Charles Lewis. Goodbye forever. If from now on you interfere with federal investigations, you will be in serious trouble, do you understand? Forget your important and lofty friendships. If you continue to meddle in the investigation we will be carrying out on Charles Lewis and his gang, you will be arrested. You are not part of any institution, but only a vigilante who has created a paramilitary group in search of revenge, so be careful in the future."

Henry was deeply impressed by Maria's ardor and courage. Thus, he decided to do something he had been thinking about since his arrival.

He passed by Tonio and suddenly grabbed the man's revolver kept on his right side, in a holster. Then Henry slammed Tonio against the wall and put the weapon in his mouth, shouting, "Never dare to threaten us again! Tonio the grim! Or I'll break your bones one by one! Piece of crap."

Dawnin opened the gun, dropping the cartridges on the ground, and at the same time gave a strong slap to the already stunned face of the ugly fellow, who was totally astonished. Tonio's companions were about to intervene, but a blatant gesture by Fuentes blocked them before they went into action.

Then Rodrigo began to clap his hands, exclaiming sarcastically, "Bravo! Bravo! Bravo! Dawnin! Do you feel better now after this little petty show? Do you feel more like a true, tough man?"

"You must thank God for being disabled, because if you weren't, I would have kicked you in the mouth and in the ass. However, I will give you some advice. From now on, stay away from me because if I find you or any of your henchmen still on my trail, I will kill you, Fuentes. You have my word," Henry replied enraged.

"So! Do you want to start a war between us? Dawnin." Fuentes said with a self-sufficient, arrogant tone while grinning amused.

"Yes! That's right! I don't see any difference between you and Charles Lewis. You are two peas in a pod, you are both criminals."

After that Henry and Maria left the villa.

Fuentes, from the threshold of the door of the house, saw the bike move further and further away.

Suddenly Rodrigo shouted furiously, "Poor crazy people! How the hell do you dare act against me? Don't you know I can crush you like ants?"

Then Fuentes turned to Tonio and with a serious tone said, "I do believe you would like to get revenge against mister Henry Dawnin, and let him pay for the affront he did to you, don't you, Tonio?"

"Yes, sir," replied the man with malice.

"Good! In the future if you see Dawnin around, kill him."

"Of course, Mr. Fuentes with immense pleasure."

"Perfect! I leave it to you to choose how to do it. I hope you surprise me."

"You can count on it."

"Luis! I want you to help Tonio in this operation."

"You can consider Dawnin already chastised, Mr. Fuentes."

Meanwhile, Henry and Maria had exited the gate of the villa, when she said worriedly, "You know what this means for us, don't you?"

"Of course, I know! From now on, my friend Mr. Fuentes will also plot revenge against us, and I would not be surprised if he tried to kill us. Am I right?"

"Yes! That's right. I also think I can say goodbye to my career. Fuentes has too many influential friendships that I can't fight against."

"Do you remember, Maria, what I told you some time ago about Seattle? Well! I think now is the right time to go there, to settle the old score once and for all. We must leave this place as soon as possible, as staying in Puerto Vallarta now is too dangerous for us."

"I agree. Too bad! I really liked the apartment by the ocean."

"Oh yes! I liked it too, but patience," Henry replied.

Henry's motorcycle had left Fuentes's villa less than twenty minutes, when a priest rang the intercom of the house.

"Yes! Hello! I would like to see Mr. Fuentes. Is he at home? Yes! It's an important matter."

The gate of the villa opened, and the priest drove through in his car.

XIX

Jose' Vargas, aka Henry Dawnin, landed at SEATAC Airport in Seattle.

He was with his wife Maria for a short vacation in the American metropolis. Mr. Vargas was provided with a regular and valid Mexican passport, complete with a visa stamped by the American Embassy in Mexico City. After checking his papers, the immigration officer stamped his passport and wished him and his lady a happy stay in the United States.

Henry was perfectly disguised. Even his mother would have struggled to recognize him if she had been alive. His hair was cut short and dyed black, he sported a mustache, and wore false cheekbones that altered the features of his face

Maria had also changed her look. In fact, she had cut her hair short but had not otherwise disguised herself.

They booked a room at the Westin Hotel downtown and took a shuttle to the hotel.

They entered the hotel room and finally found some refreshments and air conditioning. In fact, Seattle strangely enough at that time of summer was literally hot.

Maria took a shower. After a rest they went out to dinner as it was 7:30 and they were starving.

They sat at a small table in a luxurious Italian restaurant. Henry ordered red wine and while the waiter had gone to get the wine, they read the menu. They had gone to Seattle with the intention of stalking Lewis and associates but had not yet developed any plans to get rid of Charles and his gang.

Maria, through her connections and friendships, knew where Charles lived and worked, just as she had discovered the addresses of Tom Atkinson and Andrew Martin.

They decided to divide the tasks. Henry would follow Charles to understand his habits and daily routines. Maria would do the same with Tom Atkinson. Andrew Martin would come later.

Henry hoped to make a deal with Charles to tell him the truth, and propose another pact, as in his school days, such as leave me alone and I will do the same with you. But he had strong doubts about the eventual success of this plan. The school days were far away, very far away, and they were no longer boys.

Certainly, if Charles had accepted the proposal, it would have been the best solution for everyone. Henry hated violence and killing. In fact, he felt great remorse for killing Scott Johansen who, although he was a hardened criminal, was still a human being. Although he did it in self-defense, he felt truly disgusted.

In his heart he was already imagining that perhaps this story would end in a bloodbath. He was mainly frightened for this reason and did not know if he would be the winner or if he would be the loser and dead.

Maria saw that he was staring at the same page of the menu with a totally absent gaze, and she became worried.

"What are you thinking?" she asked with apprehension.

"Oh! Nothing special. I'm thinking a little bit about the near future, what we could do, and what might happen to us."

"Are you scared?"

"Yes, I am really scared, what about you?"

"Me too."

"First of all, tomorrow we will have to rent cars to get around. We certainly can't take a taxi every time we have to stalk someone, can we?" Henry said with a serious tone.

"Yes! You're right! It's not a bad idea, but we need to use the money wisely."

"I know! I know! I want to rent a bike, not a Ferrari."

"Henry! You're incredible!" Maria exclaimed, laughing in a slightly, mocking tone.

"Have you decided what you are going to eat?" A stocky and mustachioed waiter asked politely.

"Yes! I'll have calamari as an appetizer, spaghetti alla bucaniere and a Caesar salad." Maria replied.

"Very well! And for you sir?"

Henry had been caught off guard by the arrival of the waiter so for the first time he looked seriously at the menu. Seeing that the waiter was waiting, he said, "Can you come back in a couple of minutes? I haven't decided yet."

"No problem, sir! Take your time."

This time he read the menu carefully and opted for seafood spaghetti with mussels, and clams. When the waiter came back to take the order, he had already decided.

"Do you want anything else sir?"

"Yes! I would like a Fiorentina steak with fries, bruschetta, and potato croquettes. Yes! Who cares about the cost? Fuentes is paying."

"Please?" The waiter asked, not having understood the order.

"As an appetizer, bruschetta and potato croquettes, and then a beautiful, thick Fiorentina steak, and fries," he slowly repeated as if talking to a child.

"A little while ago you said something different, I did not understand well, pentes... vences, or something like that."

"Oh yes! You are right! I said Fuentes, but I do believe it's not on the menu. It was just a stupid joke to myself about a friend who loves me very much."

The waiter left and Maria burst out laughing.

"Was I wrong? Doesn't Fuentes love me so much?" Henry exclaimed, laughing.

The next morning Henry woke up early. Unable to fall asleep again, he decided to take a shower to fully wake up. He got out of bed and went to the bathroom, while Maria continued to sleep soundly. After a long shower he returned to the room and found her awake.

"Are we having breakfast together?" He asked.

"Of course! Give me a few minutes." Henry opened the curtains to let in some light and sat in an armchair by the window to think. Then he opened the patio door wide and went out onto the small balcony. It was a great day without a cloud in the sky.

Henry was unwell and felt extremely anxious. In fact, he hadn't slept well all night.

The idea of hunting for the wolf in his own den frightened him greatly. He feared for his life as well as for Maria. He gave his plan one-in-ten chance of success. Much of the time, his mind literally panicked, thinking of what he called a suicide mission.

However, on the other hand, he had a great desire to take revenge against those bastards Charles Lewis and Tom Atkinson for all the trouble they gave him in the past. His plan relied heavily on the element of surprise. In fact, this time it was he who would start. Unlike in the past when he was always the one to suffer his opponent's attack.

The surprise effect would be his only ally besides Maria, of course.

Meanwhile Maria had come out of the shower and after drying herself with a towel, went naked into the bedroom and to her surprise found the door completely open and Henry on the terrace, leaning on the railing, immersed in his dark thoughts.

"Good heavens! Henry! Why did you open the door? Don't you see that I'm naked?" She shouted irritated.

He did not hear Maria and continued his contemplation.

Maria understood he was in another world and noticed there were people in the opposite building, sitting out on the balconies, who were watching her. She nervously closed the curtains, and cursing, pulled clean clothes from her suitcase.

At the same time Henry saw that in the tower opposite, which was part of the same hotel, an old lady on the balcony was pointing in his direction to her husband. He did not understand what they wanted.

Then he noticed the elderly gentleman had disappeared, and then reappeared quickly after a few moments, armed with binoculars.

At the same time, he heard a noise behind him and turning around, glimpsed the curtains closing. Then looking back at the elderly couple, he noticed the man had put down his binoculars with a gesture of anger and disappointment, which Henry did not understand.

On the other hand, the elderly individual exclaimed happily to the wife, "What did I tell you Martha! Big cities offer pleasant, beautiful surprises that we only dream of at home, in Kansas."

"Look how many sluts are around here," the lady replied, disgusted.

Maria was undecided what to wear. At the end she opted to dress casually, a pair of jeans and a black shirt, so she would not attract the attention of Tom Atkinson. She had just finished dressing when Henry returned to the room with an absent look.

A little irritated she shouted, "What are you thinking? Why did you open the curtains before I got dressed? Do you want to show my body to the whole neighborhood?"

"What do you say? Ah yes! Excuse me! I didn't think about it," he replied, literally confused.

The time for action had arrived. Dawnin hadn't changed his gloomy, fearful mood.

"Please be very careful, and prudent." Maria said worried.

"Of course! But you must be careful too. Are you going directly to Tom Atkinson's house?"

"Yes! Today is Saturday, so it seems perfect to me. He will take it easy since he probably won't go to work. I just hope he didn't go out of town for the weekend. And what are you going to do?"

"I honestly don't know. I think I'll take a walk here in downtown, until I arrive at Pioneer Square, where our friend Charles has his office."

"Surely he will not be there," said Maria doubtfully.

"I know! But I want to look anyway. Think, if that thief is working after hours, I could wring his neck and end it once and for all."

"Good luck! Bye," Maria said, leaving quickly.

Left alone, Henry drank another latte before deciding to take the metro bus directly to Pioneer Square. As he approached the skyscraper, where the archenemy had his office, he bought a copy of the Seattle Times from a vending machine.

He looked at the headlines on the first page, leaning against the wall of a building, near a bus stop full of people. At a certain moment he felt a deep emotion. Henry had just looked up and, among the people on the sidewalk, he saw Charles Lewis walking briskly toward him with a worried air.

Scared to death, Dawnin stared at Charles carefully the whole time. Charles passed in front of him without recognizing him. In that moment, Henry felt an incredible desire to trip that jerk and make him fall to the ground like an idiot, hoping he would fracture some vertebra. However, his common sense prevented him from making such a move.

So, Henry simply followed Charles with his eyes as he approached the door of the building where he had his office.

"This disguise works fantastically." Dawnin murmured with enormous satisfaction.

He had just finished spying on Charles Lewis entering his office, when another violent, unexpected, emotion almost caused him to suffer a heart attack.

An Asian girl passed by him, so close that she involuntary touched him. Henry immediately recognized the woman. She was the mysterious, beautiful, Asian girl who had stalked him in Redlands, and whom Fuentes had shown in the slides without knowing her identity.

She was walking in the direction in which Charles had previously passed. Instantly he lost his apathy and carelessness towards events.

In fact, he felt excited. He never expected this series of events. So, he began to follow the woman, who continued to walk quickly until she stopped in front of the door of Charles's office. After a moment of uncertainty, she made a U-turn, passing back in front of him. Thus, Henry was forced to make a U-turn as well.

This time, Henry finally got a good look at the woman. She was gorgeous, a goddess. Tall and slender, her tanned skin was smooth as velvet, and her dark eyes looked fiery. Her features were delicate and perfect. The white cotton t-shirt and tight jeans adhered perfectly to her slender figure, highlighting her firm body and chest.

Henry, still blinded by her beauty and sensuality, hoped she was not another hostile and dangerous enemy.

So, he followed the woman.

She walked for several blocks, until she slowed down near a small black Honda Civic, parked on the side of the road. She opened the door and entered. The car must have become very hot inside, so the young woman hastily opened both windows to cool it down.

Henry slowed down but continued to observe her. He had almost reached the car when a risky idea flashed into his mind.

He pulled a city map out of his pocket and pretending to read it, approached the right door of the girl's car, which was totally open. At the same time, he took out his black sunglass case and held it in his hand, covering it with the Seattle Times.

Mixing words of Spanish with words of English, Dawnin asked her a question while she was putting on the seat belt, "Excuse me! Miss! Do you know how I can get to the Space Needle?"

"Of course! It's quite far from here, you must go...."

Quick as lightning, Henry opened the car door.

He entered and pointed the case of the sunglasses, totally wrapped and semi-hidden in the newspaper, and threatened aggressively, "I have a weapon pointed at your stomach. If you don't do what I tell you, I'll hurt you. I'm not kidding."

She was petrified, and stammering asked him, "If you want money... let me get my purse, the wallet is there... inside."

"Shut up! Turn on the car and let's immediately drive away from here." Henry replied nervously.

The woman was driving the car, when Henry grabbed the bag next to her and opened it. The first thing he noticed was an automatic gun, which he immediately took possession of. Then he found the wallet and opened it, without losing sight of her for a second.

"May I know what you want from me?" she asked, frightened.

Dawnin had picked up her driver's license, a Washington D.C. license, and reading the name that was written there, asked her, "Tell me what you want from me? Julie Sue!"

"I don't know you. I have never seen you in my life. You must be crazy."

"Do you work for Charles Lewis?" Henry asked her dryly, getting to the point.

Julie turned pale. Lewis's name showed her the man was not just any criminal passing by, but he had to know something and was involved with her investigation.

Unconvincingly she replied, "Charles Lewis? And who the hell is he?"

"Listen! I don't have time to waste. I want to know who you are. Who do you work for, and why did you follow me step by step down in Redlands?"

"Redlands?" Julie answered confused.

"Yes! Redlands right there! You followed me continuously. If you hadn't recognized me, I'm Henry... Henry Dawnin."

Julie was very surprised and no longer knew whether to be scared or not.

The man she had hunted for a long time but never caught was there, sitting in her car, with a gun pointed at her stomach. Now she could find out whether the dude was a criminal, as Dick Tolone had claimed, or whether her sixth sense had been right when she believed that Henry Dawnin was only a victim of events.

Quite excited, she exclaimed, "Christ! Henry Dawnin."

Henry noticed that since he had revealed his name, Julie seemed to have calmed down a bit. He could read it in her expression, so he decided to foster a relaxed atmosphere instead of tension.

Staring into her eyes, he said gently, "Yes! Julie! It's just me. I don't want to hurt you; I swear. What I want is clarification. To show I am not hostile I am ready to put away my gun and give yours back. Give me your word of honor that you won't try to escape or set any trap."

"You have my word of honor, lay down your gun and let's talk," Julie replied friendly.

Henry, after a moment of hesitation, took Julie's gun and put it back inside her purse in the same place where he had found it. "And now I will lay down my gun too, so we are even," Henry said sarcastically.

Then Henry quite blatantly, removed the newspaper that covered his hand holding the sunglass case and showed his weapon to Julie.

Julie had parked the car in a lot in Madrona Park, on Lake Washington, and she was walking along the shore with Henry while dozens of children swam, screaming and playing.

"I'm an FBI agent, Henry! I have nothing against you. Indeed! I hope you can clarify some obscure points and help me frame Charles Lewis and his gang of criminals."

"Incredible! Do you see? I guessed it!" He exclaimed, relaxing.

Julie recounted her version of events, including the FBI policy, her removal from the investigation, and the possible connection between some members of the federal agency and Charles Lewis. Then she pondered the possibility of him testifying against Charles at a potential trial.

Henry told his story. How he was involved in the affair, Tom Atkinson's attempt to kill him, and the man's relationship with Cindy Hyatt.

He also revealed the story about Fuentes and his organization, plus the latest events.

"My problem, dear Julie! It's that I don't know a damn about Charles and his illegal business, believe me, I'm not the person who can frame him. When he came to my house, he alluded to drug trafficking, but how can I prove he wasn't joking? Absolutely not! I'm sorry to disappoint you but that is the reality of the facts."

Julie was t. In fact, she had always believed Henry Dawnin knew something tremendously important that could incriminate Charles Lewis. Unfortunately, her hopes were miserably wrecked in a stormy sea. But what did it matter at this point? She was pleased to have found a helpful ally to go through the whole matter.

"Could you testify against Tom Atkinson and by accusing him, we could go all the way to incriminate Charles Lewis," Julie asked, trying to convince him.

"No at all! I'm sorry, Julie, I don't want to spend the rest of my life fearing some hitman will kill me, despite the help the police or FBI might give me. Charles Lewis and Andrew Martin, much more than Atkinson, have powerful and influential friends and connections everywhere. My life would not be worth a single cent, like that of Tom Atkinson the day he goes on trial. No! We must deal with this situation ourselves, even be ready to kill. I have never killed, except a few days ago for legitimate defense, therefore this prospect is terrifying. However, it's more horrible that people like Lewis and Martin continue to harm this society," Dawnin said with confidence.

"Will you help me in the investigation I'm doing?"

"Of course! We are in the same boat, and we will be together until the end."

"Good! I knew I could trust you. Do you know that you are unrecognizable? I would never have believed it was you at the beginning. However, I prefer you without the disguise, you are much more attractive," Julie said smiling.

"Great disguise, isn't it? I can be uglier, but instead you are always more beautiful and attractive than ever." Henry said blushing, after expressing what he really felt about her.

"Can I offer you something to drink?" he asked.

"Of course! With great pleasure."

"No! The pleasure is all mine."

"Don't you think that your partner might get jealous, if she knew?"

"Of what? I'm not taking you to bed, am I?"

Wish I could, he thought. "Who knows where Maria is now," he added.

Maria had rented a Dodge Colt at Dollar car rental, not far from the hotel, and headed to West Seattle, where Tom Atkinson lived. Using the city map she finally found her destination. She parked the car in front of the enemy's house and waited. The curtains were closed, and the house seemed deserted.

At first Maria believed Tom was not there, but nevertheless decided to stay and in the end she was right. In fact, after about twenty minutes she saw the curtains being opened in the living room.

Atkinson walked out the door and got into his car, leaving at a moderate speed.

He stopped in front of a bar and sat at a small table outside. Maria got out of her car and went to sit at a table not far from where her target was sitting.

Tom took it easy. He read the newspaper for a long time, sipping his coffee, but now he seemed to be about to leave.

Trying to be discreet and not arouse suspicion, Maria decided to move first and go to the car and wait there. She got up quickly, collecting her belongings, and moved towards the street. Unfortunately, she had not been careful putting the map inside her purse, so while walking at a brisk pace, the map fell out on the ground.

"Ma'am! Ma'am!" She heard a call.

Maria turned back and with immense amazement saw Tom Atkinson running towards her. She was stunned, and even a little frightened.

Tom stopped in front of Maria, staring at her from head to toe, dwelling on her chest, and said very politely, "I am sorry to bother you, madam. You dropped this map. Here it is. Please take it back."

"Oh, thank you! You are very kind, sir. Thank you very much," she replied timidly.

Maria took the map and placed it securely inside her purse. Then hastily she turned to leave, when Tom Atkinson, like a vulture on his prey, asked, "Madam! Are you a foreigner?"

Maria hesitated to respond. In fact, she hoped to go far away from the villain as soon as possible, but Tom asked her the same question again.

"If you want, I can be of great help to you. I know the city incredibly well. I can direct you to the best restaurants and private clubs around here," he added.

"I'm Spanish," she replied, biting her lips.

"Spanish! That's great! Coincidentally, my grandmother was Spanish, yes! From Lisbon."

Tom Atkinson didn't even know where Spain was, nor was his grandmother Spanish, but he was so excited to have picked up this beautiful foreign woman in the street, that he tried to improvise.

He had heard the name "Lisbon" from somewhere recently, so he put it to use. In fact, who cared if that city wasn't in Spain? It was somewhere in Europe.

Tom was really attracted to the beautiful brunette with the exotic accent, so he was ready to say any bullshit that came to his mind just to impress her. So, he started his bullshit at full throttle.

"Yes! Spain! What a beautiful country! The bullfights, the tango, the flamenco, the women, ah! How wonderful! Tell me, beautiful lady, what is your name? From your beauty, I believe it is an exotic name, a name ... romantic." Tom exclaimed with a rapturous tone.

Maria looked at Tom with disbelief, wondering why a jerk like him could make a career even as a criminal. That man was pathetic, and having almost killed Henry long ago, very dangerous.

"My name is Ma... I am Concita, yes! Concita is my name."

"Oh! Concita! Concita! Joy of my life! Can I put an engagement ring on your finger? I am enchanted by you. Your beauty has me completely captivated."

At this point Maria did not hold back, bursting out laughing. What she had seen and heard was too much. Tom Atkinson was too stupid.

However, Tom took her laugh as a round of applause for his irresistible poetry and comedy, so he got even more excited. And inflating his chest like a peacock, rolling his eyes to the sky to find inspiration said, "I am also a poet!" Tom exclaimed so loudly that everybody passing by heard him.

"Yes! I delight in writing poetry, when my many work commitments allow me to do so. You know! Concita! When someone like me, a successful businessman, with an established firm, finds only five minutes of free time, it is like a miracle."

"What is your name and what do you do?" Maria asked, being careful not to laugh in his face.

"Oh yes!' It's true! How careless. I was so impressed by your beauty I forgot to introduce myself. I'm Tom, Tom Atkinson, a famous businessman in the area."

"Great! What is your business, Mr. Atkinson?" She asked with a slight hint of malice.

"Oh! I work in import/export. I buy goods from abroad and sell them here in the United States, or vice versa."

"What kind of goods do you deal with?"

"It depends on the period and the availability in the market. However, my company deals with everything profitable." Tom replied without getting too specific.

"Good!" Maria exclaimed, having nothing more to say.

However, Tom seemed unstoppable and added, "You know! I had an important work commitment this morning. We had to buy a stock of timber from Brazil, for 30-35 million dollars. Nothing big! Small amount! But that idiot I was supposed to meet canceled. Okay! It means I won't do the deal with him, who cares about million plus million minus." Tom stopped talking for a few seconds as Maria was ready to move away from him.

Then he proudly added, "And then I have ships that will arrive on Thursday and will bring millions to me, ah yes! We're talking about $100-150 million."

Maria began to be annoyed. She tried to cut the conversation short and politely said, "I'm sorry to leave you Tom! I have an appointment downtown with my husband and I'm already late. I really must go. Pleased to meet you."

"Why don't you call him, saying you will be back a bit late? I would like to offer you something to drink or eat. We could go to a nice restaurant, what do you think?" Tom exclaimed with a charming smile.

"I'm sorry, I just can't." Maria answered, being tired of him.

Tom realized his attempt to pick up this woman was miserably crumbling down. So, he decided to make a last, desperate attempt to persuade her, saying more of his usual bullshit.

"Look! You are going to miss a lunch with Tom Atkinson. You could be one of the lucky ones to have gone out with me."

Maria was fed up, irritated and replied, "But who cares! Goodbye."

Having said that, she quickly turned away and continued to walk towards her car, moving away and leaving Tom Atkinson standing like an idiot, on the other side of the road, with his mouth open.

Seeing the woman leaving, Tom realized his failure to woo and seduce her. Thus, cursing with anger, he said with malice, "Fucking slut! You don't know what you have lost. I would have satisfied you more than, that short dick of your husband."

Atkinson got into his car and kept thinking about Concita. Something about that woman was familiar and he was certain he had seen her before. Yes! He was really convinced of it, although couldn't remember where.

Meanwhile, Maria was moving as far away as possible from West Seattle and the wolf's den. She was very disappointed because it couldn't get any worse. What she had tried to avoid had unfortunately happened. Tom Atkinson not only noticed her but also approached and spoke to her. By now her cover had been definitively compromised, so she could no longer continue to stalk him.

Thinking of him, a deep hatred flowed from her heart. Maria had never met a worse being in her whole life, a brash, arrogant, conceited, and ignorant person. The worst kind.

Returning to downtown Seattle, she grabbed a bite to eat, took a stroll and visited different shops. Then she visited the Public Market, where she was distracted and quite amused.

Maria spent several hours wandering around downtown, but at 5.30 she began to get tired and opted to return to the hotel. The day was particularly hot, and she regretted wearing a black shirt that attracted the sun's rays and made her sweat. So, her biggest desire now was to take a nice refreshing shower.

When Mariae finally arrived in the room, she found a great surprise.

Henry was sitting there in an armchair and a woman was half lying on the bed. Maria recognized her. She was that mysterious brunette who had followed Dawnin in Redlands in the past.

Seeing Maria coming, Henry got up from the armchair and introduced his guest.

"Maria! This is Julie," he exclaimed, not holding back emotion. The two women greeted each other, shaking hands and looking at each other suspiciously. Especially Maria, who was surprised by the visit.

Fortunately, the atmosphere became more friendly.

"I'm not surprised at all! It's in the style of Tom Atkinson. He's always been a jerk and a blowhard since he was a boy, however I think today he surpassed himself." Henry exclaimed dumbfounded, having just heard his partner's story.

"Is the FBI involved in an investigation of Charles Lewis and associates?" Maria asked with keen interest.

"No! Not officially. It seems the FBI wants to stay as far away from him as possible. It was an initiative started by my colleague Dick Tolone, and myself. I hope to bring Dick here as soon as possible, so he can help us. The two of us started our own investigation, after sensing something shady in Lewis's dealings. However, we didn't find anything that could incriminate him. Then I personally hoped for Henry's input, but even that didn't work, did it?"

"Well! As I told you, I can't be of much help to you," Dawnin replied almost justifying himself.

"What did intrigue you? What did you think was wrong?" Maria asked Julie.

"The financial position of Charles Lewis in the first place. Lewis is very rich, but his import/export firm does not earn even a tenth of his income. So where does the rest of the money come from? Then I was intrigued by another even more important fact from several years ago. Now I will tell you about those events, please pay attention. Charles Lewis lived in Chicago until a few years ago. He later moved here to Seattle following his godfather, Andrew Martin. This happened in Chicago. Charles was accused of rape seven years ago by Ann Smith, the maid, who cleaned his house twice a week, did you know that?"

"What!" Henry and Maria responded in chorus.

"Yes! My dear friends! An official complaint that did not go very far, indeed. It was dropped immediately."

"What happened?" Maria asked.

"Ann was found dead the same night she filed the complaint. Isn't that crazy? And Lewis had a solid alibi, being in the company of Andrew Martin, a local senator, and the Chicago police chief himself, at the time of the girl's death. Her death was labeled as a suicide and not a murder. The girl had died of a heroin overdose. Charles's, versions of events stated Ann Smith had filed the complaint in revenge for being fired two weeks earlier. He claimed to have fired her because he had discovered she was using drugs in his home. In fact, returning from work, he had found her collapsed in the corner of the kitchen after a shot of heroin."

"Bravo Charles! Having labeled the girl a drug addict, her eventual death by overdose could be considered plausible. The man is not stupid," Henry exclaimed disgusted.

"Not only is he not stupid, but he is also untouchable! I just hope that sooner or later Charles will make a mistake," he added.

"That's what we are hoping for. That's why I decided to go and have a chat as soon as possible with Charles's current secretary, a certain Sharon Miller. Who knows if she has something interesting to tell me? You know that motto that says: The wolf loses its fur, but not its vice," Julie replied.

"28th of September 1968." Suddenly Henry shouted, surprising the women.

"What?" Maria asked, confused.

"Of course! September 28, 1968," he yelled again louder and continued his speech, seeing that Julie and Maria were totally confused.

"There was a similar case on this date. Two girls from my school, friends of mine, Ashley Duncan and Leslie Johnson, were found dead after being tortured, and at that time Charles was also among the suspects. However, he had a solid iron alibi, as always. Do you understand the connection?"

"I don't understand what connection you are referring to?" Julie asked puzzled.

"It's easy! What in the world! Why haven't you in the FBI, who have everything computerized and cataloged never thought about it? To nail Charles Lewis, you must drastically focus on the "sex crimes" he committed in the past. It is useless to try to find evidence of illicit trade, weapons, drugs, and unpaid taxes. That man is a perverted maniac, who likes to prey, rape, and hurt women, don't you understand?"

After the discussion, Julie left their room.

Maria in a suspicious tone asked him, "Beautiful girl! Isn't she?"

"Oh yes! Julie is beautiful and nice." Dawnin replied naively and not wisely.

Hearing this and the tone in which he had said the words, the jealous Maria asked him, "Who knows what you did here in the bedroom? Alone."

"What do you mean? Maria."

"I'm saying that when one is alone with a beautiful girl, in a bedroom, well! Every now and then, something strange can happen. Don't you think so? Do you think I didn't notice how she looked at you the whole time?"

"Why? How did she look at me?" Henry said uneasily.

"I think Julie likes you, and she likes you a lot."

"So don't you like Julie?"

"No! I have nothing against her. But it is better that she stays away from you, and I don't like surprises." Maria exclaimed with a suspicious tone of voice.

"Yes! OK! I have a terrible confession to reveal." He replied in a teasing tone.

"What?" Maria exclaimed nervously.

"Yes! You're right. I am guilty! I probably got her pregnant just with one of my dirty looks." Henry exclaimed laughing.

XX

Sunday

The next day, taking advantage of Sunday, Charles had gone to visit Uncle Andrew, to talk about the latest events and to stay in his company.

Charles entered the gigantic mansion between Madrona and Madison Park, on Lake Washington, and parked his BMW in the shade of a large tree.

His uncle was in the garden watering the roses.

"Hey! Hello Uncle! How are you doing?" Charles greeted him affectionately.

"Charles! What a nice surprise! It's a pleasure to see you."

"I came to talk to you, to get out of the house, and to have a rest. Do you have any commitments?"

"No! No commitment. You did well to come, I'm happy to see you. I also want to have a chat about important matters." Andrew replied cheerfully.

Uncle Andrew was in a great mood.

Charles was surprised to find him that way. In fact, the events had become particularly complicated, and aggravated, in the last period, and the death of Scott, Ramon, and Greg had been a serious alarm bell.

Despite everything, Martin seemed not to care about those events.

That intrigued Charles.

"Beautiful day, right?" Andrew asked him, unleashing his thirty-two-carat smile.

"It doesn't feel like you're in Seattle either. The newspaper reported it will be ninety-five degrees today," Charles replied.

"And maybe it will be true. How about taking a nice ride?"

"Of course! On a boat?"

"No! We will leave the boat alone today. I have a surprise. Come on, let's go! I will show it to you," Andrew exclaimed rather excitedly.

Charles boarded the new flamboyant seaplane his uncle had just bought and kept moored in his private marina, along with four motorboats and three sailboats.

They had been flying for some time, taking a ride around the lake. Then Martin diverted to Kirkland, until he reached Lake Sammamish, where he landed for a short stop.

"I'm worried! Uncle! Things don't seem to be going so well. On the contrary, they are going very badly indeed." Charles said pessimistically.

"Are you referring to the death of those three idiots?"

"Yes! Why? Are you not worried?"

"No! Charles! I am not. On the contrary. I think that events are improving considerably. What did I tell you the day you received that odd phone call? I told you it was a trap and... I was right. The loss of those three guys is not a great thing. We can find hundreds of men as good as them, if not much better."

"I would like to know if it was Henry Dawnin who killed them, or someone from that phantom organization?" Charles asked, perplexed.

"It was Dawnin, along with that girl." Andrew replied with certainty.

"How do you know?"

"The winning weapon of our organization is that each of us has men, and trusted collaborators. I can assure you that I have informants you don't even know. Well! I learned from one of them that it was Dawnin and the girl who killed them. However, going back to what I said before, I am not at all worried because I have discovered something new about the organization that has been hunting us for some time now. However, it's still too early to talk about it."

"Why? Don't you trust me?"

"Don't say nonsense! Of course, I trust you, but you know how I am. I only speak when I am very sure. Have you warned others of the death of those three morons?"

"No! Not yet! Not even Cindy knows."

"Well! Warn them, it's time to know, and... Munro?"

"For a few days he has not been around or called, so certainly he has no news to report. This is between us, Uncle, I think Munro is no longer what he used to be. By now he should have retired. I honestly think we're wasting our money on him."

"Why do you say this?"

"For several reasons. Tell me what good he's done since we hired him?

Nothing, absolutely nothing. He killed the two prisoners he had captured without discovering anything concrete. Now he disappears from circulation without giving any news or explanation. That man is an old ruin. I'm very disappointed with him." Charles said enraged.

"Well! Charles! We all get older sooner or later. Maybe you're right, Munro has become too old for this job. Don't gnaw your liver! You'll see that things will settle down soon."

Andrew Martin stepped off the seaplane, gave Charles a pat on the back and said, "Now let's forget the problems and enjoy life. I ordered Sebastiano to prepare a special lunch for you. Do you like the idea?"

"Yes! Uncle! I am looking forward to it, I'm starving!" Charles replied smiling.

MONDAY

Despite Uncle Andrew's optimism, the next day Charles just couldn't rest easy.

Still, the thought of the deaths of his three men at the hands of Henry Dawnin was driving him insane.

Although Uncle Andrew thought they could easily be replaced, he had worked with them for years and trusted them blindly.

Charles began to have a boundless hatred for Dawnin. He considered him the cause of all his recent troubles, a real jinx, a cancer to be eliminated. He would give away all his money to personally detach Henry's head.

While waiting to meet with Tom Atkinson in his office, Charles pulled out the photos of Henry he had received anonymously. He was staring at them one by one, angrily, when Sharon, after knocking, warned him of his friend's arrival.

"Have him come in right away," he roared.

Charles was deeply irritated, and even disappointed with Tom.

For a long time, he had become like a superstar, always busy, never available, and with an excuse ready at hand to do nothing. That really bothered Charles. In fact, Tom had a solid position thanks to him, but he seemed not to care about it. On the contrary, he often behaved coldly and unfriendly towards him. Charles had noticed this fact on several occasions, and he had reached his endurance limit.

So, having to meet this guy bothered him very much.

Even this time Tom behaved as usual. He entered the room, and greeted Charles coldly, almost snubbing him.

"How are you doing? Charles! Is there anything new?" Tom asked with an air of annoyance.

"Scott, Ramon and Greg are dead. That's what's new!" Charles replied loudly in the most dramatic tone possible, intending to frighten Tom.

"What?" Tom exclaimed, surprised.

"You heard it right! They were killed by Henry Dawnin and his friend," Lewis shouted aggressively.

"Are you sure it was Henry who killed them?" Tom asked with great skepticism.

"One hundred percent. Reliable sources revealed this to my Uncle Andrew, it was Henry, along with a girl that I believe is this one here." Charles replied, as he passed the photos of Henry and Maria to him. The same ones Charles had shown him a few days earlier.

Tom Atkinson turned pale.

In fact, he recognized the woman he had met two days earlier at the bar. Of course! It was her. In the photos she had long hair, while her hair was short when he met her.

That's where Tom saw that woman! In the photos of Charles. Those photographs he had believed were just a stupid trick to cheat his idiot of a boss.

Suddenly he felt a great panic.

Tom was looking petrified at one of the photos of Maria when Charles shouted at him, "What's going on? Are you enchanted?"

"What are you saying! I was just looking at this woman. She is very beautiful! One of those women that the two of us like! Ah! Look at her body, she is gorgeous, don't you agree?" Tom exclaimed, trying to keep calm and make the conversation a joke, so he could hide his true feelings of fear.

"Beautiful my dick! That fucking slut killed three of my best men. I hate her! If I find this woman, I will smash and rape her in my own way." Charles shouted angrily.

Tom was about to reveal he had met her in the city, but in the end, decided not to.

"No! I must not tell this to Charles." He thought very confused.

Tom Atkinson had left Lewis's office a few minutes ago, refusing again to go to lunch with him. This time it was not an excuse; he was seriously sick.

When Charles brought those photos to the meeting, Tom did not give a damn about looking at them. In fact, he thought it was a bluff of that organization to confuse Charles and make fun of him.

Thus, at the time he was convinced those photos had been taken some time ago, when Henry was still alive. Neither he nor Cindy believed in their authenticity, not even for a second, because they thought Dawnin was dead.

He killed him.

But after that meeting, he began to think that Henry had not died at all, or someone was trying to avenge him. The meeting with his beautiful brunette friend had not been accidental.

That woman knew who he was, and probably had been stalking him all morning.

No! Things had suddenly gotten very bad, and he would never have believed it.

His plan, which seemed so perfect, was failing miserably. Tom would never have thought of such a reality.

For this reason, he had taken it easy by staying in Seattle. He had never feared such an event could happen.

He believed that after months, or years, of uselessly hunting for Henry, Lewis would finally abandon the search, so Tom could retire and move to the tropics.

Now his plan had backfired on him.

If Henry was alive, he could become the most dangerous witness. For this reason, he did not reveal to Charles that this woman was in Seattle. Perhaps she was spying on Charles too.

If Charles managed to capture her, that would be a tremendous boomerang against him.

Unfortunately, time was running out, but Tom still thought he had a good chance of making it.

He had to leave Seattle as soon as possible, as Cindy had often suggested, in fact, he had the money and ... insurance. Yes! It was the insurance that could save his butt and life. Because he hadn't thought about it before. He could gain a considerable advantage by using it, and now it was time to do so.

Meanwhile, in his office, Charles was profoundly irritated by Tom Atkinson.

In fact, when he invited Tom to go out and have a drink together, Tom replied that he felt nauseated. He always had an excuse ready, that asshole. Now Charles's endurance was exhausted.

Tom had become an ungrateful stranger, who always exploited and taken him for a fool. Now it was time to cut off that false friendship.

To forget about Tom, he decided to call Bruce Munro and find out what that other idiot was up to. It had been almost a week since Bruce had shown any signs of life, while Charles was continuing to pay his big salary.

As usual, Munro was not available, so Charles left another message on the answering machine, this time without much patience.

"Munro! It's me! Charles! I want to see you as soon as possible. I hoped to have some news from you. You know! I have no more time or money to waste. I am always looking for you without success, why am I paying you if you aren't doing anything. Give me your news immediately, got it? Goodbye."

"I knew! This piece of shit is no longer capable of doing anything, I am the idiot who hired him." Charles cursed violently when he hung up the phone.

Meanwhile Henry had decided to follow Andrew Martin, despite it being very dangerous. It was more curiosity than anything else.

He wanted to meet and, if possible, talk briefly with the man who was the real chief and brains of the organization.

Henry knew he was benefiting from a good disguise, and from never having met Andrew. For this reason, he was certain Martin would never recognize him, even if Charles had showed his photograph. Therefore, he left Maria with Julie and drove the rental car, heading to Bellevue, where his enemy had his office.

It seemed luck had given him a hand.

Henry had just parked the car near Martin's office when he saw Andrew walking down the street with two more people. He followed them at a distance to an outdoor bar, where the three men sat down to have coffee.

Henry sat down at a small table next to them. While drinking a coffee, he watched his target very carefully.

Andrew Martin was certainly a charming and charismatic guy.

He had a beautiful dazzling smile, a dynamic and intelligent look. He was very elegant, and even from his manners it was clear he was kind and caring, a real gentleman. If Henry hadn't known who Andrew really was, he would have voted for him in the next election. Henry was also impressed by his eyes: they were blue and shiny; he had never met a person with such distinctive eyes.

Andrew chatted affably with the other people who were probably businessmen. Suddenly the two men got up and thanking him cordially, left.

Andrew remained at the table to finish his latte.

Opening a copy of the Seattle Post-Intelligencer, Andrew was reading the headlines on the front page, when he heard, "Very hot, today, isn't it?"

Martin looked up and asked, "Excuse me! What did you say? Sir."

"I said it's quite hot today. And I've heard that in the next few days it will get much hotter than it is now."

"Are you sure? I heard it would get colder instead." Martin replied politely as he stared at Henry.

"Listen to me! It will be much hotter than now. You can count on it! Anyway! I wish you a good day" Henry said politely, as he got up from the table.

"Good day to you too, sir!" Andrew replied perplexed. He was struck by the man's eyes but his face was totally unknown to him, but the eyes….

In the end he thought it was just his imagination. However, he had the curiosity to look at the weather forecast to know which of them was right, and read: Tuesday, Wednesday, and Thursday, rain with a decrease in temperature of about ten degrees.

That man was completely wrong.

Meanwhile, Henry had gotten into the car and was returning to the hotel. Perhaps it might have seemed senseless what he had done, but it had been a great satisfaction to have met Andrew Martin personally.

Henry had finally met the man who was Fuentes's greatest fear. He remembered how Rodrigo had described Andrew: the devil who came down to earth. In appearance Martin looked more like an angel than a devil.

However, he agreed with Fuentes that Henry was a truly capable person. His own intelligent gaze proved it.

TUESDAY

Munro listened to the brief but concise message Charles had left on the answering machine and panicked.

It was true that Bruce had taken it quite easy recently, lazing around instead of working. But what could he do about it? There had been no new developments, and everything seemed to have crystallized.

So, to save his job and butt, Munro decided it was time to give Charles the compromising photographs of Cindy and Tom.

"Business is business, and I can't allow a stupid infatuation with a beautiful woman to ruin my career and reputation." Bruce murmured to himself while dressing.

On the contrary, those photographs now proved he had always been vigilant and on the job during this period. He just had to exaggerate a little the difficulty of his... mission.

So unhappy, Munro finally called Charles Lewis.

"Hello! It's Charles Lewis talking, who is this?"

"Charles! Hello! It's Munro."

"Munro! Where the fuck have you been? Is it possible you are never reachable or available?" He screamed angrily.

Charles was incredibly nervous and aggressive, and Munro resented this. To be able to silence him, Bruce had to shout more than he did.

"If you're in the office I will come by. I have some important news to reveal. I've been working like crazy, day and night this whole week, for you, Charles. I haven't even slept at night, and this is your thank you." Bruce (lied) trying to create as much drama as possible, and counterattack Charles.

"Yes! I'm in the office, come fast, because I'm busy." Charles yelled, still irritated.

"Good! I'm on the way."

Having said that, Munro abruptly hung up the phone, interrupted the conversation, and exclaimed, "Yes! I'm coming! To communicate that you are a big cuckold, piece of shit."

A short time later Bruce arrived at Charles's office.

Sharon made him sit in the waiting room and went to let Charles know his appointment had arrived.

Munro noticed the woman was wearing a light, white silk shirt, without wearing a bra underneath. His intuition was confirmed when the woman returned to call him. Munro was pleasantly attracted to that vision.

Upon entering the office, he excitedly exclaimed, "Hey Charles! Do you know that your secretary is not wearing a bra this morning?"

"Of course, I know! She never wears it."

"Wow! And who expected it! A cool lass, indeed." The exterminator said cheerfully.

"Not at all! I was the one who imposed it on her. If Sharon wears a bra in the office a single time, I will beat her to death." Charles said proudly with a satanic look on the face.

"Christ! Are you serious? Look, that is sexual harassment. You can get in trouble."

"By whom? From her? Are you joking? She knows what will happen to her family, and to herself, if she dares to make such a gesture. No! That woman is in my total power. My personal slave. Anyway! I don't think you came to talk about my secretary, did you?"

(Even Bruce Munro, the exterminator, thought Charles Lewis was an odd sod. He felt happy not to be a woman. Bruce was a killer, and he knew his job well, which is why he recognized a killer look while talking with Charles Lewis. Charles had serious issues with women, and Bruce was certain that he had killed women before, he would bet on it).

"No! I don't want to talk about her. I have some important news to give you. Well! Let's say it's a rather delicate matter," the exterminator replied a little embarrassed.

"Why hesitate? Spill the beans, come on." Charles asked anxiously.

Without answering, Munro gave him a sealed yellow envelope.

"What is it?" Charles asked puzzled.

"See for yourself."

Lewis opened the envelope and pulled out the photographs and negatives that showed Tom and Cindy in sweet love and tenderness. He looked at them one by one and was totally shocked. Eventually, his face became red, the veins of his throat swelled, and the scent of adrenaline was in the air. Then he got so mad that it frightened even Munro.

Charles swore, threw everything in his hand into the air, and slammed his fists violently on the table, shouting, "That big whore! That fucking slut! She has betrayed me. And that piece of crap Tom is dead, bastard. I will kill him. I swear! I swear."

After this outburst he covered his face with his hands, trying to calm down.

Five minutes of absolute silence passed. Munro had not dared to say a single word and had tried to distract himself by looking around the office, remaining motionless as much as possible.

Suddenly Charles, trying to have a civil demeanor, asked, "What were we talking about?"

"Well! I don't know... we were talking... of..." Bruce stuttered, striving to find something to say, when Charles interrupted.

"Ah yes! From this moment I want you to be ready to act 24 hours a day. All right? So, make yourself always available."

"Okay! Charles! As you wish."

"I have some bad news to give you. Scott and the others have been eliminated by Henry Dawnin," Charles said in a solemn tone.

Munro frowned, but didn't speak. He seemed a little intimidated and rather thoughtful.

"Can you give me one of those pictures of Henry Dawnin with that mysterious woman," he asked after a few seconds.

"Okay! Take this one."

"Charles! Do you need a hand to fix Tom?"

"Oh no! That's my private business. But stay nearby because I'll need your help later."

"OK! As you wish." That said, Munro left the office.

Charles remained to meditate on his misfortunes for a few minutes. He covered his face with shame and disappointment.

How could it be possible that he, the number one, the winner, had suffered a checkmate of this magnitude? He thought of Cindy, the woman who was about to become his wife, the one for whom he had done and given everything. The only woman he had respected in his entire life, the only one.

Why had Cindy betrayed him? Why did she have an affair with that pig, Tom?

They grew up together. That dude had spent his youth in Charles's home and had become rich thanks to Charles and his father.

Thinking about what Tom had done to him, he found no excuse. He had to pay, and he had to pay with... his life. He started banging his fists on the desk again in another nervous breakdown perhaps worse than the first.

Was it possible that he was no longer anyone? But yes, he was! He was still powerful.

He pulled cocaine out of his desk and snorted a generous amount to try to make his brain clear. After doing this, he felt good. The cocaine always worked. Now he was ready to implement the second part of the plan. Something that could distract him a little bit from his misfortunes, making him feel good and powerful.

"Sharon! Sharon!" He screamed.

When Sharon arrived, to ask what he wanted, Charles grinning said to her, "Come in, close the door, and remove your clothes."

After this last umpteenth insult, Sharon Miller left Charles's office and went to the bathroom to compose herself, determined not to cry this time. She felt internally emptied of all feelings and energy. Her mind did not want to think anymore. Her movements were slow, automatic, and drowsy.

Sharon stared at herself in the mirror for a while, totally confused. Then she returned to her desk, and carelessly answered phone calls.

She stayed an hour trying to stay calm. But suddenly her apathy turned into an almost uncontrollable frenzy. While her boss was in a meeting, she knocked on the door and timidly walked in.

"I don't feel well, Mr. Lewis! I need to go home to rest." Sharon said, interrupting the business meeting.

Charles replied with a concerned tone, "Of course! Sharon! Go home to rest, and if you're okay, I'll see you tomorrow, but if you feel bad, don't worry, stay home. I hope to see you soon. Good afternoon."

Sharon thanked him timidly and walked away quickly. She would not return to that office the next day. She swore this to herself and began to walk down the street, deeply immersed in dark thoughts.

She felt so alone and felt the urge to confide her misery to someone.

Perhaps her husband when he got home in the evening, or perhaps she should accuse Charles. But, before going to the police, she quickly dismissed that idea. First, she wanted to confide in her husband, get his support and develop a plan.

Sharon was also willing to change her name and city. Charles Lewis had to pay for what he had done. She was no longer afraid for herself. The only fear she had was for her little Jane. In fact, before taking any steps, she had to be sure her child did not face any risk.

As soon as she returned home, she went to take a shower, to clean and purify herself once again. In front of the mirror, she noticed large bruises and even scratches on her buttocks and back. Sharon came out of the shower and had just put on her bathrobe when she heard the doorbell ring.

Meanwhile, little Jane, who was downstairs in the living room watching cartoons on television, went to open the door.

"Hello! Dear! Can I talk to your mother?" A lady asked her kindly.

"Yes! Sure! But mom is in the bathroom and...."

"Who is it? Jane," Sharon interrupted, appearing after a few seconds.

Sharon walked to the door and saw a beautiful Asian woman who greeted her affably.

Thinking that the woman was a street vendor, or something like that, she said, "I'm sorry! Madam! I don't need anything."

"Are you Mrs. Sharon Miller?"

"Yes! Why?"

"I didn't come here to sell you anything. My name is Julie Sue, I'm an FBI agent. This is my badge. I don't want to waste your time, I would like to ask you a few questions about your boss, Charles Lewis."

Sharon suddenly turned pale and began to tremble. Julie noticed her reaction and smiled at her as courteously as possible.

Stammering, Sharon asked, "What is it? What's going on?"

"It's a very delicate matter. Can we talk about it in a place that is a little quieter and more private? I guarantee you it will be a strictly confidential meeting."

Sharon seemed to hesitate at first, but after a few seconds replied, "Okay! Come in, please."

Sharon accompanied Julie to a small family room, leaving the child watching cartoons on television.

After asking Julie to sit down, she said, "Just give me a few minutes to get dressed and I'll be with you right away."

"Of course! Don't rush, take your time." Julie replied, still trying to be as sweet as possible. Her sixth sense was telling her that Sharon knew something important about Charles. She believed the woman was terrorized. She had gotten that feeling in the few seconds she had spoken to her.

Sharon dressed as quickly as possible and returned ten minutes later.

"Tell me! What's going on?" Sharon spoke timidly.

"Mrs. Miller! We have been investigating your boss, Charles Lewis, for a long time. We are looking for evidence that could frame him in the illicit trafficking of drugs and weapons. The more we investigate him, the more certain we are that he is hiding some dirty secrets. I know it may sound absurd, have you ever seen anything unusual, or suspicious, working for him?"

"No! I don't … think… so." Sharon stammered frightened.

"Are you sure? Please! Try to remember any strange event that happened since you have worked with him. Even something of little importance."

"No! I assure you I have never seen anything suspicious; I swear. My job is to answer the phone, open the door, make appointments, and write letters for the company. As you can see it is a simple job and very... well paid. I have never attended any meetings with Charles and his clients, nor have I opened letters addressed to him or done any accounting. Charles Lewis... is very private in his business."

Julie observed that each time Sharon mentioned the name of her boss, she did so with hatred. So, she asked similar questions again which Sharon answered in the same tone, without giving any important information.

At that point Julie, understanding she wouldn't get any further, suddenly decided to ask her something more specific, private, and painful, "I know this could be an embarrassing question, Sharon, please be sincere. Has Charles Lewis... well... how to say... has ever... touched you?"

"What do you mean?" Sharon exclaimed surprised.

"Well! Has he ever sexually abused you?"

Sharon paled even more, started to tremble, stunned by the question. In the end, she seemed not to know how to respond or was afraid to do so.

Julie, having noticed her hesitation, politely confided to her, "I'm here to help you, Sharon! If you have anything that bothers you, please tell me. I will use all the means at my disposal to help you. I didn't ask this question to embarrass you. From my research it appears that some time ago, in Chicago, Charles Lewis was accused of rape by one of his workers, a lady who was working part-time as a maid in his house. Let me repeat the question to you. Did Charles Lewis ever sexually abuse you, against your will?"

"Yes!" The woman replied, after a few long moments, bursting into tears. All the tears Sharon had held back the whole day gushed out.

Julie went to console, hugging her lovingly and said, "You are no longer alone! Sharon! You will see that Lewis will pay for his crimes. It is a promise. I will put you into the custody of the FBI as soon as possible, so you will be safe and protected. As soon as you feel a little better, please tell me what that wicked man has done to you."

Julie left Sharon Miller's home after more than half an hour.

During that time, she had heard Sharon's confession and had tried to console, reassure, and encourage her to cooperate with justice.

Julie was horrified, disgusted, and shocked by what that sadistic character had done to Sharon.

However, selfishly on the other hand, she was enormously satisfied because she had finally found something solid to incriminate him. There was now very tangible evidence to proceed against Charles Lewis.

As Julie approached a phone booth, she remembered what Henry Dawnin had told her a couple of days earlier, "In order to arrest Charles Lewis, his private life and his sexual crimes must be investigated. This was the only weak link for framing that guy."

Henry was right.

She thought about how many other cases of rape and abuse Charles could be responsible for that had never been reported or investigated. Julie started to believe that Charles Lewis could potentially be a serial killer.

She inserted the phone card and phoned Dick Tolone.

"Hey Dick! Hello!"

"Julie! Finally! How are you?" Tolone said concerned.

"I'm fine! Thank you! I found very important evidence to frame Charles Lewis, proof to throw him in jail for at least twenty years. But that's not all, I also met Henry Dawnin."

"What?"

"Yes! That's right! Henry Dawnin is here in Seattle," she exclaimed excitedly.

Julie briefly told Dick about Sharon Miller, and then how she had met Henry.

"I really need your help, come immediately." Julie said with concern.

"I'll be there tomorrow, Julie! You can count on me. The two of us against the whole world, as in the old days," Dick spoke, trying to cheer her up.

"Fantastic! Look! I changed hotels, now I'm staying at the Westin, room 513."

"Perfect! I'll see you tomorrow, bye."

"Bye," she replied.

Meanwhile, Henry and Maria returned the rental car, which they had been using, replacing it with another car of a different brand and color. Unfortunately, Dawnin had given up the idea of renting a motorcycle, because the weather had gotten worse.

Once this was done, they headed together to the area of Charles's office, to check what the scumbag was doing.

For a couple of hours, they wandered around, pretending to make purchases, or spending time at the bar for a coffee. At half past five, they entered a used bookstore in front of the door of their enemy's office.

Suddenly Henry called Maria, who was reading a book.

"What's happened?"

"Look there," he exclaimed excitedly. She moved towards her partner and saw Charles on the other side of the street, standing with an umbrella in hand.

"What is he doing?" Maria asked.

Henry noticed that a couple of empty taxis were passing through the street, but Charles had not called them.

Quite excited, he replied, "He's waiting for someone. Here's what we do. Quick! Go get the car while I continue to watch him."

He was right. After a couple of minutes, a blue Ford pickup truck stopped. He recognized Doug driving the vehicle. Charles got on board, and the pickup left quickly.

Maria arrived a moment later.

"Shit! We lost them." Henry cursed, getting into the car.

"That's not true! They're stopped at that traffic light, three blocks ahead of us."

"Ah! Good!" Dawnin exclaimed relieved. They followed the vehicle at some distance in the pouring rain.

After about fifteen minutes, Maria said with certainty, "I know where they are headed! They are going to Tom Atkinson's house."

"Well! There will be a meeting... of criminals," Henry ironically replied.

At the same time Tom Atkinson was carefully packing his suitcase.

In fact, he had decided to leave the city the next day, foreseeing big troubles coming. He would be joined by Cindy, sometime later, at things settled, in a secret location they had established together.

Among his belongings, Tom had a leather briefcase with 400,000 dollars inside, and his famous insurance. In fact, he had decided the time had come to use the insurance, since he wanted to get Charles into trouble, and gain an advantage by disappearing as far away as possible.

He had sealed the mysterious contents in a yellow cardboard envelope. The next day, before leaving, he would send it to a well-known local television station, when he would already be far away on the road.

Tom had just finished writing the address on the envelope, when he heard a noise of car brakes coming from the street. Out of sheer curiosity he glanced out the window and saw Charles coming out of the pickup followed by Doug.

He was very surprised by this unexpected visit. Why was he coming to his house?

Tom thought Charles had some big news about the mysterious organization.

However, as a precaution, he hid the briefcase and the yellow envelope under his bed. Then he returned to the living room waiting for the two to ring the bell.

Charles aggressively rang the doorbell three times.

"He's coming," Doug said, before Tom opened the door.

"Good! You know what you must do." Charles exclaimed with malevolence.

"Hey! Boys! Good to see you! Why are you here? Do you have any news?" Tom greeted them with a false smile.

"I have some important news to tell you, really important." Lewis coldly replied.

Tom was struck by his icy tone.

While he was about to answer Charles, he noticed Doug was closing all the curtains.

"Hey Doug! What the hell are you doing? Do you want to leave us in the dark? There is still light outside! Don't you see?" Tom exclaimed in amazement.

"Let him do it," Charles answered always in that strange tone of voice.

Atkinson was disoriented and confused. He did not grasp what was happening and had not yet understood why both men wore gloves.

"What is this about? Charles! What's going on? Are there any problems?" Tom asked, trying to understand what was happening.

Charles did not answer and pulled out a yellow envelope. He removed the contents, and finally replied, "I received this."

Tom saw the handful of photographs and... recognized himself with Cindy. Charles quickly showed some of the most explicit and compromising photos. Atkinson remained dumbfounded, and before he could say or do anything, he found himself immobilized by the deadly grip of Doug, who had grabbed him from behind and prevented him from moving a single inch.

"It's not what you think! Charles! Don't be fooled by those photos." Tom pleaded.

"Oh yes! Explain to me why I should not be deceived? You are fucking my woman and I'm deceiving myself? Are these photographs a trick, a mere invention? What the fuck are you saying? Piece of shit, asshole. You fuck her and... what should I think? Well! I believe you are having an affair with her, and you are messing with the wrong person, me. But this time you have made a huge mistake, Tom," Charles replied with irony.

"Charles! This is not true. I've been with Cindy one time, but it was a mistake and... ah."

Tom was interrupted by a powerful punch to the stomach that the betrayed boyfriend had thrown at him with anger. Then he received a more powerful punch on his nose that began to bleed.

"Charles! Charles! Hold on. Stop! Stop. Please! Let me... explain." Tom implored, trying to make him think and hoping the beating would stop. But the other man seemed to take pleasure in punching him. Within minutes, Tom Atkinson was covered in blood.

Tom understood it was the end for him, thus as a last attempt at revenge, and with his last strength shouted at Charles, "Yes! You're right! Bastard! I fucked your woman, and I didn't do it once, but hundreds of times, and it was amazing. Every time I thought about you, and how each day you became more cuckold. You little pathetic piece of crap. Think about it, Cindy and I were in bed all day. And I must confess she is excellent at making love."

Hearing this, Charles became a fury and started to strike Tom repeatedly until the man passed out.

While Tom was unconscious, Doug tied him tightly. Charles went to the kitchen and took a full bucket of cold water which he unceremoniously poured on the face of his former friend. Quite slowly Tom regained his senses. When he looked around, he saw Charles's sadistic face bent over him.

"I didn't expect that from you, Tom! I thought you were like a brother. Why did you do this to me? Answer me." Charles said with an irate, yet puzzled tone.

"Because I hate you! Charles! Because I hate you. I have always hated you, all my life." Tom answered brutally.

"Son of a bitch!" Lewis exclaimed, slapping the man's already bleeding face.

"Yes! I hate you! You've always considered yourself number one, not because you really are, but because someone else made you the chief, Charles! You are the dirty result of nepotism, an incompetent who has always performed the functions of the boss and master not for merit, but for luck. You are a loser, a failure, and I wish you the end you deserve as soon as possible." Atkinson shouted in rage at him.

Charles bit his lips with anger just listening to the insults. He stood still, but inside he was like a volcano about to explode.

He beckoned Doug, who bent over him and gagged Tomc

After that Lewis approached until his face was about six inches from Tom's and looking into his eyes with the most treacherous tone said, "You arrived, where you have arrived, thanks to me, ugly bastard! And see how you thanked me. But I created you and I will destroy you."

After saying this, Charles grabbed a large, sharp, dagger and repeatedly stuck it in Atkinson's stomach. Tom closed his eyes and with an extreme grimace of pain, totally released his muscles and fell to the ground.

"What should I do? Make him disappear or create chaos, as if someone robbed and killed him?" Doug asked his boss, who had gone to the kitchen to wash the dagger.

"No! Do nothing! Let's go away. The mere sight of this piece of shit, even if dead, makes me nauseous. I will call Munro and tell him to get rid of the corpse immediately. At least he can do the gravedigger's work for what I pay him."

Charles and Doug opened the door, and carefully looked around, everything was quiet in the street. The two men left as quickly as possible from their victim's home.

Unfortunately, everything was not as simple and smooth as they had predicted.

In fact, Henry and Maria arrived at almost the same time and had parked their car not far from Tom's house.

Henry was very intrigued by the sudden closing of the curtains. He decided to go and find out what was happening, leaving Maria in the car, ready for a quick escape. Cautiously, he approached the house, until he arrived under one of the main windows. He was certain those three were plotting something shady.

He was alarmed by the commotion, noises, and shouts inside the house. Whatever was happening was certainly not friendly. Through a small gap in the curtains, he could see Charles from behind, as if he were arguing or even beating someone. Unfortunately, the gap did not allow a full view of what was happening.

For this reason, he decided not to risk being discovered and moved away from the dangerous area, hiding behind a hedge on the other side of the house. He waited there for Charles and Doug to leave, wanting to find out what had happened inside.

A couple of minutes after his enemies left the scene, Henry walked to the front door. As a precaution, he rang the bell a couple of times, thinking of a good excuse to invent in case Tom opened the door.

No sign of life.

Henry rang the bell a couple more times, but still nothing. Eventually, he decided to look inside. He turned the knob and opened the door.

He was dumbfounded that it had not been locked.

"Is there anyone home?" No one answered.

Dawnin entered the living room, and at one point suddenly froze. Behind a couch, by the fireplace, Tom Atkinson was lying in a pool of blood, gagged, and tied up.

"My God!" He exclaimed, frightened.

Immediately Henry ran towards him. When he reached Tom, he discovered he was still alive, and quickly removed the gag from his mouth.

"Who the hell are you?" Tom whispered.

"Don't you recognize me? I'm your old friend Henry Dawnin. I am disguised in this way to hide my identity and protect myself from motherfuckers like you and your fucking mates." Henry yelled bitterly, cursing, and looking disgusted at the dying man.

"You! Then... it's true... you're still alive." Tom exclaimed, surprised.

"Yes! I'm still alive Tom! Of course, no thanks to you." Henry replied with anger and contempt.

Tom with his last energy, stuttering, and spitting blood at the same time, confided to him, "Have you seen the friends... that I have? Henry. I have... very important... evidence which can frame Charles. Go... in my room, under... the bed… there is a yellow envelope... with …the address... of a TV... station... and… That said, Tom died in Henry's arms.

"Dear Tom! Those who sow wind, reap a storm." Dawnin said, moving away from the body to go to the bedroom.

There he found the yellow envelope and next to it a briefcase. Intrigued, he opened it and saw a mountain of dollars. Henry grabbed the briefcase together with the yellow envelope, still sealed, and quickly left the house, closing the door and reaching Maria.

"Drive fast! Let's get out of here," he shouted after getting into the car.

"What happened? Why are you so tense?"

"Tom Atkinson is dead, killed by Charles."

"Really! And what is in that briefcase?"

"I'll tell you later. Now let's get away from this area as soon as possible."

Maria parked the car on a deserted street many miles from Atkinson's house.

Henry opened the briefcase, and she was stunned.

"A lot of money, isn't it?" He exclaimed with satisfaction.

"Do you think we should reveal the existence of this money to Julie or the FBI?"

"I think it's a serious mistake, Maria! Why should we do that? No one knows about the existence of this money, and it can be useful in case things get bad, don't you agree?"

"You're right! We must keep this money in a safe place until we leave."

"We'll think about that later," he replied, cutting her short.

"However, the surprises are not over. "Now look at this." Dawnin added, pulling the yellow envelope out of his pocket and opening it.

"What is it?" Maria asked with curiosity.

"I have no idea! Tom Atkinson, before he died, revealed that this envelope includes extremely important evidence to indict Charles."

That said, Henry grabbed the contents, which was an old Super Eight film wrapped in a transparent plastic bag, and a hermetically sealed letter. A piece of adhesive paper was stuck to the plastic wrap that covered the film.

"Look! There are directions for use." Maria exclaimed, surprised.

Then Henry started reading.

"This material is of immense value. I strongly recommend watching the film first and then reading the letter, Tom Atkinson."

"Well! I think we must respect the last wishes of the deceased; don't you? Maria."

"What the hell will it be?"

"I don't have the slightest idea. I think it is appropriate to show this film to Julie. She will be extremely curious to find out what's in it."

Meanwhile, Charles had just returned home, accompanied by Doug. Before leaving, Doug asked thoughtfully, "Do you need more help, chief?"

"Oh no! Go home and be ready for tomorrow. I have family affairs to urgently fix today" Charles replied angrily.

"As you wish! Bye."

"Bye! See you tomorrow." Charles closed the car door and walked toward the house.

Entering the house, he saw Cindy running towards to hug him saying, "Oh Charles! My love! Where have you been? Sweety! I looked for you in the office, but no one answered, let me give you a kiss...."

Paff! A powerful slap hit her left cheek, and surprised, she screamed, "Are you crazy? What do you..."

Smack! Another even stronger slap hit her, this time on the right cheek.

"Oh my God! Go away! Enough...."

A third slap followed by a strong kick in the ass hit Cindy, before she managed to run away, causing her to fall and roll onto the floor.

After that, Charles grabbed her by the hair and leaning over shouted, "Ugly whore! Do you think I'm an idiot, a fool you can cheat at your leisure."

"What do you want from me? Charles! You're crazy, leave me alone." She begged.

"Do you reckon I don't know you've been shagging Tom all this time. That you betrayed me with him, day after day." Charles shouted furiously.

"What are you saying? It's not true at all, you're mad." Cindy replied terrified.

"Fuck you, bitch!" Charles screamed, pulling out the photos and slamming them in the woman's face. "I'm crazy! And these photographs are the fruit of my madness." He shouted with all the breath he had in his lungs.

136

Cindy, terrified, burst into tears when she saw the photos. "When did you find out?" She asked sobbing.

"A few days ago, I have big news for you. Tom Atkinson will never be available again for sultry, sexual performances, so I recommend you find another lover who satisfies you, ugly slut."

"What... what have you done to Tom?"

"Nothing! Tom left ... for the other world, with a one-way ticket." Charles answered with an evil sneer.

"Bastard! Dirty killer! I'll tell the police, the newspapers, you're a kil...."

"Smack! Another powerful slap interrupted the woman's series of curses. Then Charles said in an uncompromising tone, "I advise you not to talk anymore. If I hear even one word, I'll kick you in the mouth, do you understand?"

Cindy got up from the floor crying and locked herself inside the bathroom.

Meanwhile, Henry and Maria had found Julie and revealed the latest news. All three headed to Ballard, a neighborhood not far from downtown to a film/video production studio, to watch the film.

They asked to have a private room.

Julie told them what she had discovered from Sharon Miller, without dwelling on the details.

"I cannot believe this creep abused and raped even this poor woman, Sharon. I wonder how many other women Charles Lewis has hurt in all these years." Henry commented sadly.

"It's the same thought I had before. I believe Charles Lewis is a serial killer. However, finally we may proceed against him. I doubt Sharon Miller will testify against him. You cannot believe the anguish I felt while listening to her story. She is such a delicate, fragile, and terrified lady. Sharon literally trembled continuously in front of me during our meeting. Let's hope what Tom Atkinson said is true. In this film there will be solid evidence to indict Charles, and will send him to jail, for the rest of his days." Julie said.

After that, Julie told them about the arrival of Dick Tolone.

"I hope we can trust him." Henry said, not hiding his suspicions.

"Of course! Dick is a good friend of mine. He will help us; you can count on it. He is a great guy and totally trustworthy." Julie exclaimed with confidence.

"Will he come alone?" Maria asked.

Julie didn't answer right away, then in an uncertain tone said, "I have no idea."

In fact, she thought about the possibility that Dick would bring someone with him. Her fear was that if Dick had warned Collins, he would probably send Jeff Wilson too. Julie tried not to dwell on that hypothesis. If Jeff Wilson arrived, it would be the end. She was utterly convinced Jeff was rotten from head to toe.

They entered a small room where there was a Super 8 projector and a large white canvas screen. Maria locked the door and inserted the film into the projector. Everyone was excited and curious to see the footage. Henry had put the letter, still closed, on the table, ready to be opened at the end.

The projection began. The footage was old and silent. The beginning was a disaster. The first part of the film showed the floor of a room, then the ceiling, and the floor again. Everything seemed without a logical thread. Perhaps the operator didn't know he was filming at that moment, or maybe he was dazed, drunk, and confused.

The first thirty seconds were useless, only a dark environment was shown. Suddenly a girl appeared dancing far away, then the operator recorded a different area on the other side and filmed two people sitting on the sofa. Suddenly he shakily zoomed over to them.

"My God! That's the old Ray Brown, with Leslie Johnson." Henry exclaimed dumbfounded.

The film showed the two people for a few seconds. Leslie, totally stoned, was seen passing a joint to Ray, who was drinking gin from the bottle, like it was soda pop.

"My God!" Henry continued to exclaim, foreshadowing something nefarious and terrible.

Suddenly, the camera operator moved to the girl who was seen dancing earlier. He approached her and zoomed in.

"Oh my God! It's Ashley! Ashley Duncar!" Dawnin shouted astonished.

Ashley was beautiful, indeed gorgeous, and sensual as always. Henry, with deep emotion, watched her dancing. She wore very tight jeans, and a white shirt tied with a knot, instead of buttoned, which left her belly uncovered.

The operator dwelt a lot on Ashley, attracted by her beauty.

Then he returned to Leslie and Ray.

Old Ray had fallen asleep, and Leslie had almost fallen asleep too.

The cameraman stayed a few seconds on the two, then seeing there was no action, he returned to Ashley who had not stopped dancing.

Then suddenly he changed direction and framed a person who was adjusting the stereo system. At first it was too distant, and the low light did not allow anyone to see who it was. Suddenly the guy moved towards Ashley and the operator zoomed in on him and they recognized Charles Lewis.

Charles was also totally stoned and drunk as he could be seen staggering when walking. He approached Ashley, told her something. She smiled.

Then he passed her a reefer.

Charles got closer and closer to her. Suddenly he leaned in to kiss her, but Ashley rejected him, continuing to dance as if nothing had happened. He did not give up and tried again. Even this time she chased him away. Charles tried a third time, this time putting his hands in her blouse and trying to tear it off.

The operator followed the scene with particular interest, trying to catch some spicy moments.

Ashley appeared to be asking Charles to leave her alone while he urged her to take off her blouse. She shook her head, saying no, and urged him to leave.

To this answer Charles put his hands on her, even more violently than before.

Ashley slapped him.

Charles totally lost control of himself and violently attacked Ashley, causing her to fall to the ground. Then he brutally squeezed her throat, strangling her.

The film ended with a close-up shot of Ashley's face, and she was clearly dead.

When Julie turned on the light in the room, they all looked like three corpses. Especially Henry who knew the girls personally and liked them.

"It's not possible! It is not possible! This time Charles Lewis must pay for it. He must pay for his crimes." Dawnin shouted, banging his fists on the table, after a few endless moments of silence.

"Come on Henry! Courage! Think that this time we have solid evidence to incriminate and send this son of a bitch jail." Julie said, approaching and patting him on the back.

"Well! I don't know! This bastard always slips away like an eel. Let's see if he will pay for his crimes this time or will get away with it again?"

Henry replied in a pessimistic tone, while quickly drying the tears on his face, hoping that nobody had seen his act of weakness.

Maria opened the letter that Tom Atkinson had carefully sealed and read.

"On September 28, 1968, I witnessed the double murder that Charles Lewis committed by killing Ashley Duncar and Leslie Johnson. The events unfolded in this way.

Charles Lewis, Ray Brown, and I took the girls to Charles's house for a drug party with music and alcohol. Charles was very interested in Ashley and his goal was to get the girl high, so she could be more easily conquered. For the occasion I had brought an old Super Eight camera, without sound, to capture the party. We got off to a great start having beer, gin, whiskey, rum, weed and cocaine. We all got high, especially the host, Charles, who had done several sniffs of cocaine and was really stoned. Truthfully, even the old Ray Brown was high.

However, in the beginning, the evening went quite well. The situation changed drastically when Charles, after making many attempts with Ashley, was refused for the umpteenth time. For this reason, he became furious and attacked her violently to the point of strangling Ashley, as seen in the film. However, the story doesn't end there.

Having realized that Ashley was dead, Charles could not leave Leslie as a witness, so he decided to kill her as well. Charles was even more ruthless with Leslie. She was sleepy, sitting not far from the old

Ray. Charles got the biggest and sharpest kitchen knife and moved toward Leslie with hostile intents. He went close and woke her up. Leslie did not know what had happened before, and innocently smiled at him. Charles smiled at her too, while hiding the knife. Before doing anything, he asked Leslie to take her clothes off for a quickie. Leslie thought he was joking and sent him to hell. Charles asked again without smiling this time. Leslie started to become uneasy, and looking around, saw the dead body of Ashley on the ground. She became frantic and started to scream, and the fury of Charles Lewis was unleashed. He tore off her clothes and raped the girl in front of me. After that, Leslie tried to run away, but Charles grabbed her from behind, and stabbed her in the liver, immediately stopping her escape.

Leslie fell to the ground, screaming loudly but still alive and bleeding profusely. Charles then, like a vulture, bent over Leslie and slit her throat. While he knew he could trust me blindly, given the solid friendship we had, he did not trust Ray Brown. Thus, we came up with a ploy to neutralize him. Seeing him asleep and snoring, we put in his hands the knife Charles had used to stab and kill Leslie. Then we laid her bleeding body next to him. When that was done, we woke him up.

Ray Brown always knew he was the one who killed Leslie Johnson, and that Charles had killed Ashley to protect him and not have her reveal his horrible crime. Charles had achieved his purpose, as from that moment Ray Brown had to be grateful to him for life. I decided to keep this film and use it as life insurance in case the relationship between Charles and I deteriorated. In fact, in front of him I burned the other two films I had shot that evening, but not this third one. Charles was always convinced that the film that had shown him in action was destroyed that same night. Sincerely, Tom Atkinson."

"What sons of bitches! What motherfuckers, sons of bitches." Henry shouted angrily.

"Not only did they kill those two innocent girls, slaughtered like pigs, but they also destroyed the existence of poor old Ray Brown, who bore the burden of guilt for something he did not do. I personally have seen how Charle changed into the worst man, starting from that time. The old Ray always was a troubled man, but since then, he became the most sad, gloomy, unhappy man I ever met in my life. It's incredible! It's incredible!" Henry added with disdain.

XXI

WEDNESDAY MORNING

Charles had slept in the guest room because the mere sight of Cindy nauseated him. He used the guest bathroom to take a shower and after getting dressed, in the early morning, left the house without saying anything to his partner.

Meanwhile Cindy had remained in the bedroom, but did not sleep all night.

She was terrified, having learned about Tom's death, and above all, the idea that something similar could happen to her, tormented her.

She got out of bed and rushed to the bathroom to vomit. Her stomach churned, and her head throbbed. Looking in the mirror, she looked shockingly pale as a white sheet, with a haggard face and several bruises from the beatings she had received from Charles the previous day.

She stepped into the shower, staying there for a long time, reflecting on the whole situation. It felt like the entire world had collapsed on her. Without Tom, she felt lost, and her relationship with Charles was certainly over. Cindy decided it was time to disappear from circulation.

As she dressed, she had the idea to go to Tom's house to try to find the money. In fact, she believed he had kept some of the stolen money. The last time she met him, Tom told her he would take part of the loot and would transfer the rest to an offshore bank. Charles must still have been unaware of the existence of that money, otherwise he would have interrogated her in his own way.

Cindy decided to hit the road. She planned to go to the bank, pick up what she needed, pass by Tom's house to look for the money and run away to the farthest possible destination from Seattle, and Charles.

She quickly took a couple of suitcases, where she packed some of her best clothes. In a large bag she put part of her jewelry. Then she walked to the front door, having left the car in the street and not in the garage.

Cindy opened the door to go out but suddenly froze.

Bruce Munro, the exterminator was there in front of the door, motionless as a statue, watching her sternly. Did he want to kill her?

"Are you in a hurry, my beautiful lady?" Bruce asked her, taking a fleeting look at the suitcases.

Cindy was terrified. She didn't know what she could say or do. Her escape had been blocked from the beginning.

She had to try to stay calm, to reason, not to give up. She watched that ugly monster staring at her from head to toe with a mischievous eye. But yes! Why not! Why not try to deceive him? Thus, Cindy tried, to be natural and not seem surprised by him, on the contrary, she looked glad.

"Hi Munro! Good to see you. "What are you doing around here?" She said smiling, trying to be spontaneous and sweet.

"Charles has ordered me to stay close to you, so that you will not make, well, let's say an impulsive, foolish, or regrettable decision." Bruce replied frankly.

"What do you mean? Munro." She replied with her phony smile.

"Well! I guess that leaving, running away suddenly, could be considered a stupid, foolish move by Charles." The exterminator said calmly.

"Then you have not come to kill me?" Cindy asked him, grinning like it was a joke, while instead she was trembling with fear.

"Kill you! Ah! Ah! Is that a joke? What are you saying? I could never kill a woman as beautiful as you!" Bruce replied gallantly.

Hearing those words, Cindy felt like she was reborn, so she relaxed, and began to start thinking of a good strategy to get out of this jam.

"Would you like a cup of coffee? Bruce."

"Yes! Of course."

"Good! Then come in."

Bruce Munro was tired of burying bodies he had not personally killed. He had made Tom Atkinson's body disappear the previous evening, and Tom had already been the second person he did not kill. In fact, he felt like the undertaker of the organization, and he did not like that job.

However, when Charles Lewis called and told him to check on his sweet companion, the situation was different.

Munro dreamed of that beautiful lady, day and night and being able to remove even a callus from her left foot, was like having an orgasm for him.

When Cindy invited him to get a cup of coffee, inside her home, his heart began to pound hard. Bruce just had to keep his cool, that was his only problem, because he felt Cindy was attracted to him. But Bruce was a tough man, first she had to meow like a cat, then he would give her what she was asking for.

Cindy was deeply irritated by her mistake in offering him coffee. That ugly monster, sitting in the living room, was wasting her precious time. On the other hand, she was overjoyed when she discovered Munro had no hostile intentions. Now it was up to her to get rid of him.

While she was making coffee, she unfastened two buttons of the blouse she was wearing.

She put two cups of coffee on a tray and went to the living room.

"Here's the coffee," she exclaimed smiling, as she bent over him, and the blouse gaped open.

Munro was struck by this vision.

She sat in an armchair in front of him and said, "How come a handsome man like you does not try to enjoy life more?"

"I don't understand what you're referring to, Miss Cindy." Bruce answered, frowning and blushing like a little innocent kid.

"What can I tell you? From the first time I saw you, I fell in love with you. Munro! Do you understand that you are a man, with great charm."

Bruce Munro, feeling flattered by Cindy, who had always been the dark object of his most recent desires, no longer knew how to behave, or act. He was paralyzed by her great beauty.

"Why don't you try to change your life and profession?" Cindy asked with a serious tone.

"What are you alluding to?" Bruce answered puzzled.

"Munro! Let's not act like children, you know what I mean. Explain to me why a man like you works and takes orders from someone like Charles Lewis. Don't you feel frustrated?"

"Well! Everyone takes orders from someone else, don't they?"

"It's true! But you take orders... to kill."

"What?"

"You got it right! You are a killer! A killing machine, but haven't you gotten tired of it?" Cindy said bluntly.

Munro was totally surprised by what she was telling him and above all, he did not grasp what she meant. He did not answer, but just waited to learn more.

"Pay attention! Because I'm going to offer you something that could change your life in the future."

Having said that, Cindy got up from the armchair and leaned closer to Bruce, giving him an even clearer view. Seeing the empty cup of coffee in his hand, she asked, "More coffee?"

"Yes!... Yes thank... you!" Munro answered stammering.

She went to the kitchen again and while filling the cup, opened the third button on her blouse.

The fish was about to fall into the net.

"Here's the coffee." Cindy said, coming back and slowly bending over him.

"Thank...you, very much!" Bruce stuttered, not knowing whether to look at Cindy's face, or the rest of her.

"So! What we were talking about, Bruce?" Cindy asked, as she was still leaning in his direction.

"I don't remember." He exclaimed with embarrassment, opting for a third way. He did not look her in the face or anywhere else, but instead he stared at the chandelier.

"Come on! Munro! Look me in the face! Let's talk as serious people."

Munro turned to look at her, giving a fleeting glance at her face and moving to the rest. When satisfied, Cindy got up and went to sit in the same armchair as before.

"I'm talking about $10 million."

"I don't understand?" Bruce answered totally confused.

"You got it right! $10 million! To be divided between you and me. Henry Dawnin never stole Charles's money; Tom and I did."

"What?"

"Yes! I'm not kidding. Dawnin never took a single cent of Charles's money, and now that money is hidden somewhere in Tom's house. I am proposing, as good friends, to divide it in half, and not only this, but you will earn more, you will have me. I don't think I'll stay with Charles in the future." Cindy told him smiling.

Bruce Munro got into his van with Cindy next to him as a passenger. The mere idea of owning that woman, even for a single minute, made him so excited. He was almost not interested in taking possession of his share of the money. Bruce quickly headed to Tom Atkinson's house, where he had already gone the previous day.

They entered the house and Cindy told him, "I have no idea where Tom hid the money. Look in the living room, while I go to the kitchen and bedroom. I'm sure it must be somewhere."

Munro started looking, moving aside all the cushions in the armchairs and sofa, when he felt a sudden sharp pain in his back. Before Bruce could turn around, he felt another intense pain this time in his liver.

He turned around completely and saw Cindy, with a kitchen knife in her hand, about to stab him a third time. Munro used all his strength to stop her before she could stab him again, pushing Cindy several feet away.

Munro instinctively pulled his silenced gun out, from his holster.

When Cindy angrily charged him, he fired three shots, hitting her in full, but not stopping her. Cindy fell over him, and hit Bruce's chest, and the man collapsed to the ground not far from her.

Cindy died instantly; Bruce was seriously injured.

He reached toward Cindy's lifeless face and shouted at her, "Why? Why did you do this? Stupid woman! You were the last person in the world I would ever kill. Idiot! We could be happy together."

Then with his last remaining energy, Bruce slowly placed his lips on her lips, kissed her and before dying said, "You were a real, beautiful woman! Cindy! You...idiot. I loved...you from the first moment I saw you."

Having said that, Bruce Munro, the exterminator, took one last wheezing breath and died. The man who had killed dozens and dozens of dangerous and powerful people had been killed at the hands of a fragile woman.

WEDNESDAY AFTERNOON

Dick Tolone arrived at SEATAC airport at noon.

After collecting his luggage, he took a shuttle and went directly to the Westin Hotel. He looked for Julie in room 513, but unfortunately, she was not there.

Dick loitered in the lobby. He drank a coffee, got a magazine to pass the time, and sat in one of those comfortable armchairs, where he could observe everything.

After about twenty minutes he noticed Julie entering and heading to the front desk.

He promptly got up and went to meet her.

"Hey Julie! I'm here," Dick exclaimed cheerfully.

"Oh! Hello! How long have you been there?"

"Not too long."

"Did you have a good trip?"

"Yes, enough! Let's go and sit down. I have some news to tell you." Tolone said with a serious tone.

They sat on the couch and Dick revealed to her, "Collins and Jeff will arrive on a three o'clock flight."

"What?"

"You got it right! Just them."

"You're crazy! Why did you warn Collins?" Julie exclaimed, irritated.

"Listen Julie! We can't frame Lewis alone. I told him the news you gave me by phone, and after shouting, he was satisfied, very satisfied. I think it was the first time in my life that I ever saw him in that way. Collins confided that after what you discovered, he would put you back on duty as soon as possible.

"So, the big boss is coming in person? Why?" Julie asked puzzled.

"I have no idea. Maybe he wants to check the evidence we have to indict Charles for himself. If Collins signs an authorization to proceed against Charles, we can put the handcuffs on that scumbag in a matter of hours." Dick exclaimed gladly.

"I think Collins will do it immediately, if he has the balls, especially after what we found out last night."

"What's new? Anything important?"

"Yes! I have solid evidence of a double murder Charles Lewis committed against two poor girls about twenty years ago." Julie answered proudly.

"Oh my God! This is dynamite. Fantastic! Finally! This time we will arrest Charles Lewis. I am looking forward to personally putting handcuffs on him and dragging that asshole to a federal prison." Tolone said, very satisfied.

"Precisely! Dick."

"Why is Jeff Wilson coming along with Collins? You know what I think of that man." Julie asked nervously, after a couple of seconds.

"I have no idea why Collins is bringing him, but we must be very careful with Wilson. In fact, I agree with you, Jeff is dirty. That is the sore point of the story," Tolone replied concerned.

So! Jeff is dirty, and he is coming here. What do we do now? I am not happy at all about this. Have you discovered anything wrong with that dude?" Julie asked unhappily.

"No really! I had a couple of odd episodes with him. One time, I was passing close to his desk, he was on the phone, and he gave me a dirty look, and stopped the call immediately. I was intrigued by this and kept an eye on him. After I left, he started to talk to someone again on the phone. I passed by again and heard: everything is going as planned. We will know the result soon. And I will alert you if anything is discovered, I am keeping an eye on them. The woman is su… At that point Wilson saw me passing by again and stopped the call immediately."

"This is very peculiar, but there is nothing tangible and definitive in that conversation. "We cannot draw any conclusion." Julie said thoughtfully.

"I totally agree with you, nothing solid, however if you were there you would have some doubts too. It was strange how the man acted, like he had something to hide, and looked so annoyed by my presence. Unfortunately, I could not hear the last part, but the last words: I don't know where that rogue agent is.... I am wondering if the rouge agent could be you because you are suspended and don't follow protocol. I could be wrong. For the rest I did not find anything to incriminate Jeff Wilson." Tolone said worriedly.

Dick went to eat at the hotel restaurant, while Julie looked for Henry and Maria to share the news. She found them in their room lying lazily in bed.

"You seem down to me, Julie! What happened?" Maria asked, observing her unhappy face.

"You are right! I'm down."

Julie told of the unexpected arrival of her boss Matthew Collins and Jeff Wilson, the person who according to her was linked to Charles Lewis and his organization.

Henry did not say anything, merely looking at Julie and listening to her story.

Then in a worried tone he said, "I don't like this story; I don't like it at all. I think the time has come for Maria and I to get out of here. Now that you FBI have concrete evidence to indict Charles and throw him in jail, it's your case."

"Listen! Henry! Tonight, when the others arrive, I will show them the footage of the murders of Ashley and Lesly. I would like you and Maria to be present."

"I'm sorry! We can't ever talk about it."

"Please! It could be important."

"Why?"

"I don't know! Maybe Dick or Collins will have questions for you that I haven't thought of. Please come," Julie pleaded.

Henry looked at Maria who also seemed thoughtful, then replied, "If Maria agrees, we will come. However, tomorrow morning, we will go as far away as possible from this place, and I don't want to hear a single word of this story anymore."

"Very well! I will tell you later what time the meeting is." Julie exclaimed, satisfied and left the room.

After Julie left, Henry and Maria were puzzled and did not talk for a while, until she said, concerned, "I agree with you. Something is fishy. The arrival of these agents scares me. Especially if Julie herself doesn't trust one of them, we must leave, Henry! As soon as possible."

"And we will. However! Let's clean and load our guns so we will be ready for action. I really feel confused. I don't know what we can do. Part of me is saying to leave here immediately. On the other side, everything we can do to harm Charles Lewis will be useful. Think if finally, this nightmare will be over, and tomorrow we can toast and celebrate the end of Charles Lewis and his organization."

Dawnin replied thoughtfully.

"But let's be prepared for a plan B too, in case of trouble," he added.

The fateful moment came.

At half past five they met at the same place, where they watched the footage the previous evening. Julie arrived with Dick Tolone, while Collins and Jeff arrived in different vehicles.

They went inside the room, after facing heavy and pouring rain.

The atmosphere was tense and nervous.

Julie introduced them to Henry and Maria, a brief handshake, a couple of jokes, and they entered the little room to watch the film.

Before the screening began, Henry got up from his chair and said, "I'm sorry gentlemen! I can't watch this dreadful film for a second time, I'll wait for you outside." And he left the room.

After a few seconds Maria followed and found him leaning against the wall, immersed in deep thought. Something about those men had struck him. Henry couldn't remember what it was, but he was sure it was something important.

Maria approached and asked concerned, "Are you still upset about this film?"

"No! Not only for that, Maria. There's something important that is bugging me. However, I can't remember what."

"Think! Tomorrow we will be light years away from this place and we will forget all these nefarious events. Now all this will be FBI business." Maria exclaimed, trying to be positive.

"Yes! But we are still here," he replied with pessimism.

A few minutes later the light in the room went on and the door opened. Henry and Maria walked in and noticed that Collins was complimenting Julie.

"It's also thanks to them," Julie revealed to her superior, pointing to the newcomers.

"Nice job! Mr. Dawnin." Exclaimed Matthew Collins, energetically shaking Henry's hand to congratulate him.

Jeff Wilson also joined the group and taking Julie aside told her, "Well done! You have done a terrific job! Congratulations! I apologize to you for my behavior in the past and I hope you can forgive me."

Julie shook his hand reluctantly, yet the man's words seemed sincere, so probably all her fears were wrong. However, she still felt uneasy about him.

"What did I tell you? Finally, everything has been resolved! We don't need to worry anymore. The fate of Charles Lewis is decided, he can't escape this time. The evidence is overwhelming. The reality is that Lewis will get life in prison for these murders. Now you can relax, my dear." Dick Tolone said cheerfully.

"What do you think about Jeff Wilson?" Julie exclaimed thoughtfully.

"Frankly, we have no evidence linking Jeff Wilson to Charles Lewis, our suspicion were all assumptions. Probably Jeff is just an unfriendly asshole, but he is clean. And anyway, now Collins will take care of the matter. We are off the hook and deserve a nice vacation in a tropical resort." Dick said satisfied.

Collins left first, with the film in his briefcase. Before leaving, he again complimented Henry and Maria.

Then it was Jeff Wilson's turn to say goodbye.

Dick was the last to leave them.

"It has been a pleasure to meet you, Henry. I hope to see you again in the future." He exclaimed, stopping in front of him.

"The pleasure is mine." Dawnin replied, shaking Dick's hand vigorously for several seconds.

"Guys! See you later, okay!" Julie exclaimed, leaving with Dick.

Dick and Julie slowly walked out of the building, chatting, and joking.

Henry and Maria stayed inside.

Henry seemed upset, at one point exclaiming loudly, "Oh my God! Oh my God! Damn."

"What's going on?" Maria asked with apprehension.

"Oh! My God! My God! What a terrible mistake. We should never have come here."

"Talk? What is bothering you?"

"Maria! We are ruined! Doomed. Why didn't I think about this before? We must leave immediately; we have been deceived."

"Tell me, why?"

Henry was about to answer when he heard footsteps approaching, so he waited.

Jeff Wilson appeared suddenly, walking quickly towards them.

After seeing the two, he said with an enigmatic grin, "I forgot my umbrella in the room."

Jeff had just finished talking when Henry, taking the man by the collar, violently slammed him against the wall, and at the same time, put his revolver in Jeff's mouth.

"Son of a bitch! Are you thinking you can fool me? Do you and your friends want to kill me? Well! I will send you first to the creator."

Dawnin shouted in one of those moments when the beast inside him was coming out, and he could hardly restrain himself.

"Henry! What's going on? Chill out." Maria cried out.

"Stay calm! Henry! Don't make any impulsive moves, you might regret and listen carefully to me. It is crucial." Jeff spoke calmly and friendly.

Dick Tolone drove slowly, talking with Julie about different topics.

Suddenly, he moved away from the main road, and drove for a mile, until he parked the car on a narrow deserted, dark, road in the middle of nowhere. He stopped the engine and looked at Julie, while whistling.

Julie was intrigued and asked, "Why did we stop here? What's going on?"

"I must make a confession to you, Julie." Tolone exclaimed with an odd tone.

"What is it?" Julie asked wondering.

"Well! I'm worried."

"Why? Everything seems fine, don't you think?"

"I'm sorry! Julie! I'm very sorry."

"Why are you worrying? I don't understand you?"

Without answering, Dick suddenly pulled out a gun with a silencer from his pocket and pointed it at her.

"Have you gone crazy?"

"I'm sorry! I didn't think you would get so far in the investigation. I was hoping that after a couple of days, you would be back in the office, totally unsuccessful, like the first time, and the whole affair would be trashed once and for all."

"Dick! What are you saying? Are you mad? It's me! Julie! Julie Sue. Your friend." Julie said shocked, on the verge of crying.

"I know! Julie! And that's why I'm sorry, I would never want to do it, but business is business, you must understand." Tolone answered cold and cynical.

"Oh… my… God! Do you work for Charles Lewis? No! I can't believe it." Julie exclaimed, stuttering with a thready voice.

"In fact, don't believe it! I don't work for Charles Lewis. I work for Andrew Martin. I have never met Charles Lewis in my life. He has no idea of my existence." Dick answered still with that icy tone.

"So, you want to kill me, Dick! Are you sure? Is this want you really want to do?"

"Yes! Julie, goodbye."

A moment before Dick was to shoot Julie, Jeff Wilson, appeared suddenly, and pointed his gun at Dick's temple through the window, shouting, "Throw the gun to the ground! You are under arrest. Get out with your hands up." Tolone turned to him and without answering dropped the gun on the ground.

"Now get out of the car, slowly, with your hands up."

He obeyed the command.

However, as he walked out of the door, with his left-hand Dick drew a gun he had in a holster, on his left calf, and quickly fired a couple of shots at Jeff, who, despite being injured, shot back.

Although Dick was injured in the shoulder, he managed to hit Jeff again with another pair of bullets, and Jeff fell to the ground dead.

After that Tolone turned back to look for Julie.

He was surprised that she had run away from the car.

"Julie! It is useless for you to hide from me. You know! You can't escape me, and if you do fool me, you won't escape another hitman who works for the organization. Come on! Give up. It will be painless; I will shoot you directly in the heart. I guarantee a quick death, I promise." Tolone said cruelly.

"Throw the gun! Dick! And move slowly, otherwise I'll kill you instantly. My gun is pointed at you," Julie shouted from behind him.

"What do you want to do? Kill me?" Dick replied ironically.

"Have you ever killed someone? Julie! I don't think so! You know! It's hard to do, especially the first time," he added maliciously.

"Throw the gun on the ground."

"Then it's even harder to do it against someone you know well."

"Throw the gun, or I'll shoot, Dick," she shouted as loud as possible.

"But you will not shoot! Right, Julie?"

Slowly Dick Tolone was turning towards her, holding the gun tightly in his hand.

Julie, frightened and confused, continued to keep him in sight.

"Think of all the good times we spent together, the laughter we had. Do you really want to shoot me?"

"The truth is that you started all this crap, and if it weren't for that poor Jeff Wilson, I would have already died. I repeat to you for the last time, throw the gun." Julie yelled this time with an aggressive tone.

Tolone had completely turned around towards her and slowly pointed the weapon at Julie. She panicked and pulled the trigger a couple of times, but to her surprise the gun did not fire.

"To shoot, a gun must be loaded with cartridges," Dick told her laughing.

Pulling out the cartridges from his pocket, he added, "Never leave the bag in the car, with strangers, not even to go to the toilet for a moment."

"I thought you weren't a stranger," Julie replied wistfully.

"Unfortunately! You are totally wrong, my beautiful girl and ex-partner. Anyway, our conversation ends here, goodbye Julie. I will bring flowers to your grave. Again, farewell my honey."

For the second time Dick Tolone was going to pull the trigger, when he heard a voice behind him, "Never pretend to be a priest when you are not, nor shake hands with strangers."

Dick turned around surprised and found Henry aiming his 38 special revolver at him.

"Now the game is over, Dick! Throw the gun! My revolver is loaded, and I am not in the mood to hear any more of your bullshit. You have two seconds to comply, if you don't, I will shoot."

"Dawnin! Fuck you!" Dick yelled with hatred.

Tolone did not obey and pointed the weapon at Henry who did not react immediately, but before Dick could shoot, he was riddled by bullets from Maria's gun.

In fact, Maria was hidden behind a tree a few feet to Henry's right.

"Next time try to be quicker to shoot, John Wayne! If not, someone will kill you easily." Maria shouted nervously, seeing that Henry stood still like a moron, without reacting.

"You know I'm not familiar with guns." He replied trembling.

Maria approached Julie to comfort her because she was scared to death.

"How are you, Julie? Are you injured?"

"I could be better! Anyway... I'm still alive." She stammered.

"I cannot believe it! Who expected this from Dick? I considered him one of my best friends, and this great friend was going to kill me. How did you know about him, and why did Jeff Wilson save me?" Julie asked again in disbelief.

"Get in the car with us and I'll reveal the whole story. Unfortunately, I must warn you we are really in trouble. We must flee as far as we can, and as soon as possible." Henry, concerned, told her as they walked to the car. They got into the car and left.

"So! Tell me. I'm curious to know." Julie asked anxiously.

"When I met those men this afternoon, I was puzzled by a detail of one of them. Even though I tried to remember what it was, in the end I couldn't remember anything. However, I had this obsessive thought in my brain. Something didn't add up. At the end of the film, each of them shook my hand before leaving. When Dick Tolone greeted me, I suddenly remembered what it was.

In Puerto Vallarta, the day we confronted Charles's assassins, I met a priest who asked me for money to give to charity. When I gave the money to him, the priest shook my hand to thank me. And I noticed that he had a small, but very visible purple scar, possibly caused by a burn, on the upper part of his right hand, between his thumb and index finger.

That priest seemed to be passing through, but strangely enough he was in the same place, where Scott and the other criminals were about to kill us, and he was sitting at a table between us and the others.

Later, we discovered the existence of a fourth man affiliated with Charles's gang, who was probably ordered to check on how things were going. In fact, Greg Murphy had managed to escape, but his escape did not last long, because after a few minutes he was slaughtered in the rental car. Greg was killed by this elusive fourth man, who was unknown.

So, when shaking hands with Dick Tolone, I saw the exact same scar. It wasn't difficult to connect the whole story. Dick was perfectly disguised as a priest. I could never have suspected he was the same person. However, he had neglected a small detail, the scar. I just remembered this when Jeff Wilson came

147

back to get his umbrella. At that point, fearing he was also part of the conspiracy, I was going to beat him up, then another twist. Jeff revealed that he was an internal affair agent, and guess who he was investigating?"

"Dick! Of course," Julie replied with certainty.

"No! My darling! You're totally wrong. Jeff knew nothing about Tolone. He was investigating Collins."

"What?"

"Yes! That's right. Your superior Matthew Collins works in cahoots with Charles Lewis." Maria replied bluntly.

"Oh my God! This is incredible! Then all our efforts were wasted. That footage will never reach a courtroom." Julie exclaimed discouraged.

"It's what I believe too! Charles Lewis wins once again." Henry said gloomily.

"How did you find me? You arrived just in time to save me. How did you know I was there?" Julie asked, perplexed.

"The main credit goes to Jeff. In fact, it was he who saw where that scumbag parked his car. As soon as the story between us was clarified, we hurried to find you. For our good fortune you walked slowly to the car, so we arrived just in time to notice Dick's car leaving and the direction he had taken. We quickly got into the car following your route, but unfortunately you had disappeared. Luckily, we saw Tolone's car parked in front of a McDonald's. That stop was truly providential." Maria revealed.

"It was there that pig of Dick unloaded my gun." Julie vented angrily.

"Well! Don't think about it anymore, now that traitor can't hurt anyone." Henry said.

"I feel bad for poor Jeff Wilson, not only because he is dead, but also because I always thought he was a bad guy, instead he was not. He was just doing his job." Julie said sadly.

"I know how you feel, and I know how hard it is working undercover. I have done this task in the past. You must act and behave as a totally different person from who you are. Probably Jeff exhibited that hostile behavior towards you, to create a distance between himself and you, possibly to deceive Collins, who always disliked you." Maria spoke seriously.

WEDNESDAY EVENING

"Great job! Congratulations!" Charles exclaimed with great satisfaction, as he burned the film.

"You don't know how grateful I am, Collins!" He added smiling.

"Oh nonsense! Mr. Lewis, nonsense. I'm deeply sorry! I don't have time to meet Mr. Andrew Martin. But I must go home. Can you greet him for me?" Collins exclaimed with a servile tone.

"Yes! Certainly! Rest assured," Charles replied, shaking Collins' hand.

"Is Henry Dawnin staying at the Westin Hotel?"

"Exactly! Under the name of Vargas, Jose' Vargas. Dawnin is disguised fantastically. When you see the dude, you will not recognize him."

"Well! Have a good flight! Collins! And thank you again."

"Have you heard? Doug! My pal Henry Dawnin is staying at the Westin Hotel. He spares no expense when he uses my money, that fucking bastard."

"You should be glad that we found him. This time he can't escape, and we will get him."

Doug answered viciously.

"Of course, I am happy! First let's get Henry, and then without wasting time let's go punish my dear secretary, Sharon, big boobs, who apparently is talking too much for my taste."

"Why don't you send Munro to get rid of Sharon?"

"Because I have no idea where that idiot is. I phoned him three times this afternoon, but he did not call me back. That man is just useless! I was wrong to hire him. I hope that ugly worm is now in hell, where he belongs." Charles shouted angrily.

Meanwhile, Henry, Maria and Julie were eating together in a Mexican restaurant.

Despite drinking a few cocktails and trying to distract themselves, the atmosphere remained tense and sad. The events of the day shocked everyone, especially Julie who had been deceived all this time by Dick Tolone.

Also, Henry was depressed.

The idea of being forced to kill to survive and living among murdered people and those who wanted to kill him, did not suit him at all. Those corpses began to weigh heavily in his stomach, and on his conscience. It seemed he had entered a vicious circle and couldn't find a way out of it. Henry was the dude who had always been against violence and wore Grateful Dead psychedelic t-shirts, or shirts with the peace sign.

The quietest was Maria, who unlike the others kept her cool.

Breaking the silence that reigned among them, Dawnin, said, "What are you going to do in the future, Julie?"

"Well! To tell the truth, I don't know," she replied frustrated.

"You know! It's crazy to go back to Washington D.C. or stay here. Anyone who has seen that film will be killed without mercy." Dawnin exclaimed worried.

"Of course, I know. It's incredible! I've worked with some really trusted people, Dick, Collins" she exclaimed with much irony.

"It's certainly not your fault! Now your only goal is to try to save yourself and your butt," Maria said bluntly.

"Shit!" She cursed.

"What's going on?" Henry asked.

"We can't run away now; we are screwed because our passports are in the hotel?"

"Damn! It's true! This is very bad," Henry replied, worried.

They returned to the hotel feeling depressed.

At the entrance Maria suggested a quick final toast to be held in their room, almost like a last farewell. Furthermore, they decided to take their luggage and leave without staying overnight in the hotel.

"Not a bad idea! Let's drink champagne. I bought a bottle of Dom Perignon for my friend Lisa, but for this occasion I can sacrifice it. I'm going to get it, and will be back soon," Julie said.

The two headed to their room.

Henry opened the door, followed by his companion, but before he could turn on the light he was pushed violently forward and the same happened to Maria.

One moment later the room lit up and they saw Charles Lewis, who was sitting blissfully in an armchair with a cigar in his mouth, "Good evening Mr. Jose' Vargas, how are you?" He exclaimed in Spanish with an ironic tone.

Henry looked around and beside Charles, he noticed Doug who held a gun with a silencer pointed at them. He quickly searched and took away their weapons.

"So! Señor Vargas! Why don't you answer me? How come? I spoke to you in Spanish before, don't you understand your language?"

Henry continued to stare at Charles with hatred and without answering.

"So! Mister Vargas! What do you think of Seattle? Rainy, isn't it? It's certainly not like Puerto Vallarta, where you live and kill people. By the way! Why are you here? Do you want to steal more money from me?"

"Charles! You're more and more stupid, you are a dick head."

"Henry! Finally, I recognize you. But yes! It's you. You see it! Doug, I finally found my old friend Henry Dawnin. But look how you are disguised! You look like a scarecrow."

"I don't think you are here to greet me, are you Charles?"

"I'm here to talk about business. You know! When someone steals my money, well! I don't like it so much. Let's change the subject for a moment, who is this beautiful girl who is next to you?"

"It's not your business." Henry shouted.

"Of course, it's my business! Look at those nice tits she has! What do you think Doug? Does she have beautiful tits?"

"They look great to me, Charles."

"For me too! Check if she is wearing a bra or not."

"Leave her alone. She has nothing to do with this. It's with me that you must argue, isn't it?"

"Okay! All right! It means I will think about her in the future. Don't worry my beautiful girl! I'll fix you later, I'll open and split you in half with the big can opener I have, ah, aha, ah." Charles laughed maliciously.

"Those who boast of their big attributes are generally those who have major sexual problems, and generally have short dicks." Maria replied in a defiant tone.

Charles was surprised by Maria's answer.

To change the subject and return to what was important to him, he said, "Tell me, Henry! Where did you put my money?"

"What money?"

"The money you stole from me, ugly son of a bitch! Have you forgotten? The money hidden in the cemetery." Charles spoke with an icy tone.

"Sorry to disappoint you! But I've never touched a single dollar of your loot."

"Stop lying bastard! And tell me what you have done with my money, besides spending it at the Westin Hotel, or having fun with sluts."

"You can cut my eyes out and torture me, but you will never know where the money went because, believe it or not, I never stole it. I swear it on my mother's head."

"You are also a dirty liar, as well as a thief," Charles exclaimed, literally jumping up from the armchair, and hitting Henry with a strong punch to his stomach.

Henry collapsed to the ground in pain, while Charles hit him again with a powerful kick.

Despite the severe pain, Henry replied, "Do you want to know the truth?"

"It is important that you tell the truth, not a bunch of bullshit."

"Then open your ears wide, fucking asshole! And don't beat me anymore. I never took a penny of your money, never. You were robbed by Cindy and your good buddy Tom Atkinson."

"What the fuck are you saying, bastard!" Charles cursed, hitting him again with a violent kick in the stomach.

Summoning his strength to stay conscious, Henry gathered all his energy and shouted, "You have always been a stupid animal. You only know how to beat and never listen, poor imbecile! Beat me, beat me, while Tom Atkinson screws your woman in front of your face."

Hearing the last sentence said by his rival, an alarm bell began to ring in Charles's head.

How did Henry know this?

"What the hell are you saying?" Charles asked him, pretending not to have any idea of Tom and Cindy's love and relationship.

"You heard it right. Tom and Cindy are having a love affair, and your friend Tom tried to kill me at that mission in Mexico."

"Why do you speak in the present? You know Tom can no longer have any love affair, since he is deceased. Weren't you one of those who found that famous film at his house?"

Henry gave a fleeting and worried look to Maria; Collins had already given Charles the film.

Trying not to give weight to the news, Henry continued his story.

"I followed your instructions carefully and went to that damn cemetery. Cindy made me dig not one, but three different graves, and in each of them we found money. Suddenly Tom, emerging from a secluded place where he had hidden, approached and fired a couple of gunshots at me. Then he loaded the money and left with her. Do you want to see the scars I still carry?"

Charles began to believe Henry's story. In fact, why would he want to deceive him? Surely, he could not have known about Tom and Cindy's love affair or the existence of all that hidden money. He wondered how Cindy had found out, since she had to be the one who had organized everything. Charles grabbed the phone and called home hoping to talk to her.

But Cindy didn't answer. He cursed and slammed the handset violently.

"What do you think of all this, Doug?" Charles inquired curiously.

"I think Henry is telling the truth, Charles. You have been betrayed by Cindy, no doubt about it." Doug answered bluntly.

"Indeed, yes! I came just for you, to clarify the situation once and for all. I got tired of waiting for your hitmen to find me in some distant tropical place and take me out."

"What a noble soul! And what do you want to do? Do you want to kill me?" Charles asked ironically with a wicked sneer.

"It's not my style and you know that well. I came to tell you the truth, hoping you would leave me alone, because I am not the one who robbed you."

"Beautiful and wise words, Henry! Unfortunately, we are no longer at school and this truce is useless. You have given me a lot of trouble in the last period, pal, and have discovered some of my important and vital secrets. I'm sorry, the time for truce and reconciliation are over forever. Get ready to go to the afterlife with your beautiful friend."

Meanwhile Julie, with the bottle of champagne in her hand was getting ready to knock on the door. But she paused a moment, hearing Henry, screaming loudly, the commotion inside the room, and someone mentioning the name of Charles.

Within seconds she understood what was happening.

She began to tremble. The bottle of champagne slipped from her hands, but she managed to catch it. Instinctively she moved away from the door and hid behind a corner in the corridor. Julie had the gun with her, but didn't know what to do.

Julie waited to see if the men were leaving the room. On the other hand, she feared if she did not intervene immediately, it would be the end for Henry and Maria.

"Get ready for a nice ride, the last one you'll have in your life. Come on, let's go! Beautiful lady! Let's go! Quickly."

"If you must kill us, do it right here, don't prolong the time. Do it and that's it." Maria shouted furiously.

Doug approached Maria and gave her a strong slap in the face, yelling, "If you shout again, I'll kill you here, not in a quick way, but by breaking your bones one by one, ugly slut."

Henry seeing that Doug was beating his woman went to attack him, but Charles pulled out his revolver and shouted, "Don't do anything stupid."

"You are two cowards! Dirty cowards." Dawnin shouted.

Charles gave him another strong slap making his nose bleed, then in an uncompromising tone said, "Don't make me waste any more time, come on! Let's go."

Julie had heard Maria's loud screams.

She decided to go into action, even if she did not how. At that point she wanted to try anything that could save the lives of her friends.

Julie came out of the corner of the hallway and was approaching their room when the door opened. She quickly hid in the same place. Even without looking, she understood that Henry and Maria were being taken to the elevator.

Charles and Doug hid the weapons under their jackets and started to take their enemies to the underground garage, where they had parked their vehicle.

In the elevator Charles said, "It's odd! I'm a little sorry to get rid of you, Henry. Well! Despite everything, you and I grew up together."

Dawnin stared into his eyes with hatred, but didn't answer.

Then when the elevator had almost arrived at its destination, Henry asked Charles, "Why did you entangle me in all these troubles? Why did you get me involved in this whole damn mess?"

"I thought you were the right man to carry out the operation." Charles cynically replied.

"Bullshit! I don't believe you! You could recruit hundreds of people better than me. No more subterfuge! Tell me the truth, once and for all."

"Do you want to know the truth? Henry!" Charles answered coldly.

"Yes!"

"Okay, I'm happy to reveal the truth to you. The real reason is that I have an old score to settle with you, my dear friend!" He angrily said.

"What do you mean? I don't understand. What old score are you talking about?" Henry asked surprised.

"Nathalie!"

"Nathalie?" Dawnin asked incredulously.

"Yes! Exactly! Just her. The only woman in the world I could never own, and the one I wanted to have, but you stole her from me."

What in the world! And you did all this for Nathalie, for that story that is more than twenty years old."

"It was all your fault! Not only did you steal Nathalie from me, but you even married her." Charles grumbled.

"You're crazy! Charles! A dangerous madman. You are taking revenge for a remote and forgotten story. If you're still in love with Nathalie, why don't you visit her? It has been over for a long time between us. We're divorced, didn't you know?" Dawnin said surprised.

"Now it's too late! Someone like me, cannot suffer insults from a starving bum like you. I am a winner! Everything I've done in my life proves it, while you are a failure, a dirty loser who has never done anything good."

"Ah yes! You are a winner! You have accomplished great things in life! How are you not ashamed to say that? What good have you done in your existence? Nothing! You raped and killed innocent girls, murdered people and sold weapons and drugs. You piece of shit! You have made your career as a criminal because someone else helped you, otherwise you wouldn't have been good at that either. You are a perfect example of nepotism. Your father was a scumbag, and a crook, and you as his son are the same."

Charles struck him violently in the stomach with a punch, causing Henry to fall to the ground in the middle of the deserted garage.

Meanwhile, Julie had checked where the elevator was going and realized that Henry and Maria were being taken to the underground garage. She was waiting for the elevator, unfortunately it arrived slightly late.

Julie began to fear she would not arrive in time to save them. Her fear grew when the elevator stopped on the ground floor for a useless stop.

No one came in. Julie nervously presses the closing button. Finally, the doors closed. She reached the desired floor and rushed out like a fury.

Everything was deserted. Walking into the garage, she saw the men far away. Grabbing her gun, she ran in their direction, hiding behind a row of parked cars.

"Get up sissy!" Charles shouted with contempt.

Henry, in pain, slowly got up, while Charles furiously shouted at him, "I will not kill you immediately, because this is not the right place. After what you said, I will make your ending slow and painful. You can count on it, bastard."

Henry looked at Maria who seemed terrified. Then he watched Doug, who stood by her side, holding the gun firmly in his hand.

He was the cornerstone of everything. Charles put his revolver back in his holster and seemed anxious to get to their vehicle as soon as possible.

Maria gave Henry a worried look, as if to tell him, "If we do not try to do something immediately, we are doomed."

Henry understood the silent message and tried to come up with something, but nothing came to mind. However, he approached Charles.

"I must act immediately," Henry murmured to himself.

"Come on, come on!" The evil enemy screamed at him.

Charles had just finished saying that, when they heard footsteps getting closer and closer.

Julie had almost caught up with them, running very fast, with her weapon in hand.

Doug, turning in her direction, saw Julie coming and quickly pointed the gun at her.

Suddenly, Maria attacked him with desperate force. Doug fired a couple of shots at Julie, but with Maria clinging to his back and fighting furiously, he could not take aim.

Using his immense strength, Doug did not have much trouble getting rid of Maria, who literally flew into the air. That moment of struggle was fatal to him. In fact, after shoving Maria off his back, he pointed the gun back at Julie, but she was ready to shoot him with the entire magazine of the gun, hitting him squarely.

Doug collapsed to the ground, dead.

Meanwhile, Charles had not remained idle during Julie's attack and tried to draw his revolver when Henry attacked and blocked him.

A violent scuffle ensued.

In the end Charles managed to draw his revolver, but he could not shoot anyone because Henry grabbed his hand firmly. Charles fired three shots at the roof of the garage and in a car parked in front, triggering the alarm. Suddenly the weapon slipped out of his hand, and it fell to the ground.

Charles tried to hit Henry with a couple of punches, but in vain.

At that moment the beast in Henry Dawnin came out again in the most powerful, scary way possible.

Henry was furious and hit Charles repeatedly with punches to the stomach and face.

Then Henry kicked him in the testicles, while screaming loudly, "Piece of scum this is for Ashley Duncar." Dawnin kicked him again, screaming, "This kick is for Ann Smith."

Charles collapsed to the ground with blood gushing from his mouth.

But soon as he tried to get up, Henry hit him with a third kick in the same place, shouting, "And this is for Sharon Miller, your current secretary."

Charles fell backwards. Dawnin was a fury unleashed.

While Charles was on the ground, Henry jumped on him four times, shouting angrily: "This is for Leslie Johnson, and all the people you have raped and hurt."

Charles was lying on the ground and looked dead. Henry turned back to the women and saw that luckily, they were alive. Maria was the most battered, with bruises on her forehead.

"How are you?" Henry asked with concern.

"We're still alive," Julie replied, wiping sweat from her forehead.

"It's over! At least for now. This bastard won't bother anyone in the future."

"Let's hope so!" Maria exclaimed.

They were about to leave when Julie, looking back, and noticed Charles, crawling slowly towards his revolver.

"Damn! He's still alive, look!" She yelled in fear.

Charles was very slow. Taking advantage of this, Maria picked up Doug's gun and hastily fired four shots that hit Charles.

Henry bent over him and felt his wrist.

Charles was dead.

"Let's go! Ladies! This time, it's over for real. Charles Lewis will not rape any more women or hurt anyone else." Dawnin exclaimed with relief.

XXII

Puerto Vallarta, A Few Months Later

Tonio the grim's white van arrived at the gate of Fuentes' villa at dawn. Tonio opened the gate with his remote control and stopped to greet a couple of men who were guarding it.

"Leave the gate open, do you understand?"

"Of course! Tonio! Don't worry."

"See you later." Having said that, he drove toward the villa at high speed.

He parked in front of the main door, and at the same time one of the Fuentes' servants opened the door of the house.

Six men in camouflage outfits quietly stepped out of the white van, with four of them moving toward the dormitories, where Coco, Roberto, Luis, and the others were sleeping deeply.

Tonio opened the door, and the men quickly entered. Moving from room to room, using daggers or guns equipped with silencers, in a few minutes they had killed all the trusted men of Fuentes. The people went from sleep to death without even realizing it.

"Nice job! Chico," Tonio exclaimed to the head cook he met in the courtyard.

"Thank you! I used all the sleeping pills you gave me," he replied proudly.

The men quickly walked to Fuentes's bedroom. They tried to open the door, but it was locked.

So, they kicked it open and entered, turning on the light.

"What the hell is going on?" Rodrigo shouted, terrorized. Then, realizing what was happening, he went to open the drawer of the nightstand, where he kept a gun, but one of the men blocked him.

"Oh my God!" Carmen Fuentes exclaimed in terror.

One of the guys pulled away the bed sheets, while another grabbed and tore off Carmen's nightgown. The men laughed and sneered wickedly, looking at her lasciviously. Once this was done, the same individual fired a gunshot in her forehead, killing Carmen instantly.

"Damn killers!" Fuentes shouted with anger and contempt. After he cursed, he was forcefully loaded into his wheelchair and securely tied up.

Suddenly Tonio, the grim, entered the room and smiled treacherously at his master.

"Tonio! May you be damned for eternity!" Fuentes screamed with all the breath in his lungs.

"Business is business! Mister Fuentes! You should know this." Tonio replied with a satisfied tone and a wicked smile.

"I believed you were one of my most trusted men."

"I'm sorry! But your time has come," Tonio answered with malice.

"May the blood of myself, my wife and of all those whom you have treacherously killed, fall on your head, damn you!" Fuentes spoke angrily.

Meanwhile, three other vehicles arrived at the villa, two jeep station wagons and a white limousine. Ten men got out of the jeeps. The driver of the limousine, together with a sturdy young man, went to open the rear door of the car.

ANDREW MARTIN got out of the car, elegantly dressed as always, in one of his many white Armani suits. Escorted by his men, Andrew went inside the house.

Meanwhile, Fuentes was taken away from his room by a couple of men, who forced him into his wheelchair and took him downstairs.

Martin appeared suddenly, coming from behind Fuentes's back, and stopping about four feet in front of him.

"We haven't seen each other for a long time, have we? Montgomery! Or now must I call you Fuentes, Rodrigo Fuentes? What do they call you around here?"

"Andrew Martin! You!" Fuentes exclaimed in horror, opening his eyes wide.

"Yes! Just me, my dear! You know until recently I thought you were dead. Then a big, surprise, my friend Montgomery is not only alive and well, but even plots revenge behind my back."

"Damn! How did you find me? Tell me! Bastard."

"Hey Montgomery! What is this foul language? I do not recognize you anymore. Did you know that you have become rude and crude?" Andrew answered with one of his 24 carat big smiles.

"Tell me how you found me?" Fuentes repeated this time more calmly.

"Don't worry! I'll tell you, rest assured! But later. Now I have some important chores to do."

That said, Andrew nodded to his men and two of them began pushing Fuentes's wheelchair out of the house.

Tonio the grim had witnessed the whole discussion, along with the others, and seemed to be enjoying the scene a. Andrew, noticing the man's wicked smile, moved towards him.

"You did a great job, Tonio! Congratulations!" Andrew said satisfied.

"Thank you! Mister Martin! See! You won't regret hiring me." Tonio replied, smugly.

"You're right! I won't regret it; you can count on it." Andrew answered in an enigmatic tone. At the same time, he pulled out his forty-four Magnum from the holster and shot Tonio in the face.

"I'm sorry Tonio! There is no place for traitors in my organization. If you have betrayed once, you could do it a second time, with the difference that I am not your Mr. Fuentes, I am a very different person." Andrew exclaimed, putting his weapon in the holster.

Unfortunately, Tonio could not answer because he lay dead on the floor with his head exploded.

A few drops of blood had stained Martin's immaculate white jacket. One of his men gave him another similar jacket.

Then a cry was suddenly heard from the upper floor.

Luisa, the little daughter of Fuentes, terrified, had seen everything that had happened. Martin gave a nod to one of his men who immediately went to get her. When he reached Fuentes, who was being guarded by a couple of men, they were at the edge of the courtyard, near the road leading to the gate.

"Here we are! Dear Montgomery! What were we talking about?"

"Tell me how you found me? Pig! Tell me." Fuentes shouted scared to death.

"Okay! Okay! If you don't swear. Now I will tell you everything. Open your ears wide because I will speak only once." Andrew exclaimed harshly.

"You must know, dear friend, that your organization gave us a real hard time in the beginning. I did not know who the hell was manipulating the whole situation. Unlike my nephew Charles, who seemed to be very concerned about it, I kept my cool. In fact, I was firmly convinced our phantom adversaries would sooner or later make a mistake, a misstep. And I was right.

When Charles told me that he had received an anonymous phone call, saying that Henry Dawnin was in Puerto Vallarta, well! You cannot imagine my joy. Because I was sure that whoever had created that trap, was around here. While Charles sent some of his men, without saying anything to anyone, I sent one of mine. A man whom no one in the gang knew. His job was simple, just watch over my men, it was not Dawnin he was looking for, but the head of that mysterious organization.

The pinnacle of success came the day Henry Dawnin and his girlfriend eliminated Scott and his companion. My man killed Greg Murphy, who had become a liability, and he followed Dawnin when he came to see you. The rest is history. That's who that man was." Andrew said with another smile.

Fuentes watched in disbelief as Andrew took the photograph of the priest and showed it to him.

After a few seconds Rodrigo said, "You were always wicked and diabolical, Martin."

"How can you dare to speak, the man who does not hesitate to terminate his own men when they do not carry out a mission. Or the man who betrayed Dawnin's good faith by using him as a lure. Shut up! Montgomery! You are not better than me," Andrew shouted angrily.

A moment of silence reigned among them, then Fuentes in a pleading tone exclaimed, "Please! Spare my daughter! She's just a little girl. Please! Try to be human."

"There is a big black market for organs to transplant, and your daughter looks very cute and healthy. The eyes, liver, spleen, kidney have immense value. Oh yes! Your little one is worth a lot, don't you think?" Andrew replied in an icy tone.

"Damn! May you be cursed! I hope you go to hell for all eternity."

"Well! Go there first! Montgomery! And be careful not to get too burned."

Having said that, Andrew Martin, released the brake and pushed Fuentes' wheelchair with all his strength to where it rolled down the hill and ended up slamming violently into the closed gate.

Rodrigo Fuentes was immediately crushed and died.

"Now it's just you, Dawnin! It's just a matter of principle." Andrew murmured, as he pulled out a letter from his pocket, received several months earlier with a Seattle stamp.

He read it for the umpteenth time.

"Dear Mister Martin! You were right. I was wrong about the weather conditions. However, even though it rained, and the weather cooled down in Seattle, I was still correct in predicting it would have been much hotter, under different circumstances. This is particularly relevant to you and your organization of criminals and murderers. Regrettably, I cannot meet you again, to send you straight to hell, where you belong. You would stay in the company of your worthy friends Charles, and Harold Lewis. Patience! Unfortunately, it seems the worst people never die in this world."

The letter was signed by Henry Dawnin.

Andrew placed the letter in his pocket, thinking of Henry. The only person who had fooled and harmed him in his entire life. Then Andrew walked toward one of his men, and he said, "No one saw me! I've never been here; did you get it?"

"Yes, sir," replied the guy.

Before Andrew was leaving, one of the men approached him, and asked, "Sir! What do we do with the child? Do I kill her now, or what?"

Andrew turned around and saw the child terrified and trembling. He walked toward her, until he reached Luisa. Then he bent down and gently touched the face of the crying girl and smiled at her. Then he moved away and ordered his man, "Leave her alive, take the child to a monastery of nuns, where they take care of orphans."

After saying that, Andrew, walking slowly, and said farewell to his men, who stood up immediately.

The driver opened the rear door of the limousine, Andrew got inside, and the car left the villa, disappearing into the horizon.

XXIII

On Some Remote Pacific Island, Four Years Later

Henry Dawnin was on the beach, with a cigarette in his mouth, and a fishing rod next to him. He was reading an old copy of the New York Times, almost two months old.

Henry was stunned and outraged to read a long article the newspaper reported on its front page. The article described the inauguration of the Harold and Charles Lewis Museum of Contemporary Art in New York. The newspaper gave ample space to Senator Andrew Martin, who had personally financed the whole project.

Several celebrities from the world of politics, art, music, and cinema took part in the inauguration. Among the famous guests was the president of the United States with the first lady.

Henry stared at the photograph of the president amicably shaking hands with Andrew Martin. After describing the social event, the newspaper published a long interview with Senator Martin.

Dawnin read the interview extensively.

Andrew Martin was proud to have dedicated the museum to his friends, unfortunately deceased, Harold and Charles Lewis. Two valiant, courageous, upright gentlemen, who had always worked for the good of the community, a better society and for a better America.

Martin recalled the "sacrifice" of Charles Lewis, who died in the prime of his life to fight the evil, the cancer of this society. The man had sacrificed his young life to fight against a gang of drug traffickers and murderers led by the notorious criminal Henry Dawnin, well known to the FBI and CIA for his many crimes.

Dawnin was a very dangerous murderer who in his career as a criminal had killed more than thirty people. Among them, he had mercilessly killed Charles's Lewis girlfriend, Cindy Hyatt, a good, chaste, and honest housewife. And he had killed Charles's secretary, Sharon Miller, after raping and torturing her, along with her entire family.

The senator dwelt on his intention to fight organized crime, so that these atrocities would not be repeated. He would fight with all the means at his disposal to protect the honest and the weak.

At the end of the article, Martin announced he would not run in the next presidential election, but perhaps in the next four years he might change his mind.

Dawnin stayed frozen, staring at the article, when he heard, "Henry! Henry."

He turned around and saw Maria arriving at the beach, beautiful and tanned, with little Valerie, just two years old.

"Say hello to Dad," Maria asked.

"Hello! Daddy," Valerie exclaimed smiling.

Henry, laughing, took her in his arms and said, "I see you have a new bucket and a yellow shovel."

"Yes! It's a gift from mom," she replied with happiness.

"Go and build castles with the sand, but don't go too far. Soon I will come help you," he said to Valerie.

The little girl ran away to play on the shoreline.

"What's going on? I see you are very upset?" Maria asked concerned.

"Have you read this article in the newspaper?"

"No."

"Good! Then read it! And you will be upset too."

Henry passed the newspaper to Maria who began to read it carefully.

After finishing, she exclaimed astonished, "It's incredible, absolutely incredible! Definitely, they put false data in the computer and archives creating your criminal record and accusing you of a series of crimes you never committed."

"What I think too."

"How can they do these things?"

"Powerful people like Andrew Martin can do anything they want in this world, it's ordinary people, idiots like us who pay the price for everything."

"Henry! Did you read that they killed Sharon Miller? Charles's secretary."

"Of course! According to everybody, I was the one who killed her, more than five thousand miles away, perhaps with a postcard. Sharon was a liability, one of those people who knew the truth about Charles Lewis. She could not be left alive, poor woman."

"I wonder what happened to Julie?" Maria exclaimed with concern.

"I hope she's still alive, I hope so with all my heart," he replied.

Henry grabbed the newspaper, crumpled it and threw it away.

Then arm in arm they walked toward little Valerie, who was having fun playing the sand.

"Let's enjoy this beautiful sunny day and this lovely place without thinking about anything negative. Do not let the wicked win again," Henry exclaimed in a philosophical tone.

As a gentle sea breeze blew around them, Henry and Maria walked slowly, hand in hand, along the white shoreline of their tropical beach in paradise.

Made in United States
Troutdale, OR
11/14/2024

24751152R00093